T0350941

Get the eBooks FREE!

(PDF, ePub, Kindle, and liveBook all included)

We believe that once you buy a book from us, you should be able to read it in any format we have available. To get electronic versions of this book at no additional cost to you, purchase and then register this book at the Manning website.

Go to https://www.manning.com/freebook and follow the instructions to complete your pBook registration.

That's it!
Thanks from Manning!

Enterprise Java Microservices

KEN FINNIGAN

MANNING
SHELTER ISLAND

For online information and ordering of this and other Manning books, please visit www.manning.com. The publisher offers discounts on this book when ordered in quantity. For more information, please contact

Special Sales Department
Manning Publications Co.
20 Baldwin Road
PO Box 761
Shelter Island, NY 11964
Email: orders@manning.com

Manning Publications Co.
20 Baldwin Road
PO Box 761
Shelter Island, NY 11964

Development editors:	Karen Miller and Susanna Kline
Technical development editor:	Nick Watts
Review editor:	Aleksandar Dragosavljević
Project manager:	Deirdre Hiam
Copy editor:	Sharon Wilkey
Proofreader:	Elizabeth Martin
Technical proofreader:	John Clingan
Typesetter:	Gordan Salinovic
Cover designer:	Marija Tudor

ISBN 9781617294242
Printed in the United States of America
1 2 3 4 5 6 7 8 9 10 – SP – 23 22 21 20 19 18

brief contents

contents

preface

Since the beginnings of developing a framework for Enterprise Java microservices at Red Hat, I've known it's a critically important topic to disseminate to the wider developer community. Lots of useful information can be lost behind buzzwords, and a book was needed to present the information that developers need to get the job done.

My sincerest hope is that *Enterprise Java Microservices* succeeds at taking existing Enterprise Java developers on a path from traditional application development to developing microservices. It's not always an easy road to travel, because moving from traditional development requires a different mindset, but my desire is for this book to provide that bridge of knowledge to help you take those initial steps into microservices.

acknowledgments

As this book took longer than expected to complete, I'll be forever indebted to Erin, my wife, for her continued understanding and support throughout the entire process. Without her strength, guidance, and perseverance, I'd probably still be writing and reworking chapters today. I'd also like to thank my sons, Lorcán and Daire, for understanding the continued absence of their dad for play on the weekends, while I was buried in a computer working on this book.

To Karen Miller and Susanna Kline, my development editors, thank you for being so understanding about my often slow pace of writing and for pointing out places where I could do better with the content. In addition, I'd like to thank all the reviewers: Alexandros Koufoudakis, Andrea Cosentino, Andrew Block, Benjamín Molina, Christian Posta, Conor Redmond, Damián Mazzini, Daniel MacDonald, David Pardo, Eric Honorez, Gary Samuelson, John Clingan, Justin McAteer, Kelum Senanayake, Miguel Paraz, Peter Perlepes, Rinor Maloku, Rohit Nair, Sergiy Pylypets, Siva Kalagarla, and Tony Sweets. Also, a thank you to the entire Manning team for all their effort on the project.

about this book

Over the last seven or eight years, the term *microservices* has exploded in its use, not always to the betterment of developers trying to understand what it means. During the latter part of that time, developers have sought to bring their existing Enterprise Java knowledge to microservices, not always with the best of success. *Enterprise Java Microservices* is written with the goal of helping existing Enterprise Java developers bridge the gap between traditional application development and microservices.

As part of my job at Red Hat, I've seen the explosion of microservices first hand. That explosion was a contributing factor in a colleague and me forming the WildFly Swarm project in 2015. We saw the need for developers with existing Enterprise Java knowledge to create microservices, and with nothing focused on the Java EE space at the time, we created WildFly Swarm. Much has changed since then, and the current landscape for microservices makes it seem like a lifetime has passed.

Since I began writing this book, changes have continued to occur rapidly with Enterprise Java—in particular, the Thorntail project that I lead, and with microservices more generally. As best as I can, I've endeavored to update the book as those changes occurred.

It should be noted that this book isn't intended to delve deeply into all aspects of microservice development; it would be many times longer than it is now if that were the case. Where appropriate, links to additional reading are provided if you choose to delve into a particular topic in greater detail.

Who should read this book

This book is for any Enterprise Java developer with at least four years of experience. These developers may have basic knowledge of microservices and may even have tried microservices with Node.js or other non-Enterprise Java technologies, but haven't learned to develop Enterprise Java microservices.

How this book is organized: a roadmap

The book is split into two parts. Part 1, chapters 1 through 5, discusses the overall architecture of microservice and distributed systems, along with the concept of slimming application servers, testing, and cloud native development. Part 2 delves into the nitty gritty of microservice development such as service registries, fault tolerance, and security.

Chapter 1 introduces the reader to Enterprise Java—in particular, what a monolith is and how it came about. Then the chapter introduces distributed architectures and microservices by covering what they are, what the term means, and other processes that go hand in hand with the switch to microservices. Lastly, it introduces patterns that can be applied to migrating from monoliths to microservices, and when each might apply.

Chapter 2 introduces a microservice by developing RESTful endpoints for managing a list of categories for a shopping site. The chapter also introduces the Cayambe monolith, which will be converted to a hybrid and have additional microservices developed for it throughout the book.

Chapter 3 introduces the concept of a Just enough Application Server (JeAS) runtime and showcases the differences between the frameworks available to support such a runtime.

Chapter 4 covers how unit and integration testing differ now that we're developing microservices, and the tools available to make testing easier. The chapter also introduces a new concept of consumer-driven contract testing, which is critical to success in architectures with many microservices collaborating and communicating.

Chapter 5 talks about the cloud and the different service models used in different cloud environments. We also discuss cloud native development and how that fits into the microservices world. Next, we use tools at our disposal for local cloud development, and you'll see how these tools can be used for testing.

Chapter 6 discusses the libraries available for consuming external microservices, and the levels of abstraction they provide. We cover fairly low-level libraries like java.net and Apache HttpClient before investigating libraries with a higher level of abstraction such as JAX-RS and RESTEasy clients.

Chapter 7 extends chapter 6 by adding the necessary pieces for our microservices to be able to discover what they wish to consume. Without being able to register a microservice, or discover it, there's no way to reliably consume one.

Chapter 8 dives into a critical topic for distributed architectures and microservices—failure and how to mitigate against it. We briefly cover the typical types of failure we can encounter with microservices, before covering how the various parts of the Hystrix framework enable us to provide a means for our microservice to account for failures that might arise.

Chapter 9 discusses security for our microservices and how to achieve it with Keycloak. From what is required to secure microservices, to retrieving tokens within a microservice for calling secured microservices, and, lastly, authenticating a user within a UI for consuming secured microservices, this chapter covers it all.

Chapter 10 revisits the Cayambe monolith by showing how it can be run in its unmodified form. You'll then be taken through the steps to switch Cayambe to be a hybrid that has monolithic parts, but that also consumes microservices to expand and distribute its functionality.

Chapter 11 introduces the topic of data streaming with Apache Kafka by reducing the duplication of data between hybrids and microservices. You'll use data streaming to enable real-time updates to disparate data to simplify distributed architectures.

About the code

All the code from the book can be found in the source code files that accompany the book. The source code can be downloaded free of charge from the Manning website (www.manning.com/books/enterprise-java-microservices), as well as via the following GitHub repository: https://github.com/kenfinnigan/ejm-samples. All the sample code is structured as a series of Maven modules for each chapter or part of a chapter.

All source code in listings or in the text is in a `fixed width font like this` to separate it from ordinary text. In many listings, the code is annotated to point out key concepts.

Book forum

Purchase of *Enterprise Java Microservices* includes free access to a private web forum run by Manning Publications, where you can make comments about the book, ask technical questions, and receive help from the author and from other users. To access the forum, go to https://forums.manning.com/forums/java-microservices-in-action. You can also learn more about Manning's forums and the rules of conduct at https://forums.manning.com/forums/about.

Manning's commitment to our readers is to provide a venue where a meaningful dialogue between individual readers and between readers and the author can take place. It isn't a commitment to any specific amount of participation on the part of the author, whose contribution to the forum remains voluntary (and unpaid). We suggest you try asking the author some challenging questions lest his interest stray! The forum and the archives of previous discussions will be accessible from the publisher's website as long as the book is in print.

about the author

 KEN FINNIGAN has been a consultant and software engineer over more than 20 years for enterprises throughout the world. He leads the Thorntail project, which seeks to make developing microservices for the cloud with Java and Java EE as easy as possible. He previously served as the project lead for LiveOak, along with other JBoss projects.

about the cover illustration

The figure on the cover of *Enterprise Java Microservices* is captioned "Girl from Lumbarda, island Korčula, Croatia." The illustration is taken from the reproduction, published in 2006, of a 19th-century collection of costumes and ethnographic descriptions entitled *Dalmatia* by Professor Frane Carrara (1812–1854), an archaeologist and historian, and the first director of the Museum of Antiquity in Split, Croatia. The illustrations were obtained from a helpful librarian at the Ethnographic Museum (formerly the Museum of Antiquity), itself situated in the Roman core of the medieval center of Split: the ruins of Emperor Diocletian's retirement palace from around AD 304. The book includes finely colored illustrations of figures from different regions of Dalmatia, accompanied by descriptions of the costumes and of everyday life.

Dress codes have changed since the nineteenth century, and the diversity by region, so rich at the time, has faded away. It is now hard to tell apart the inhabitants of different continents, let alone different towns or regions. Perhaps we have traded cultural diversity for a more varied personal life—certainly for a more varied and fast-paced technological life.

At a time when it's hard to tell one computer book from another, Manning celebrates the inventiveness and initiative of the computer business with book covers based on the rich diversity of regional life of two centuries ago, brought back to life by illustrations from collections such as this one.

Part 1

Microservices basics

What are Microservices? A *microservice* consists of a single deployment executing within a single process. How do microservices differ from traditional Enterprise Java applications? In what situations is it appropriate to use microservices? These are just some of the questions that we'll address in these first five chapters.

Part 1 also explores the runtime options available for Enterprise Java microservices, before finishing with how to test microservices and deploy them to the cloud.

Enterprise Java microservices

This chapter covers

- Enterprise Java history
- Microservices and distributed architecture
- Patterns for migration to microservices
- Enterprise Java microservices

Before you dive in, let's step back and discuss what I hope you achieve during the course of this book. We all know that there's no such thing as a *free lunch*, so I won't pretend that microservices are easy. This chapter introduces microservices—their concepts, benefits, and drawbacks—to provide a basis on which you can build your technical knowledge. Chapters 2 and 3 provide an example of a RESTful endpoint microservice and cover some of your runtime and deployment options for Enterprise Java microservices.

So what is an *Enterprise Java microservice?* In a nutshell, it's the result of applying Enterprise Java to the development of microservices. The latter part of this chapter and the remainder of the book explore in detail what that means.

After you've learned the basics of microservices, you'll delve into tools and techniques for use in Enterprise Java to mitigate the drawbacks and complexity of microservices. Being more familiar with microservices, you'll then look at an existing Enterprise Java application and how it could be migrated to take advantage of microservices. The last few chapters touch on more advanced microservice topics related to security and event streaming.

1.1 Enterprise Java—a short history

If you're reading this book, you're most likely already an experienced Enterprise Java developer. If you aren't, I appreciate and applaud your desire to broaden your horizons into Enterprise Java!

1.1.1 What is Enterprise Java?

For those who are new to, or need a refresher in, Enterprise Java, what is it? *Enterprise Java* is a set of APIs, and their implementations, that can provide the entire stack of an application from the UI down to the database, communicate with external applications via web services, and integrate with internal legacy systems, to name a few, with the goal of supporting the business requirements of an enterprise. Though it's possible to achieve such a result with Java on its own, rewriting all the low-level architecture required for an application would be tedious and error prone, and would significantly impact the ability of a business to deliver value in a timely manner.

It wasn't long after Java was first released more than 20 years ago that various frameworks began to crop up to solve the low-level architecture concerns of developers. These frameworks allowed developers to focus on delivering business value with application-specific code.

> **Enterprise Java**
>
> Many frameworks have come and gone, but two have remained the most popular through the years: Java Platform, Enterprise Edition (Java EE), and Spring. These two frameworks account for most development by an enterprise with Enterprise Java.
>
> Java EE incorporates many specifications, each with one or more implementations. Spring is a collection of libraries, some of which wrap Java EE specifications.

1.1.2 Typical Enterprise Java architecture

In the early days of Enterprise Java, our applications were all *greenfield* development, because no preexisting code was being extended.

> **DEFINITION**   *Greenfield* refers to the development of an entirely new application without any preexisting code that needs to be taken into consideration, excluding any common libraries that might be required.

Greenfield development presents the greatest opportunity to develop a *clean* layered architecture for an application. Typically, architects would devise an architecture similar to that shown in figure 1.1.

Here you'll likely recognize familiar pieces of architectures you've worked on in the past: a *view* layer, a *controller*, possibly using a reusable *business service*, and finally, the *model* that interacts with the database. You can also see the application packaged as a WAR, but many combinations of packaging for each layer could be applied, including JAR and EAR. Typically, the *view* and *controller* are packaged in a WAR. The *business service* and *model* are packaged in JARs, either inside a WAR or EAR.

As the years passed, we continued developing greenfield applications with Enterprise Java using such a pattern, but there reached a point where most enterprises

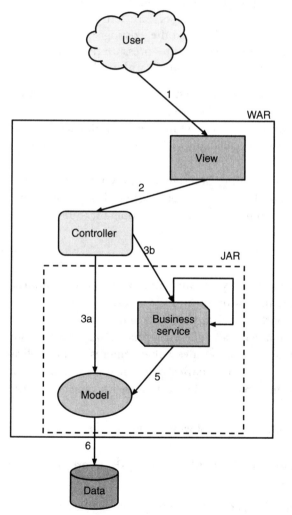

1 A *user* makes a request from a browser specifying which *view* of an application they wish to see.

2 The *view* calls out to a *controller* to retrieve whatever information might by required to construct itself.

3 The *controller* can retrieve the information in one of two ways:
3a Directly interact with the *model* of the application to retrieve an object model populated with data.
3b Call one or more *business services*, possibly to aggregate data from different sources.

4 A *business service* can also make many calls to other *business services*. It all depends on how the business features have been architected.

5 The *business service* calls a *model* to retrieve the data it needs. This step is equivalent to 3a.

6 *Model* classes provide the mapping onto physical data storage, and are often passed back up through the layers of the application.

Figure 1.1   Typical Enterprise Java application architecture

were, for the most part, enhancing existing applications. From that day, many Enterprise Java applications became a legacy burden on enterprises by virtue of the maintenance work required—not because of a flaw or deficiency in Java, though there have been several, but because developers aren't the best at architecting changes to existing applications and systems. This is complicated further for enterprises that have hundreds of architects and developers pass through their doors, each bringing their own preferences and patterns to extending existing applications.

> **NOTE** I'm not sitting in an ivory tower disparaging developers. Many times I've made decisions about how a feature should be implemented without fully grasping existing functionality—not through any intent or malice, but because those who wrote the code are no longer employed at the enterprise and therefore can't be asked about the code, and because documentation may be lacking or nonintuitive. Such a situation means developers are left to make a judgment call as to whether or not they've understood the existing system sufficiently to make modifications. Throw in some deadline pressure from management, and such a situation becomes even more fraught with problems.

Over time, many Enterprise Java applications diverged from the clean architecture shown in figure 1.1 and became a mess of spaghetti more closely resembling figure 1.2. In figure 1.2 you can see how clear boundaries between functionality within a layer have become blurred, resulting in components in each layer no longer having a well-defined purpose.

This situation is where many enterprises find themselves today. Only a few applications of an enterprise may fit this mold, but this mess of spaghetti is a problem that must be solved in order for an application to foster future development without significant costs being incurred each time.

1.1.3   *What is a monolith?*

What defines an Enterprise Java application as a monolith? A *monolith* is an application that has all its components contained within a single deployable, and that typically has a release cadence of 3–18 months. Some applications may even have a release cadence of two years, which doesn't make for an agile enterprise. Monoliths typically evolve over time from attempts to make quick iterative enhancements to an application, without any concern for appropriate boundaries between different parts, or components, within it. Indicators of an application being a monolith can include the following:

- Multiple WARs that are part of a single deployment, due to their intertwined behavior
- EARs that contain potentially dozens of other WARs and JARs to provide all the necessary functionality

Is figure 1.2 a monolith? It most certainly is, and an extremely bad one, because of the blurring of functional separation between components.

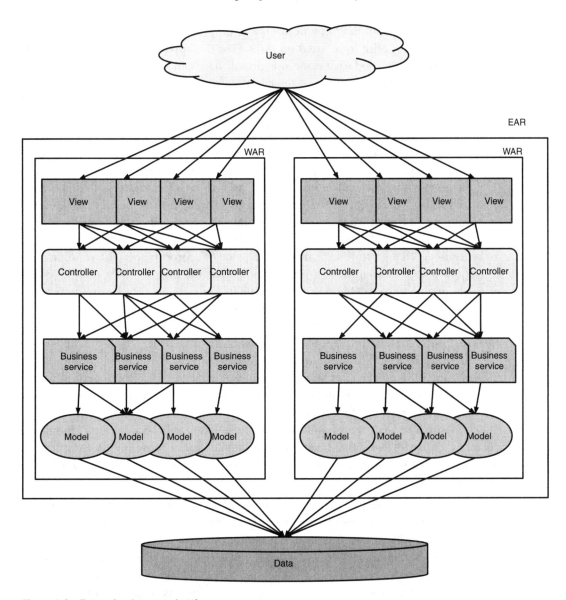

Figure 1.2 Enterprise Java spaghetti

Why do the preceding factors make an application a monolith? A single deployable for an application is perfectly fine when you have a small footprint, but when you have potentially thousands of classes and dozens of third-party libraries, an application becomes infinitely more complex. Testing even a minor change to the application would require large amounts of regression testing to ensure that no other part of the application was impacted. Even if the regression testing were automated, it'd still be a mammoth task.

Whether an application is a monolith is also determined in part by its architecture. Classifying as a monolith isn't based on the size of the application on disk, or the size of the runtime being used to execute the monolith. It's all about how that application has been architected with respect to the components within it.

Release cadence is a forcing function for enterprises. If an application is released only every 3–18 months, the business (unknowingly or not) will focus on larger feature changes that take significant time to develop. No incentive exists to request a minor tweak that could be made and released in a few hours, or days, when even the most simple change won't reach production for months.

Release cadence dictated by the time it takes to develop and test changes has a direct impact on the ability of an enterprise to be agile and respond to a changing environment. For instance, if a competitor were to begin selling the same widget as your enterprise for 15% less than you do, can you react? Taking several months to make a simple change to reduce the selling price of a product could have disastrous consequences for the bottom line. If that widget was the biggest seller, and the enterprise was unable to compete on price for three months, it may even be on the verge of going out of business by the time a price change was released.

Along with release cadence, it's critical to note that discussions around *micro* versus *monolith* don't have any relation to constraints on size. You could have a microservice that's 100 MB in size, or a monolith that's only 20 MB. The definition is more about the coupling of dependencies between components, leading to the benefit of updating a single component without needing to cascade updates across many components. This decoupling is what allows for a faster release cadence.

Though it appears that monolithic Enterprise Java applications are all gloom and doom, is that really the case? In many situations, it makes sense for an enterprise to continue with, or develop, a monolith. How do you know if you should stick with a monolith?

- *Your enterprise may have only a few applications that it actively develops and maintains.* It may not make sense to significantly increase the development, testing, and release burden when you have so few applications.
- *If the current development team has a dozen people, splitting them into one- or two-person teams for microservices may not provide any benefit.* In some cases, that split will be detrimental. Basecamp (https://basecamp.com/) is a perfect example of a monolith that's fine the way it is, developed by a team of 12.
- *Does your enterprise need multiple releases a week, or even a day?* If not, and the existing monolith has a clear separation of components, reducing the release cadence may be all that's required to derive increased business agility and value.

Whether staying with a monolith is the right thing for an enterprise varies, depending on the current circumstances and the long-term goals.

1.1.4 *What are the problems associated with monoliths?*

In general, an architectural design akin to the one in figure 1.1 is a good idea, but drawbacks exist as well:

- *Inability to scale individual components*—This may not seem to be a major problem, but certain factors can alter the impact of poor scaling. If a single instance of the application requires a large amount of memory or space, scaling that out to a not-insignificant number of nodes requires a large investment in hardware.
- *Performance of individual components*—With a single deployment containing many components, it's easy for one component to perform worse than the rest. You then have a single component slowing down the entire system, which isn't a good situation, and the operations team won't be pleased.
- *Deployability of individual components*—When the entire application is a single deployment, any changes require a deployment of the entire application, even if you have a single-line change in one component. That's not good for business agility and often results in release cadences of many months to include many changes in one updated deployment.
- *Greater code complexity*—When an application has many components, it's easy for the functional boundaries between them to become blurred. Blurring the separation of components further increases the complexity of code, both in terms of code execution and for a developer understanding the intent of the code.
- *Difficulty in accurately testing an application*—When the complexity of an application grows, the amount of testing and time required to ensure that any change didn't cause a regression grows. What seems like the smallest and most insignificant change can easily lead to unforeseen errors and problems in completely unrelated components.

All these issues cause great cost to enterprises, as well as slowing the speed with which they can take advantage of new opportunities. But these potential drawbacks are still small in comparison to starting from a clean slate.

If an enterprise has an application that has evolved with new features over a decade or more, attempting to replace it with a greenfield project would cost hundreds of man years in effort. This is a huge factor in why enterprises continue maintaining existing monoliths.

When it's too costly to replace a monolith with a more modern alternative, that application becomes entrenched in an enterprise. It becomes a critical application, and any downtime causes business impacts. This situation becomes ever more compounded with continual enhancements and fixes.

On the flipside, some monoliths have been running well for years and can be easily managed by a handful of developers without much effort. Maybe they're in a maintenance mode and not under heavy feature development. These monoliths are perfectly OK as they are. If it ain't broke, don't fix it.

What do you do with monoliths that are too cumbersome to replace with a green-field project, even though the enterprise knows it's costing them a great deal in business agility and expense? How do you update them to use newer frameworks and technologies so they don't become legacy? We'll answer these questions next.

1.2 *Microservices and distributed architecture*

Before delving into the definitions for *microservices* and *distributed architecture*, let's revisit how figure 1.2 might look when using them; see figure 1.3. This depiction has certainly cleared up the separation between components by splitting them into separate microservices with clear boundaries between them.

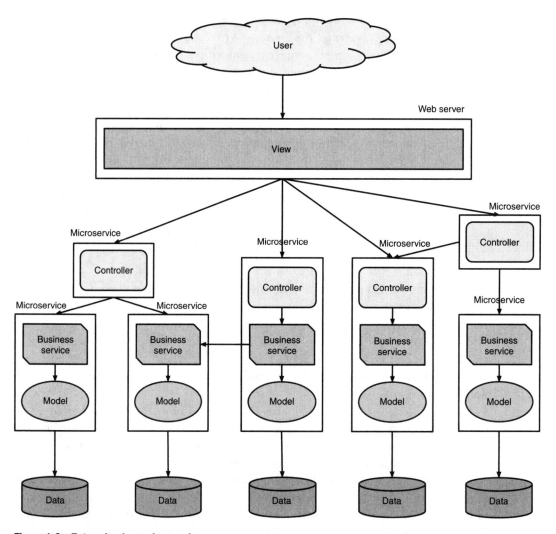

Figure 1.3   Enterprise Java microservices

So what do I mean by a microservice? A *microservice* consists of a single deployment executing within a single process, isolated from other deployments and processes, that supports the fulfillment of a specific piece of business functionality. Each microservice focuses on the required tasks within a *Bounded Context*, which is a logical way to separate the various domain models of an enterprise. We'll cover this in greater detail later in this chapter.

From the definition, you can see that a microservice, in and of itself, isn't useful. It becomes useful when you have many loosely coupled microservices working together to fulfill the needs of an application. A microservices architecture containing many microservices communicating with each other can also be referred to as a *distributed architecture.*

To make a microservice useful, it needs to be easily used from other microservices and components of the entire system. It's impossible to achieve that when a microservice attempts to accomplish too much. You want a microservice to focus on a single task.

1.2.1 *Do one thing well*

In 1978, Douglas McIlroy, best known for developing UNIX pipelines and various UNIX tools, documented the UNIX philosophy, one part of which is, *Make each program do one thing well.* This same philosophy has been adopted by microservice developers. Microservices aren't the kitchen sink of application development; you can't throw everything in them and expect them to function at an optimal level. In that case, you'd have a *monolithic microservice,* also referred to as a *distributed monolith*!

A well-designed microservice should have a single task to perform that's sufficiently fine-grained, delivering a business capability or adding business value. Going beyond a single task brings us back to the problems of Enterprise Java monoliths, which we don't want to repeat.

It's not always easy to figure out a sufficiently granular task for a microservice. Later in the chapter we'll discuss Domain-Driven Design as a method to assist in defining that granularity.

1.2.2 *What is a distributed architecture?*

A *distributed architecture* consists of multiple pieces that work with each other to make up the full functionality of an application distributed across processes, and often across network boundaries as well. What's distributed can be any part of an application, such as RESTful endpoints, message queues, and web services, but it's most definitely not limited to only these components.

Figure 1.4 shows what a distributed architecture for microservices might look like. In this depiction, the *microservice* instances are described as being in a *runtime,* but that doesn't dictate how the instance is packaged. It could be packaged as *uber jars* or Linux containers, but many other options are available. The runtime is purely for delineating the operating environment of a microservice, showing that the microservices are running independently.

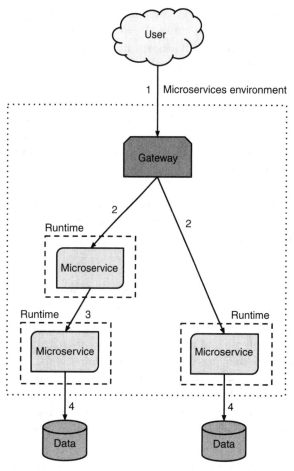

1 A *user* makes a request from a browser to interact with a particular service. This could be from a mobile device or from a UI that was previously retrieved.

2 When the request enters the *microservices environment*, it enters the *gateway*, which routes the request to the appropriate *microservice*.

3 A *microservice* receives the request and performs some of its own processing on it before calling another *service*.

4 The last *microservice* in the chain interacts with the *data* storage layer for retrieving/writing records.

Figure 1.4   Typical microservices architecture

> **NOTE**   An *uber jar*, also known as a *fat jar*, indicates that the JAR file contains more than a single application or library, and that it can be run from the command line with `java -jar`.

1.2.3   Why should you care about being distributed?

Now that you've seen a distributed architecture, let's look at some of the benefits:

- *Services are location-independent.* Services can locate and communicate with other services no matter where they're physically located. Such location independence allows services to be located on the same virtual hardware, same physical hardware, same data center, different data centers, or even a public cloud, and all act is if they're in the same JVM. The main downside to location independence is the extra time required to make the network calls between them, and by the nature of adding new network calls, you've reduced the likelihood of successful completion.

- *Services are language-independent.* Though this book focuses on Enterprise Java, we're not so naive as to believe that there won't be times that services need, or are desired, to be developed in different languages. When services aren't required to run in the same environment, you can use different languages for different services.
- *Service deployments are small and single-purpose.* When a deployment is smaller, less effort is required for testing, and this makes it possible to shrink the release cadence of that deployment down to a week or less. Having small, single-purpose deployments enables an enterprise to more easily react to business needs in a near-real-time fashion.
- *New services are defined by the recomposition of existing service functionality.* Having discrete distributed services throughout your architecture greatly enhances your ability to recombine those services in new ways to create additional value. This recombination can be as straightforward as deploying a single new service, combined with a handful of services already deployed. This enables you to create something new for the business in a shorter time frame.

Sounds awesome—how can you develop distributed applications right now? You need to pull back on the reins a bit here. Yes, being distributed does improve a lot of the issues that we've had with Enterprise Java over the years, but it also introduces its own challenges. Developing distributed applications is in no way a silver bullet, and you can easily shoot yourself in the foot.

You've seen some benefits of being distributed, but there's never a free lunch with most things—and definitely not with distributed architecture. If you have a bunch of services that interoperate through communication and no coupling, what problems can that introduce?

- Location independence for services is great, but how do they find each other? You need a means of defining services logically, regardless of what their physical location or IP address might be. With a means of discovery, you can locate a service by its logical name and ignore wherever it might be physically located. Service discovery serves this purpose. Part 2 of this book covers how to use service discovery.
- How do you handle failure without impacting customers? You need a means of gracefully degrading functionality when services fail, instead of crashing the application. You need service resilience and fault tolerance to provide alternatives when services fail. Part 2 covers how to provide fault tolerance and resilience for your services.
- Having hundreds or thousands of services, versus a handful of applications, places additional burdens on operations. Most operations teams aren't experienced in dealing with such a large number of services. How do you mitigate some of this complexity? Monitoring needs to play a major part here—in particular, automated monitoring. You need to automate the monitoring of hundreds of services to reduce the burden on operations, while also providing information that's as near to real-time as possible about the entire system.

1.2.4 *What can be done to assist in developing microservices?*

Microservice development is hard, so what can you do to make it easier? There's no panacea for making it easy, but this section covers a couple of options for making microservice development more manageable.

1.2.5 *Product over project*

Netflix has been a major proponent of the product-over-project idea for its microservices since rewriting its entire architecture under the leadership of Adrian Cockroft.

All these years, we've been developing projects and not products. Why? Because we develop an application that meets a set of requirements and then hand it over to operations. The application might require two weeks or two years to develop, but it's still a project if, at the end, the application is handed over and the team disbanded. Some team members may be retained for a period to handle maintenance requests and enhancements, but the effort is still considered a project followed by lots of mini projects.

So how do you develop a *product?* Developing a product means that a single team owns it for the entirety of its lifespan, whether that be 2 months or 20 years. The team will develop it, release it, manage the operational aspects of the application, resolve production issues—pretty much everything.

Why does the differentiation between a project and a product matter? Owning a product engenders a greater sense of responsibility about the way an application is developed. How? Do you want to be paged in the middle of the night because an application is failing? I know I don't!

How does a shift of focus from project to product help with developing microservices? When you're seeking a release cadence of a week or less, as is typical for true microservices, it's hard to reach that release frequency with developers who aren't familiar with the codebase, as would be the case with a *project* approach.

1.2.6 *Continuous integration and delivery*

Without continuous integration and delivery, developing microservices becomes a great deal more difficult.

Continuous integration refers to the processes that ensure any change, or commit, to a source repository results in a new build of the application, including all associated tests of that application. This provides quick feedback on whether or not changes broke the application, provided the tests are sufficient enough to discover it.

Continuous delivery is a reasonably new phenomenon that has come from the DevOps movement, whereby application changes are continuously delivered between environments, including production, to ensure expeditious delivery of application changes. A manual step may occur to approve a build going into production, but not always. Having a manual step is likely for critical user applications and less so for others. Continuous delivery is usually offered by means of a build pipeline, which can consist of automatic or manual steps, such as a manual step to approve a release for production.

Continuous integration and delivery, referred to as *CI/CD*, are key tools in facilitating a short release cadence. Why? They enable developers to find possible bugs earlier in the process in an automated manner. But more important, CI/CD significantly reduces the amount of time between determining that a piece of code is ready for production and having it live for users. If a release process takes a day or two to complete, that isn't conducive to releasing multiple times a day or even once a day.

Another important benefit of CI/CD is the ability to be more incremental in delivering functionality. The goal isn't just to be able to physically release code faster; being able to deploy smaller pieces of functionality is crucial for minimizing risk as well. If a small change reaches production that causes a failure, backing out that change is a relatively easy task.

1.3 Patterns for migration to microservices

You've looked at Enterprise Java with its existing monoliths and you've learned about microservices in a distributed architecture. But how do you get from one to the other? This section delves into patterns that can be applied to the problem of splitting an existing monolith into multiple microservices.

1.3.1 Domain-Driven Design

Domain-Driven Design (DDD) is a set of patterns and methodologies for modeling our understanding of the domains in our software. A key part of this is the Bounded Context pattern (https://martinfowler.com/bliki/BoundedContext.html), which enables you to segregate parts of the system to be modeled at a single time.

This topic is far too broad to be covered in a few small paragraphs in this book, especially because many books are already dedicated to DDD. But we'll cover it briefly here as another piece in the puzzle of developing with microservices. DDD can be used both in greenfield microservice development and in migrating to microservices.

A sufficiently large application or system can be divided into multiple Bounded Contexts, enabling design and development to focus on the core domain of a given Bounded Context at any one point. This pattern acknowledges that it's difficult to come up with a domain model for an entire enterprise at any one time, because too many complexities exist. Dividing such a model into manageable Bounded Contexts provides a way to focus on a portion of that model without concerning yourself with the remainder of the, likely unknown, domain model. Figure 1.5 is an example to help you understand the concepts behind DDD.

Say you have a store that wants to develop microservices, and its domain model consists of an order, items within an order, a product, and a supplier of that product. The current domain model combines the different ways a Product can be defined. From the perspective of an Order, it doesn't care who supplies the product, how many are currently in stock, what the manufacturer price is, or any other information that's relevant to only the administration of the business. Conversely, the administration side isn't necessarily concerned with how many orders a product may be associated with.

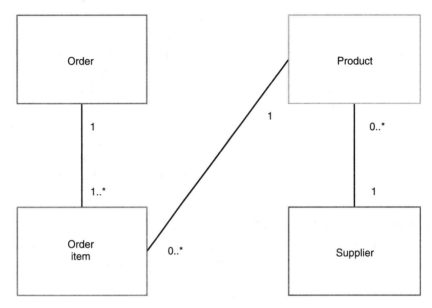

Figure 1.5   Store domain model

Figure 1.6 shows you now have Product in each Bounded Context; each represents a different view of a product. The Order Bounded Context has only information such as a product code and description. All the product information required by the business is within the Product Bounded Context.

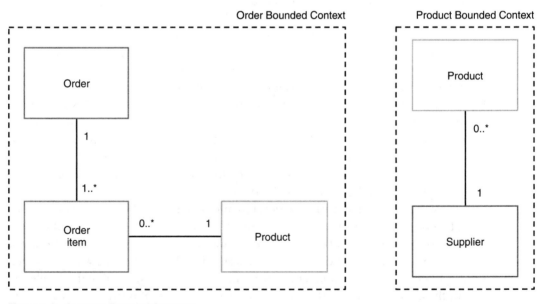

Figure 1.6   Separate Bounded Contexts

In some cases, a clean split will exist in the domain model of a Bounded Context, but in others there will be commonality between the separate models, as in the preceding example. In this situation, it's important to consider that although a part of the domain model is shared between Bounded Contexts, one domain can be classed as the *owner*.

Having defined the owner of a piece of the domain, it becomes necessary to make that domain available to external Bounded Contexts—but in a way that doesn't implicitly tie the two Bounded Contexts together. This does make it trickier to handle the boundary, but patterns such as Event Sourcing can help with this problem.

> **NOTE** *Event sourcing* is the practice of firing events for every state change in an application, which is usually recorded as a log in a certain format. Such a log can then be used to rebuild entire database structures, or as in this case, as a way to populate a piece of a domain model that's owned externally.

How do all these Bounded Contexts fit together? Each Bounded Context forms part of a greater whole, a context map. A *context map* is a global view of an application, identifying all the required Bounded Contexts and the way they should communicate and integrate with each other.

In this example, because you've split Product into two, you'd need such a data feed from the Product to Order Bounded Contexts to be able to populate the Product with appropriate data.

As you saw in our example, one side benefit of shared domain models in Bounded Contexts is that each can have its own view of the same data. An application is no longer forced into viewing a piece of data in the same way as its owner does. This can provide huge benefits when a domain needs only a small subset of the data in each record that the owner might hold. For additional information on Domain-Driven Design and Bounded Contexts, I recommend *Functional and Reactive Domain Modeling* by Debasish Ghosh (Manning, 2016).

1.3.2   *Big Bang pattern*

The *Big Bang pattern* for migrating to microservices in an enterprise is by far the most complicated and challenging. It entails breaking apart every single piece of an existing monolith into microservices, such that there's a single cutover from one to the other.

Because deployment is a single cutover—a Big Bang—to production, developing for such a change can take just as long as developing on a monolith. Certainly, by the end of the process, you've moved to microservices, but this pattern would be a bumpier road for most enterprises than other patterns for migrating to microservices—especially when considering the internal process and procedure changes required to move between the two deployment models. Such an abrupt change would be traumatic and potentially damaging to an enterprise.

The Big Bang pattern isn't recommended for most enterprises as a means of migrating, and most definitely not for those who aren't experienced with microservices already.

1.3.3   *Strangler pattern*

The *Strangler pattern* is based on the Strangler Application defined by Martin Fowler (www.martinfowler.com/bliki/StranglerApplication.html). Martin describes this pattern as a way to rewrite an existing system by gradually creating a new system at the edges of the existing one. The new system slowly grows over several years, until the old system is strangled into nonexistence.

You may find a similar end result as the Big Bang pattern—not necessarily a bad thing—but it's achieved over a much longer time span while still delivering business value in the interim. This approach significantly reduces the risk involved, compared to the Big Bang pattern. Through monitoring progress of the application over time, you can adjust the way you implement microservices as you learn with each new one implemented. This is another huge advantage over the Big Bang pattern: being able to adjust and react to issues that might arise in processes or procedures. With a Big Bang approach, an enterprise is tied into its processes until everything has cutover.

1.3.4   *Hybrid pattern*

Now that you've seen both the Big Bang and Strangler patterns, let's look at the *Hybrid pattern*. I feel this pattern will become the predominant pattern for enterprises migrating to and developing microservices.

This pattern begins life in a similar fashion to the Strangler. The difference is that you never fully strangle the original monolith. You retain some functionality within a monolith and integrate that with new microservices. Figure 1.7 shows the path of a request through an existing Enterprise Java monolith and a new microservices architecture:

1   A user makes a request from a browser specifying which view of an application they wish to see.
2   The view calls out to a controller to retrieve whatever information might be required to construct itself.
3   The controller calls a business service, possibly to aggregate data from different sources.
4   The business service then passes the request into the microservices environment, where it enters the gateway.
5   The gateway routes the request to the appropriate microservice based on routing rules that have been defined.
6   A microservice receives the request and performs some of its own processing on it before calling another microservice.
7   The last microservice in the chain interacts with the data storage layer to read/write records.

An architecture such as that in figure 1.7 provides a great deal of flexibility for growth and delivering business value in a timely fashion. Components that require high performance and/or high availability can be deployed to the microservices environment.

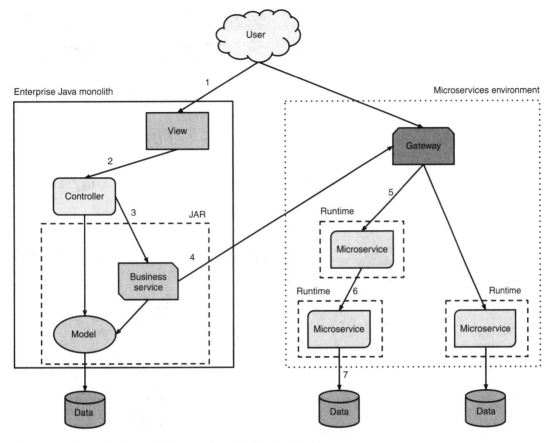

Figure 1.7 Enterprise Java and microservices hybrid architecture

Components that are too costly to be migrated to the new architecture can remain deployed on an Enterprise Java platform.

You'll focus on the Hybrid pattern later in the book, when you migrate an existing Enterprise Java application to use microservices.

1.4 *What are Enterprise Java microservices?*

As I mentioned at the beginning of the chapter, Enterprise Java microservices are purely microservices developed with Enterprise Java. So let's take a look at a simple example to see it in practice.

Let's create a simple RESTful Java EE microservice that uses CDI and JAX-RS. This microservice exposes a RESTful endpoint to greet the user by name; the message returned is being provided via a CDI service you inject (listing 1.1).

Listing 1.1   CDI service

```
@RequestScoped
public class HelloService {

    public String sayHello(String name) {
        return "Hello " + name;
    }
}
```

CDI annotation that says you want a new HelloService instance for each servlet Request made. In this instance, because you're not storing state, it could easily have been @ApplicationScoped instead.

Service method that takes a single parameter and returns it prefixed "Hello"

The preceding service defines a single `sayHello()` method that returns `Hello` combined with the value of the `name` parameter.

You can then `@Inject` that service into your controller.

Listing 1.2   JAX-RS endpoint

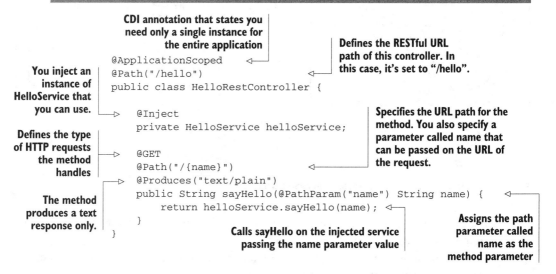

CDI annotation that states you need only a single instance for the entire application

Defines the RESTful URL path of this controller. In this case, it's set to "/hello".

You inject an instance of HelloService that you can use.

Defines the type of HTTP requests the method handles

The method produces a text response only.

```
@ApplicationScoped
@Path("/hello")
public class HelloRestController {

    @Inject
    private HelloService helloService;

    @GET
    @Path("/{name}")
    @Produces("text/plain")
    public String sayHello(@PathParam("name") String name) {
        return helloService.sayHello(name);
    }
}
```

Specifies the URL path for the method. You also specify a parameter called name that can be passed on the URL of the request.

Calls sayHello on the injected service passing the name parameter value

Assigns the path parameter called name as the method parameter

If you've developed JAX-RS resources before, you'll recognize everything in the preceding code. What does that mean? It means that you can develop microservices with Enterprise Java just as if you were developing an Enterprise Java application. The ability to develop a microservice with existing Enterprise Java knowledge is a significant advantage in using Enterprise Java for microservices.

This microservice example is simplified because you're dealing with only the producer side of the equation. If the service also consumed other microservices, it would be more complex. But you'll come to that in part 2 of this book.

Though the preceding example was implemented with Java EE APIs, it could just as easily have been implemented using Spring instead.

1.4.1 Why Enterprise Java is a good fit for microservices

You've seen how easy it is to develop a RESTful endpoint as an Enterprise Java microservice, but why should you? Wouldn't you be better off using a newfangled framework or technology specifically built for microservices? You have plenty to choose from right now: Go, Rust, and Node.js are just some examples.

In some situations, using a newer technology may make more sense. But if an enterprise has significant investment in Enterprise Java through existing applications, developers, and so forth, it makes a lot more sense to continue using that technology, because developers have one less thing to learn in developing a microservice. And by *technology* I don't mean Java EE or Spring per se; it's more about the APIs that a technology offers and developers' familiarity with those APIs. If the same APIs can be used with monoliths, microservices, or whatever the next buzzword is to hit developer mindshare, that's far more valuable than relearning APIs for each type of development situation.

If a developer is building microservices for an enterprise for the first time, using a technology that the developer already knows and understands allows that developer to focus on the requirements of a microservice—without being concerned about learning the nuances of a language or framework at the same time.

Using a technology that's been around for nearly 20 years also has significant advantages. Why? A technology that's been around that long is almost guaranteed not to disappear in the near future. Can anyone say Cobol?

It's a great comfort to enterprises to know that whatever technology they're developing and investing in isn't going to be defunct in a few short years. Such a risk is typically why enterprises are reluctant to invest in extremely new technology. Though it can be frustrating not being able to use the latest and greatest, it does have advantages, at least for an enterprise.

Enterprises aren't the only factor that need to be considered when choosing a technology for developing microservices. You also need to consider the following:

- *Experience and skills of developers in the marketplace*—There's no point in choosing a particular technology for microservice development if you don't have a sufficiently large pool of resources to choose from. A huge pool of developers have Enterprise Java experience, so using that is advantageous.
- *Vendor support*—It's all well and good to choose a technology for developing microservices, but if no vendors are offering support of that technology, it's difficult. It's difficult because enterprises like to have a vendor available 24/7 for support problems with a technology, usually in a production situation. Without vendor support, an enterprise needs to employ those who work directly on that technology to guarantee they can resolve any issues of their microservices in production.
- *Cost of change*—If an enterprise has been developing with Enterprise Java for a decade or more and has a stable group of developers who have worked on

projects over that time, does it make sense for an enterprise to abandon that history and carve out a new path with different technology? Though in some cases, that does make sense, the majority of enterprises should stick with experience and skills even if moving to microservices.

- *Existing operational experience and infrastructure*—In addition to developers, the convenience of having years of operational experience with Enterprise Java is just as critical. Applications don't monitor and fix themselves, though that would be nice. Having to hire or retrain operations staff on new languages and frameworks can be just as time-consuming as doing it for developers.

Summary

- A microservice consists of a single deployment executing within a single process.
- An Enterprise Java monolith is an application in which all its components are contained within a single deployment.
- An Enterprise Java microservice is a microservice developed using Enterprise Java frameworks.
- An Enterprise Java monolith isn't suitable for a fast release cadence.
- Implementing microservices isn't a silver bullet and requires additional consideration to implement successfully.
- Migrating to microservices from a monolith can be best achieved with the Hybrid pattern.
- An enterprise's history of Enterprise Java development shouldn't be disregarded in the decision to implement microservices.

Developing a simple RESTful microservice

This chapter covers

- Introducing the Cayambe monolith
- Developing a simple RESTful application
- Packaging your simple RESTful application as a microservice
- Understanding development with Enterprise Java for microservices

This chapter will introduce you to the Cayambe monolith. The Cayambe monolith will assist as we develop Enterprise Java microservices throughout the book, with each microservice becoming a part of a new Hybrid monolith in chapter 10.

2.1 Cayambe monolith

Cayambe is an e-commerce application that hasn't been maintained for the last 15 years and needs serious modernization. It's easy to see from the homepage in figure 2.1 that it doesn't quite have the same look as modern websites do today.

©2002 Cayambe

Figure 2.1   Cayambe homepage

As you can see in figure 2.2, Cayambe is an EAR deployment that consists of three WARs, a common JAR for the UIs, and a JAR containing the EJBs (Enterprise Java-Beans) and DAOs (data access objects) for interacting with the database.

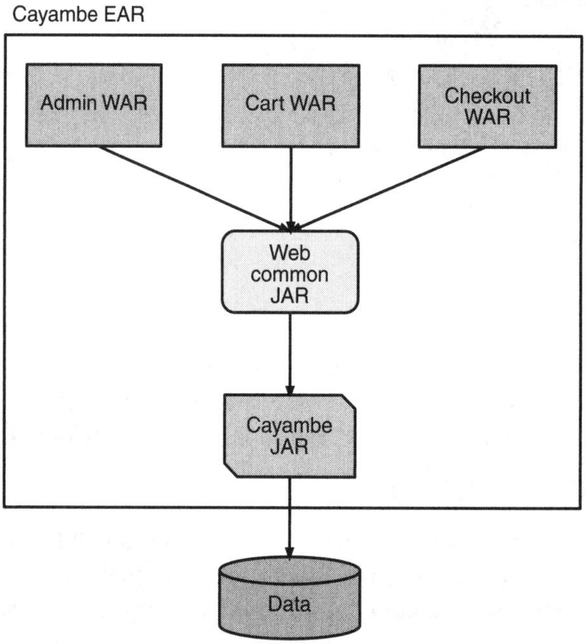

Cayambe EAR

```
Admin WAR     Cart WAR     Checkout
                             WAR

              Web
              common
              JAR

              Cayambe
              JAR

              Data
```

Figure 2.2   Cayambe monolith architecture

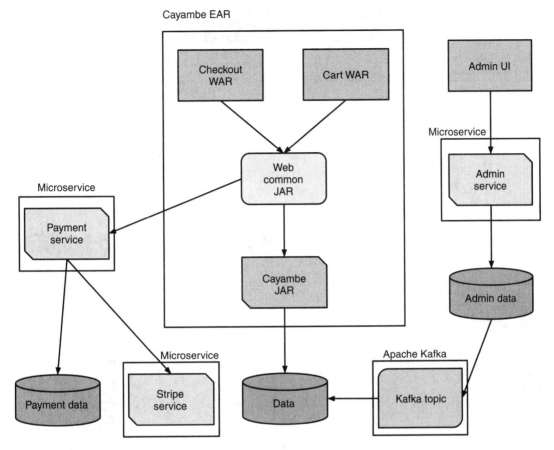

Figure 2.3 Cayambe future architecture

Throughout the book, you'll work toward moving Cayambe to a series of deployments, as represented in figure 2.3. Chapter 10 outlines additional details of Cayambe; in that chapter, you'll integrate the monolith with the microservices you develop over the coming chapters.

2.2 New administration site

As part of modernizing Cayambe, you'll split out the administration of the site, enabling the customer aspects of the site to be scaled without also scaling the administration aspects.

The first tasks are to develop a JAX-RS RESTful microservice to provide the necessary administration endpoints, and to develop a new UI for it by using ReactJS. For those already familiar with JAX-RS, you'll see some repetition of prior knowledge.

Figure 2.4 is the current administration interface for Cayambe. Viewing or updating categories in the UI isn't possible except for the main category Transportation.

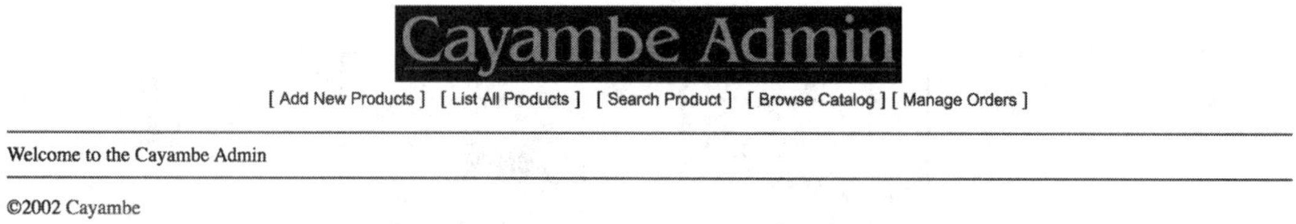

[Add New Products]   [List All Products]   [Search Product]   [Browse Catalog] [Manage Orders]

Welcome to the Cayambe Admin

©2002 Cayambe

Figure 2.4   Old Cayambe administration interface

This is far from an ideal situation, so you'll begin by developing a new administration site and microservice to handle managing the product categories.

Figure 2.5 shows the new administration interface with ReactJS, along with the category data displayed as a tree.

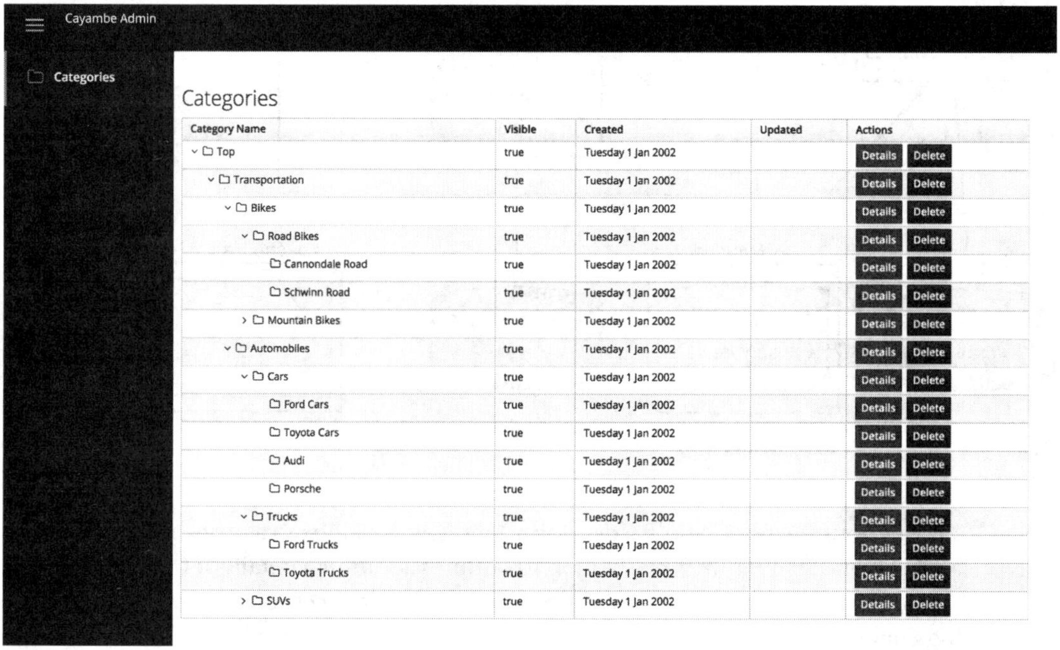

Categories				
Category Name	Visible	Created	Updated	Actions
⌄ ☐ Top	true	Tuesday 1 Jan 2002		Details Delete
⌄ ☐ Transportation	true	Tuesday 1 Jan 2002		Details Delete
⌄ ☐ Bikes	true	Tuesday 1 Jan 2002		Details Delete
⌄ ☐ Road Bikes	true	Tuesday 1 Jan 2002		Details Delete
☐ Cannondale Road	true	Tuesday 1 Jan 2002		Details Delete
☐ Schwinn Road	true	Tuesday 1 Jan 2002		Details Delete
› ☐ Mountain Bikes	true	Tuesday 1 Jan 2002		Details Delete
⌄ ☐ Automobiles	true	Tuesday 1 Jan 2002		Details Delete
⌄ ☐ Cars	true	Tuesday 1 Jan 2002		Details Delete
☐ Ford Cars	true	Tuesday 1 Jan 2002		Details Delete
☐ Toyota Cars	true	Tuesday 1 Jan 2002		Details Delete
☐ Audi	true	Tuesday 1 Jan 2002		Details Delete
☐ Porsche	true	Tuesday 1 Jan 2002		Details Delete
⌄ ☐ Trucks	true	Tuesday 1 Jan 2002		Details Delete
☐ Ford Trucks	true	Tuesday 1 Jan 2002		Details Delete
☐ Toyota Trucks	true	Tuesday 1 Jan 2002		Details Delete
› ☐ SUVs	true	Tuesday 1 Jan 2002		Details Delete

Cayambe Admin — Categories

Figure 2.5   New Cayambe administration interface

Figure 2.6 shows where the RESTful microservice you're developing in this chapter will fit into the new Cayambe architecture when you're finished with the book.

Let's dive into creating the RESTful microservice you need in order to enable the new interface to work.

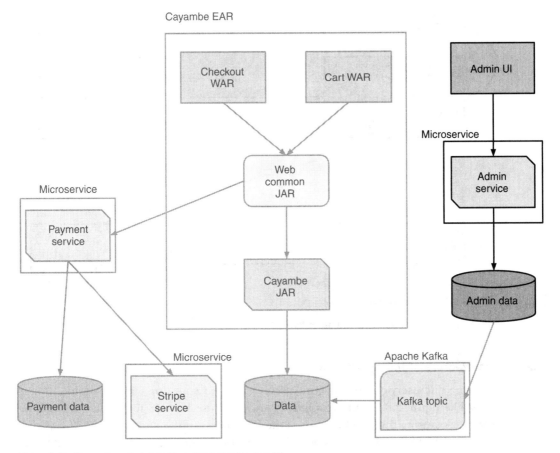

Figure 2.6 Cayambe administration microservice and UI

2.2.1 Use cases

For this chapter, you'll focus on developing the category management parts of the administration, but you'll want to migrate the other aspects from the previous administration site at some point as well. Doing so simplifies what you're learning to a single problem domain instead of many, focusing on the code required to make category management possible.

As part of category management, you need to support Create, Read, Update, and Delete (CRUD) operations on the categories. This process certainly isn't the most interesting part of developing RESTful endpoints, but most services will need some type of CRUD at their core.

The UI will call the CRUD operations on the microservice for maintaining categories. The microservice RESTful endpoints could be called from any client, but you'll show them operating with your UI. Figure 2.7 details the states and transitions between them for managing the categories within the UI.

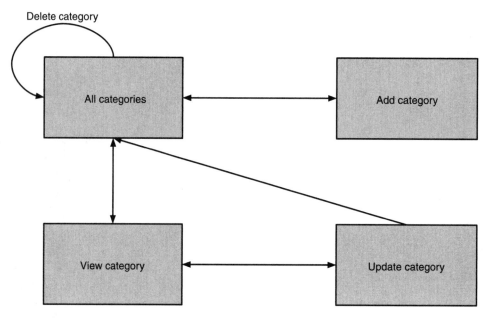

Figure 2.7   Category management state flow

2.2.2   *Architecture of the application*

Ignoring microservices for now, the architecture for your application will look something like figure 2.8. At the *presentation layer,* you use ReactJS for the UI, though we won't be covering the development of the UI as part of this chapter. The *API layer* contains the RESTful endpoints using JAX-RS for the category. Finally, you have JPA entities of the category in your *data layer* that interacts with the physical database. The API layer is responsible for interacting with the data layer to persist record updates.

You could've separated the API layer and used services within a business layer on top of the data layer, but I chose to simplify it by removing an unnecessary layer. Typically, all these layers would be packaged within a single WAR for deployment to an application server.

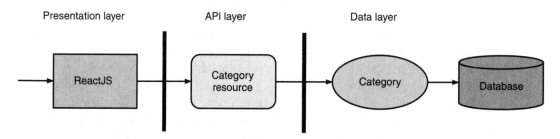

Figure 2.8   Category management architecture

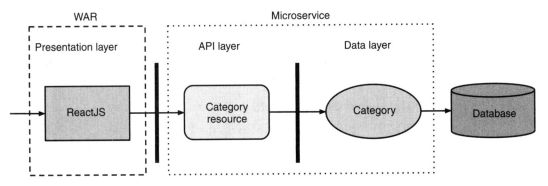

Figure 2.9 Category management microservice architecture

How does the architecture change when you shift to constructing a microservice? See figure 2.9.

Here you can see that your server-side layers are encompassed in a single microservice. Your UI then sits in its own WAR to package and deploy the UI to a separate runtime. The application architecture is now split into separate deployable pieces: the UI, a microservice, and a database.

> **NOTE** On this occasion, you choose to package the UI as a WAR, but because it's solely HTML/CSS/JS, you could've used any means for packaging and deploying static sites.

Because you've split your UI and services into separate runtimes, you need to add support for *cross-origin resource sharing* (CORS). If you don't, the browser will prevent the UI from making an HTTP request to the microservice. To do that, your microservice needs a filter.

Listing 2.1 CORSFilter

```
@Provider
public class CORSFilter implements ContainerResponseFilter {

    @Override
    public void filter(ContainerRequestContext requestContext,
            ContainerResponseContext responseContext) throws IOException {
        responseContext.getHeaders().add("Access-Control-Allow-Origin", "*");
        responseContext.getHeaders()
            .add("Access-Control-Allow-Headers", "origin, content-type, accept,
    authorization");
        responseContext.getHeaders().add("Access-Control-Allow-Credentials",
    "true");
        responseContext.getHeaders()
            .add("Access-Control-Allow-Methods", "GET, POST, PUT, DELETE, OPTIONS,
    HEAD");
        responseContext.getHeaders().add("Access-Control-Max-Age", "1209600");
    }
}
```

TIP   Keep in mind where a UI retrieves data from, and whether CORS needs to be taken into account. Not doing so can easily lead to frustrating UI bugs when RESTful calls fail for seemingly no reason. On the flip side, if your UI is using an API gateway to interact with microservices, the API gateway could offer configuration to handle CORS directly as opposed to in a microservice.

2.2.3   Creating RESTful endpoints with JAX-RS

To keep the microservice simple, you'll focus on the RESTful endpoint, the API layer, and ignore the development of the JPA entities you need for the database. You'll assume that another kind developer has already written them for you! Rest assured that this kind developer has made them available in the project code.

In addition to the JPA entities, the developer has provided a convenient `load.sql` file containing initial categories that will be used on startup to populate the database.

Figure 2.10 shows what you'll be developing in this section. The code for this section can be found in the /chapter2/admin directory of the book's example code.

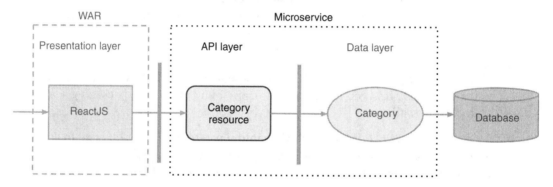

Figure 2.10   Category management—API layer

In this section, you'll develop `CategoryResource`. Your `CategoryResource` will focus on making the CRUD-style operations for category data available from RESTful endpoints. It specifies that the RESTful `@Path` for the controller is /category. You define `EntityManager` to be injected with CDI, which then provides a way to perform operations on the database.

NOTE   Though many would argue CRUD isn't appropriate for RESTful services, it's often used that way by developers as a means of bolting RESTful onto existing CRUD. Many levels of REST also are defined by Leonard Richardson in the Richardson Maturity Model. Hypermedia as the Engine of Application State (HATEOAS) is the most complex and difficult level within the model. The examples in this book don't conform to the HATEOAS level of REST, mostly because it's not what many enterprise developers are familiar with in their regular work. Take a look at http://mng.bz/vMPk and https://restfulapi.net/richardson-maturity-model/ for further information on the maturity model.

By default, all JAX-RS resource instances are active only on a per-request basis. If you don't change that, every request will spend time creating the necessary `EntityManager` instance to be injected. That doesn't have a huge performance impact, but if you can avoid it, you should. To avoid the re-creation of `EntityManager`, you need to mark it as `@ApplicationScoped`. This tells the runtime that you want `CategoryResource` to have its lifecycle managed by CDI, and not by JAX-RS. You need to define a JAX-RS application class to define the root path for your microservice.

Listing 2.2 `AdminApplication`

```
@ApplicationPath("/admin")                          ⟵┐  Defines the RESTful URL for
public class AdminApplication extends Application {  │  the root of the application
}
```

That's all you need to do for this class. Because you're asking CDI to manage the lifecycle of `CategoryResource`, you don't need to configure any singletons within JAX-RS. Now it's time to develop the RESTful endpoints you need for CRUD operations of your categories.

VIEWING ALL CATEGORIES

The main screen for your application is a tree of categories. Populating the list on the screen requires a RESTful endpoint to retrieve all the categories from the database.

Listing 2.3 `@GET` on `CategoryResource`

```
                   @Path("/")
   @GET            public class CategoryResource {
indicates that
the method            @PersistenceContext(unitName = "AdminPU")
will accept           private EntityManager em;
only HTTP
GET requests.         @GET
                      @Path("/categorytree")
                      @Produces(MediaType.APPLICATION_JSON)
   Finds the          public CategoryTree tree() throws Exception {
CategoryTree              return em.find(CategoryTree.class, 1);
instance with         }
primary key of 1
using the injected     . . .
EntityManager     }
```

Specifies the particular persistence unit, AdminPU, that you want an EntityManager for

RESTful URL to the endpoint is set as /categorytree.

Indicates that the method returns data that has been marshaled to JSON

Returns a CategoryTree as the root category. All other categories will be retrieved as children of the root.

DELETING A CATEGORY

After you have a category, you need the ability to delete an old one that isn't used. For that, you need to add a RESTful endpoint for deleting a category from the database as shown in listing 2.4.

Listing 2.4   @DELETE on `CategoryResource`

Requires a transaction to be present when executing this endpoint

```
@Path("/")
public class CategoryResource {
    ...

    @DELETE                                                    ◁─────  @DELETE indicates the
    @Produces(MediaType.APPLICATION_JSON)                              method will accept only
    @Path("/category/{categoryId}")                            ◁──     HTTP DELETE requests.
    @Transactional
    public Response remove(@PathParam("categoryId") Integer categoryId)
    throws Exception {
        try {
            Category entity = em.find(Category.class, categoryId);
            em.remove(entity);                                 ◁──
        } catch (Exception e) {
            return Response
                    .serverError()
                    .entity(e.getMessage())
                    .build();                                  ◁──
        }

        return Response
                .noContent()
                .build();                                      ◁──
    }

    ...
}
```

@DELETE indicates the method will accept only HTTP DELETE requests.

Defines that the method accepts a parameter and gives it a name of categoryId

Finds the Category instance based on the categoryId you received as a parameter

Removes the Category instance from being persisted

If you encountered an exception, returns a server error containing the exception message using JAX-RS Response

Returns an empty response if the Category was successfully deleted

ADDING A CATEGORY

Sometimes new categories need to be added. For that, you have a RESTful endpoint to add a new category into your database.

Listing 2.5   @POST on `CategoryResource`

The method also returns a Category that's marshaled to JSON.

```
@Path("/")
public class CategoryResource {
    ...

    @POST                                                      ◁─────  @POST indicates the
    @Path("/category")                                                 method will accept only
    @Consumes(MediaType.APPLICATION_JSON)                      ◁──     HTTP POST requests.
    @Produces(MediaType.APPLICATION_JSON)
    @Transactional
    public Response create(Category category) throws Exception {
```

@POST indicates the method will accept only HTTP POST requests.

Indicates that the method will accept only JSON that can be marshaled to a Category instance

```
                                              If the Category has an ID set,
                                              returns a 409 response status to
                                              indicate a conflict with the record
                                              attempting to be created
    if (category.getId() != null) {     ◁───┘
        return Response
                .status(Response.Status.CONFLICT)
                .entity("Unable to create Category, id was already set.")
                .build();
    }

    try {                                  Persists the new Category
        em.persist(category);         ◁───┘ into the database
    } catch (Exception e) {
        return Response
                .serverError()
                .entity(e.getMessage())
                .build();
    }
    return Response
            .created(new URI(category.getId().toString()))
            .build();                    ◁───┐
}                                             As part of the Response, sets the
                                              location path to the new Category
    ...                                       with its identifier
}
```

In addition, the `CategoryResource` has RESTful endpoints defined to retrieve and update a category. The code for the additional methods is available in the chapter 2 source.

2.2.4 *Running it*

Although you've indicated that your RESTful endpoint is an administration microservice, nothing in the code you've developed prevents it from being built as a WAR and deployed to an application server.

Because you're dealing with a UI communicating with only a single microservice, there isn't any difference between that and existing Enterprise Java development with WARs. The upside to the similarity is that migrating existing Enterprise Java code into a microservice is easier if no code changes are required for a microservice producer.

To give more of a microservice feel for our example, you'll package it as an uber jar with Thorntail. Thorntail offers an alternative approach to packaging your applications as a WAR or EAR and then deploying to a full Java EE application server. It allows you to choose the parts you need from WildFly and package them into an uber jar that can be run from the command line. Chapter 3 covers the features of Thorntail in detail. To run the microservice, you need to add the plugin in listing 2.6 to your pom.xml.

Listing 2.6   Maven plugin configuration

```
<plugin>
  <groupId>io.thorntail</groupId>
  <artifactId>thorntail-maven-plugin</artifactId>
  <version>${version.thorntail}</version>                    ⟵— Latest version of Thorntail
  <executions>
    <execution>
      <id>package</id>
      <goals>                                    ⌐ Run the package goal of
        <goal>package</goal>              ⟵—┘ the plugin when executed.
      </goals>
    </execution>
  </executions>
  <configuration>                                      ⌐ Specify a port offset of 1
    <properties>                                       │ so your microservice will
      <thorntail.port.offset>1</thorntail.port.offset>  ⟵—┘ start on port 8081.
    </properties>
  </configuration>
</plugin>
```

That's all you need to do to provide a way to run the microservice from the directory, as well as package it as an uber jar. So how and what do you run? Two pieces need to be run: one for the UI and one for the microservice. If you wanted to execute tests against the RESTful endpoints directly, without using the UI, you need to start only the microservice.

STARTING THE MICROSERVICE

Open a terminal, or command window, and navigate to the /chapter2/admin directory of the book example code. From that directory, run this:

```
mvn thorntail:run
```

This starts the administration microservice containing your RESTful endpoints. After the log shows that the microservice is deployed, you can go to a browser and open it to http://localhost:8081/admin/category. Your browser will load the category data and display it in JSON format. Now that you know the microservice is running, let's run the UI.

STARTING THE UI

Open a terminal and navigate to the /chapter2/ui directory of the book's example code. From that directory, run the following:

```
mvn package
java -jar target/chapter2-ui-thorntail.jar
```

This packages the UI in an uber jar, and then starts the uber jar that contains a web server with the UI code only. After the log shows that it's deployed, you can go to a browser and open it to the following:

```
http://localhost:8080
```

Your browser will load the UI containing the Cayambe category data, as shown previously in figure 2.5. Both the microservice and UI can be stopped by pressing Ctrl-C in each terminal window.

Summary

- You can develop a category management microservice with JAX-RS.
- RESTful microservices can easily be created with Enterprise Java.
- Developing RESTful endpoints doesn't change between Enterprise Java and a microservice.
- Enterprise Java experience is easily transferable to developing Enterprise Java microservices.

Just enough Application Server for microservices

This chapter covers

- What is Just enough Application Server?
- What is MicroProfile?
- What runtimes support JeAS?
- How do JeAS runtimes compare?

This chapter explores the ideas behind Just enough Application Server (JeAS) and the runtime options that we as developers have for developing Enterprise Java microservices using JeAS. We'll begin by defining JeAS and how it compares to Java EE. To aid in the discussion, a hypothetical microservice, requiring several specifications, will be described so its needs may be evaluated against what the various JeAS runtimes offer. As part of the comparison, we'll detail each of the JeAS runtimes and how they differ as we develop a Beach Vacation shopping application.

3.1 Just enough Application Server

The term *Just enough Application Server* has been used occasionally over the years, but usually in relation to customizing a full application server by removing functionality manually. Only since the popularity of microservices has JeAS become *crucial* for Enterprise Java. This section covers what JeAS means, its benefits, and what an example developed in each of the JeAS runtimes looks like.

3.1.1 What does JeAS mean?

Say you need to develop a microservice that interacts with an enterprise information system (EIS), such as SAP, to retrieve Human Resources (HR) information on employees. For this microservice, you've chosen to use JAX-RS, CDI, and JMS. If you were to develop such a microservice for deployment onto a typical Java EE application server, it'd most likely be done against the full Java EE platform, as illustrated in figure 3.1.

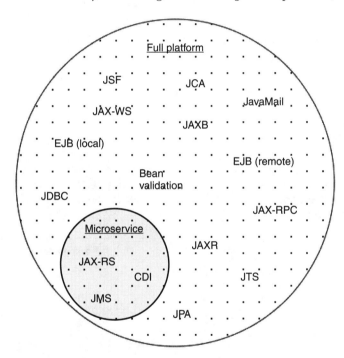

Figure 3.1 Microservice specification usage of full Java EE platform

As you can see, there are lots of specifications within the full platform that you're not using, but they're still there even though you don't require them. The full platform has 33 JSRs included within it. That's a lot of specifications that you may not always need.

Maybe there's a Java EE profile you can use to slim it down? You have only one option right now. Let's try the Web Profile and see how that works; see figure 3.2.

That results in fewer unused specifications, but now you have the problem that JMS isn't part of the Web Profile. You can still add an implementation of JMS to your microservice as part of the deployment, but it's no longer automatically part of the stack and may require additional configuration that you didn't need with the full platform.

What's the answer? Can JeAS help? And what exactly is Just enough Application Server? In a nutshell, JeAS inverts the relationship between an application server and an application, ensuring that you package only the parts of an application server that your application requires. In the case of our preceding microservice example, you know that you need JMS, so you choose the full platform of an application server. But you know your application will never use large parts of that application server.

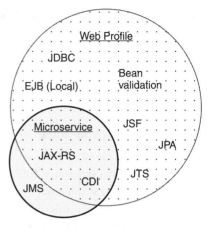

Figure 3.2   Microservice specification usage of Java EE Web Profile

Java EE profiles

Since Java EE 6, we've had one profile and the full platform available for developers to choose as their application server. Although you may not be familiar with these options, the following provides an overview of which specifications the full platform and Web Profile contain.

Feature	Web Profile	Full platform
EJB (Local)	✔	✔
JTS/JTA	✔	✔
Clustering	✔	✔
Servlet	✔	✔
JSF	✔	✔
JPA	✔	✔
JBDC	✔	✔
CDI	✔	✔
Bean validation	✔	✔
JAX-RS	✔	✔

(table continued)

Feature	Web Profile	Full platform
JSON-P	✔	✔
EJB (remote)		✔
JCA		✔
JAX-WS		✔
JAXB		✔
JMS		✔
JavaMail		✔
JAX-RPC		✔
JAXR		✔

Many application servers provide the flexibility to slim down their distribution by removing components and their associated configuration. I've worked with many customers in the past who have taken this approach. But finding the correct combination that still ensures that the application server functions properly requires somewhat of a trial-and-error approach. In some cases, there may even be a component that you'd like to remove but can't, usually because that component is a key part of the application server.

Customizing an application server for many different applications quickly devolves into a complex set of differing configurations that need to be managed and maintained. In these situations, developers typically prefer to simplify their lives and choose the full platform as opposed to spending time trying to slim the application server. They opt to accept the extra overhead that comes with not using all components of the application server.

Over the years, several application servers, such as WildFly, have worked to reduce the footprint of components that aren't being used. Though the dependencies required for various components are still on the classpath, the application server is clever enough to not load those classes into memory if the deployed applications don't require them. This can go only so far, unfortunately, because many components are too central to the functioning of the application server, no matter what an application might require.

So where does JeAS fit in with your microservices architecture from figure 1.4? Take a look at figure 3.3.

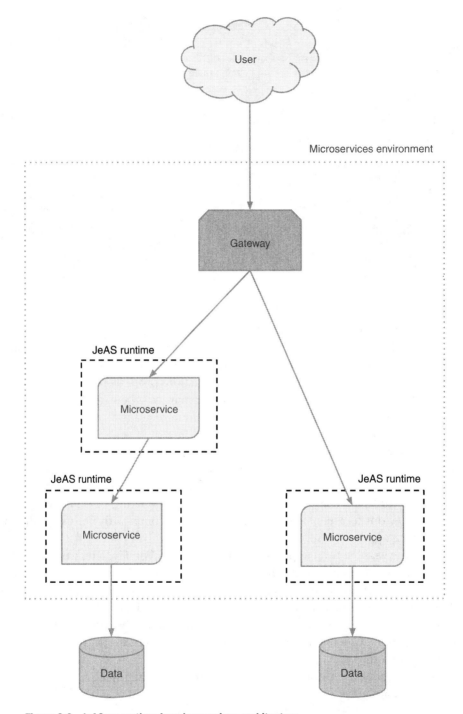

Figure 3.3   JeAS as runtime for microservices architecture

As you can see, the focus of JeAS is on the runtime needed for a microservice. A JeAS runtime aims to provide a whittled-down application server for microservices, but the way it's packaged can differ among implementations.

JeAS runtimes provide a simple and manageable way to include only the parts of an application server that your application requires. Some runtimes are more flexible than others in terms of what's included, and we'll cover those details shortly.

Which JeAS runtime is chosen can impact the packaging available to a microservice. The driving factor, however, should always be about what's supported by a JeAS runtime and not how it needs to be packaged.

3.1.2 *What are the benefits?*

In your SAP microservice from the previous section, you saw how painful it can be when your application relies on the smaller-footprint Web Profile. It requires you to bring in additional libraries and configure them to work with the rest of the application server.

As developers, we want to spend our time effectively, developing new features or fixing bugs. We don't want to spend it endlessly configuring application servers based on differing requirements between applications. More often than not, we'd choose the full platform for the sake of simplicity.

What's the big deal with using the full platform? Sure, there are lots of parts you may not use today, but you plan to one day, right? Certainly, in some cases an application will grow to include the use of one, or maybe two, additional specifications that weren't part of the original design. It's highly doubtful that an application would suddenly grow to include all specifications of the full platform. If it does, there's likely a need to redesign the application, because it contains too many features for a single application. So that leaves a large part of a full platform application server unused.

Wouldn't it be nice if application servers weren't *one size fits all?* This is one of the use cases that JeAS aims to solve, by allowing the developer to choose which features, or specifications, of an application server are required for a given application.

Why does that matter? If an application needs only servlets, it can be deployed to a JeAS runtime that has only servlets available for an application. With a JeAS runtime, if an application needs to add a feature, such as JAX-RS, a developer can choose to add that feature into the JeAS runtime as a standalone piece. It's no longer necessary to choose between only two Java EE options, or attempt to customize the application server yourself.

This flexibility means that JeAS runtimes have great benefits:

- *Reduced package size*—When compared against an application bundled with the application server it's deployed to.
- *Reduction in allocated memory*—How reduced will depend on many factors, such as the number of classes that are no longer being loaded.

- *Reduced security footprint*—Fewer ports are being opened for various features, and fewer services are running. In addition, you have a significantly reduced surface area for potential critical vulnerabilities (CVEs).
- *Greater separation between applications*—Many applications were usually deployed to a single application server.
- *Simplified upgrades*—The upgrade impacts a single application only.

Greater separation between applications can mean a great many things, so it warrants additional explanation. Over the years that Enterprise Java applications have been deployed into production, an application server rarely would contain a single application. Typically, an application server would be running anywhere from a handful to dozens of applications in a single instance.

As you can see in figure 3.4, JeAS runtimes provide a greater isolation between different microservices than applications in a traditional Java EE application server.

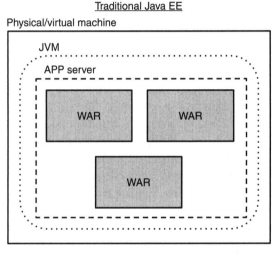

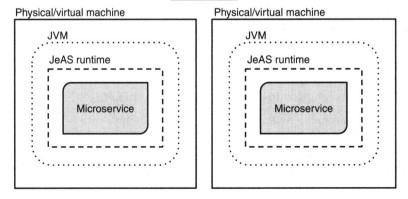

Figure 3.4 Traditional Java EE vs. JeAS runtimes

Why was this the case? Historically, the biggest reason is cost—and not just the cost of the application server, which usually wasn't cheap, but all the physical hardware that was required to run a single application server. Certainly, over the last decade, with improved virtual machines and the rise of containers in recent years, the amount of required physical hardware for production environments has dropped significantly— and along with it, the cost of production environments for enterprises.

With JeAS runtimes, it's possible, ignoring containers for now, to run many instances of them on a single piece of physical hardware. Each JeAS runtime running in its own process is isolated from the others, preventing a common problem of collocated applications in an application server: namely, that one application failure causes the whole application server, and all applications running on it, to fail in an unrecoverable manner.

3.1.3 Eclipse MicroProfile

For anyone following developments in the landscape of Enterprise Java and microservices over the last couple of years, you've likely heard about Eclipse MicroProfile. It's a community initiative to "optimize Enterprise Java for microservices" that was formed with collaboration from Red Hat, IBM, Tomitribe, Payara, and the London Java Community. Since its initial formation, the community has moved to the Eclipse Foundation.

From the first release with JAX-RS, CDI, and JSON-P forming the base Java EE technologies, we've now surpassed version 1.3, including eight new MicroProfile specifications over those versions so far. Table 3.1 details the specifications included in each MicroProfile release.

Table 3.1 MicroProfile specifications in each release

Specification	1.0 (Sep 2016)	1.1 (July 2017)	1.2 (Sep 2017)	1.3 (Jan 2018)
JAX-RS	✔	✔	✔	✔
CDI	✔	✔	✔	✔
JSON-P	✔	✔	✔	✔
Config		✔	✔	✔
Fault tolerance			✔	✔
JWT propagation			✔	✔
Metrics			✔	✔
Health check			✔	✔
Open tracing				✔
Open API				✔
Type-safe REST client				✔

The community has an aim of providing a new release roughly every quarter. The project has done well to hold closely to that schedule, though a delay occurred after the 1.0 release for the project submission to the Eclipse Foundation. Time was needed for all existing project code and documentation to be reviewed by the Eclipse Foundation, as is required by the foundation.

Eclipse MicroProfile creates specifications for Enterprise Java microservices, with the benefit that microservices become portable between JeAS runtimes that support Eclipse MicroProfile. There will certainly be JeAS runtimes that don't implement the specifications, and those that provide more flexibility than is defined. The goal isn't to cover every possible use case for Enterprise Java microservice development, but to collaborate on what an opinionated stack should contain that covers the majority of use cases.

Over the last 18 months, the MicroProfile community has delivered functionality for solving the problems of Enterprise Java, microservices, and the cloud. It has done so in a collaborative and inclusive manner, with more individual contributors and vendors joining the effort as it moves forward.

3.2 *Choosing Just enough Application Server*

Now it's time to evaluate a handful of the most popular runtimes for Enterprise Java microservices. You'll follow the development of a simple microservice example application to show the differences among the frameworks, both in the way the code differs and in the sets of features that each framework brings to the table.

The full code of the example application for each runtime is available in the source code for this book (https://github.com/kenfinnigan/ejm-samples).

3.2.1 *Beach Vacation example application*

Our Beach Vacation example application will be a simple shopping cart that has a RESTful interface and a single class representing an item in the cart. You'll pre-populate the contents of the shopping cart with items that everyone needs on a beach vacation! To keep it simple, you'll store only a name and quantity in your `CartItem`.

Listing 3.1 `CartItem`

```
public class CartItem {
    private String itemName;          ⟵── Name of the item.

    private Integer itemQuantity;     ⟵── Quantity to be bought.

    public CartItem(String name, Integer qty) {     ⟵┐ Construct an instance
        this.itemName = name;                          of CartItem with the
        this.itemQuantity = qty;                       provided name and
    }                                                  quantity.

    public String getItemName() {
        return itemName;
    }
```

```
    public CartItem itemName(String itemName) {
        this.itemName = itemName;
        return this;
    }

    public Integer getItemQuantity() {
        return itemQuantity;
    }

    public CartItem itemQuantity(Integer itemQuantity) {
        this.itemQuantity = itemQuantity;
        return this;
    }

    public CartItem increaseQuantity(Integer itemQuantity) {    ◁
        this.itemQuantity = this.itemQuantity + itemQuantity;
        return this;
    }
}
```

> **Convenience method for increasing the quantity by a specified amount**

The other piece you need is your RESTful interface. In keeping it simple, you won't be using a database to store items; the data will be held in memory only. Your `Cart-Controller` will initialize a list of items for you to use as a base for the shopping cart. Listing 3.2 is your controller code at its simplest so you can see exactly what each framework requires within the class and methods later. It provides three methods that you'll make available over REST: `all()`, `addOrUpdateItem()`, and `getItem()`. The `addOrUpdateItem()` method is the most complicated, because it handles adding quantity to an existing item in the cart or adding an entirely new item.

Listing 3.2 `CartController`

```
public class CartController {
    private static List<CartItem> items = new ArrayList<>();

    static {                                                  ◁
        items.add(new CartItem("sunscreen", 3));
        items.add(new CartItem("towel", 1));
        items.add(new CartItem("hat", 5));
        items.add(new CartItem("umbrella", 1));
    }

    public List<CartItem> all() throws Exception {
        return items;                                         ◁
    }

    public String addOrUpdateItem(String itemName, Integer qty) throws
      Exception {
        Optional<CartItem> item = items.stream()
                .filter(i -> i.getItemName().equalsIgnoreCase(itemName))
                .findFirst();                                 ◁
```

> **Populates the cart with commonly required items for a beach vacation**

> **Returns all the current items in the cart**

> **Streams all the cart items to find one whose name matches**

```
        if (item.isPresent()) {                ⟵  Checks whether you found an item by
            Integer total =                        name. If yes, then update the quantity.
    item.get().increaseQuantity(qty).getItemQuantity();
            return "Updated quantity of '" + itemName + "' to " + total;
        }
                                                 ⟵  Item wasn't found
        items.add(new CartItem(itemName, qty));      in cart, so add it.
        return "Added '" + itemName + "' to shopping cart";
    }

    public CartItem getItem(String itemName) throws Exception {
        return items.stream()
                .filter(i -> i.getItemName().equalsIgnoreCase(itemName))
                .findFirst()
                .get();              ⟵  Filters all cart items to find the
    }                                    one whose name matches
}
```

Now you've covered the two main classes you'll need for your Beach Vacation shopping application. In the following sections, you'll update these two classes for each JeAS runtime based on their particular requirements.

> **NOTE** The following examples don't always follow the proper use of REST HTTP verbs and semantics. The examples illustrate a comparison of the runtimes, rather than proper REST patterns.

3.2.2 *Dropwizard—the original opinionated Microservice runtime*

Dropwizard provides a small JeAS runtime by being opinionated about what developers need in order to build a microservice. For Dropwizard, that means the following:

- Eclipse Jetty as an HTTP server
- Jersey for RESTful endpoints
- Jackson for transforming data to/from JSON
- Hibernate Validator
- Dropwizard Metrics to provide insight into code behavior in production

Dropwizard provides additional libraries to make it easier to develop a microservice, in addition to the preceding ones. Check out www.dropwizard.io for the full list.

If your application requires libraries that Dropwizard doesn't include for you, you need to add the necessary Maven dependencies to your project, adding whatever configuration those libraries might require as well.

> **NOTE** Dropwizard began in early 2011 and was the first project to put together an opinionated JeAS runtime for microservices. Dropwizard has now surpassed version 1.3.0.

Let's go back to the sample microservice we talked about earlier that uses JAX-RS, CDI, and JMS. Figure 3.5 shows what the microservice looks like with Dropwizard.

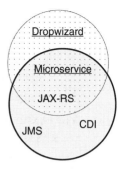

When developing microservices that use more than just JAX-RS from Java EE, it's obvious that everything else you need must be added and integrated. Though this is possible, it may not be the most practical option because it requires a lot more initial project setup before being able to develop any code.

It's for this reason that Thorntail, not Dropwizard, is my preferred runtime for Enterprise Java microservices. Dropwizard covers only a small portion of what would be required. This is especially true when converting existing Enterprise

Figure 3.5 Microservice usage in Dropwizard

Java applications into microservices, because you don't want to have to rewrite all the code to use different technologies. Ideally, you want to take an existing application and package it in a different manner for use with a JeAS runtime.

Back to our Beach Vacation shopping cart, let's create your Dropwizard project by generating a project with the Maven archetype:

```
mvn archetype:generate -DarchetypeGroupId=io.dropwizard.archetypes
➥ -DarchetypeArtifactId=java-simple -DarchetypeVersion=1.0.9
```

Now that you have your project, let's modify the basic code so it can be used with Dropwizard. The first change is easy: adding a default constructor to your `CartItem` bean.

Your `CartController` needs modification to make it RESTful. First you need to define the RESTful path that your controller will be accessible from.

Listing 3.3 `CartController` RESTful path

```
@Path("/")
public class CartController {
}
```

Now you need to add the JAX-RS annotations to your methods.

Listing 3.4 `CartController` methods with annotations

```
@GET
@Produces(MediaType.APPLICATION_JSON)           ⬅  Indicates that the
public List<CartItem> all() throws Exception {}    method supports only
                                                   HTTP GET requests

@GET
@Path("/add")               ⬅— Endpoint is accessible as /add.      Method parameters
public String addOrUpdateItem(                                      that will be passed
    @QueryParam("item") String itemName,                           on the URL, such as
    @QueryParam("qty") Integer qty) throws Exception {  ⬅—┘        /add?item=hat&qty=2
}
```

```
@GET
@Produces(MediaType.APPLICATION_JSON)
@Path("/get/{itemName}")
public CartItem getItem(
    @PathParam("itemName") String itemName) throws Exception {  ◁
}
```

Parameter defined as part of the URL path, /get/hat.

The JAX-RS annotations you've added have no surprises, because they're regularly used for RESTful endpoints. Your three methods are all annotated with `@GET`. The `all()` and `getItem()` methods both produce JSON output, so you've added `@Produces` to indicate the correct media type for JSON. The `addOrUpdateItem()` method is accessible with a URL path of /add, and you add the necessary `@QueryParam` definitions to your method parameters. It maps URL query string parameters into your method parameters on invocation based on the name you pass to `@QueryParam`. Finally, `getItem()` specifies a URL path that defines the path parameter `@Path("/get/{itemName}")`, which is then passed to your method by setting `@PathParam("itemName")` on the parameter.

> **NOTE** `CartController.addOrUpdateItem()` is defined with `@GET`, which does break normal RESTful semantics; it isn't an idempotent operation, because you're modifying data. But I've taken this route purely for simplicity, because your object model has only two fields and it enables you to call the endpoint directly from a browser URL, removing the need to use `curl` or browser extensions to `POST` data for testing.

Now you need to add custom classes so that Dropwizard knows what to run and how it's configured. First, you need to create a configuration class that specifies any environment-specific parameters that your application requires. In this example, you're not worried about environment parameters, so the class can be empty.

Listing 3.5 Chapter3Configuration

```
public class Chapter3Configuration extends Configuration {
}
```

Finally, you need to extend `Application` from Dropwizard so you can specify what needs to be run.

Listing 3.6 Chapter3Application

```
public class Chapter3Application extends Application<Chapter3Configuration> {

    public static void main(final String[] args) throws Exception {     ◁
        new Chapter3Application().run(args);
    }

    @Override
    public String getName() {
```

Used by Dropwizard to start your application.

```
        return "chapter3";
    }

    @Override
    public void initialize(final Bootstrap<Chapter3Configuration> bootstrap) {
    }

    @Override
    public void run(final Chapter3Configuration configuration,
                    final Environment environment) {
        final CartController resource = new CartController();
        environment.jersey().register(resource);
    }
}
```

> **Configure any parts of the application that need to be set up before it's run.**

> **Register an instance of your RESTful endpoint with Jersey.**

Now that you've built the application, how can you run it? By creating the project with the Maven archetype, it has added the necessary plugins to build an uber jar. The only thing you need to do is ensure that the plugins in pom.xml reference the application class you created on any configuration that needs `mainClass`. Now build the application:

```
mvn clean package
```

and run the application:

```
java -jar target/chapter3-dropwizard-1.0-SNAPSHOT.jar server
```

It's now possible to access the application by going to http://localhost:8080/ in a browser. This returns the list of current items in the cart. You can look at the details of hat in your cart by navigating to http://localhost:8080/get/hat. Update the quantity of an existing item with http://localhost:8080/add?item=towel&qty=1 or add a new item to your cart with http://localhost:8080/add?item=kite&qty=2.

Dropwizard has many other features that we didn't cover here, such as Metrics and Health Checks, so check out www.dropwizard.io/1.0.0/docs/index.html for further information.

3.2.3 *Payara Micro—slimmed Java EE app server in a JAR*

Payara Micro is similar to Dropwizard in that it provides an opinionated JeAS runtime where the stack is defined. Any additional libraries that you want to be used need to be added to the application directly.

Payara Micro also has a different deployment model than the other runtimes you'll look at, as Payara provides a distribution that can be executed directly. Payara's distribution is like a prebuilt application server, except that it can be started with `java -jar payara-micro.jar` and given a WAR to deploy with `--deploy myApp.war` as part of the same command. Without `--deploy`, the distribution starts up just as a normal application server, but with nothing deployed.

NOTE   Payara Micro came out of the work that Payara was doing in providing fixes and enhancements to GlassFish v4.x via its Payara Server. Payara Micro was first released in May 2015 as a subset of Payara Server. Payara Micro has now surpassed version 5.181.

There are certainly advantages to having a distribution that you deploy your application to, as in a traditional application server. The biggest advantage is that the Payara Micro distribution can be used as a Docker layer. This makes it possible to create a Docker image containing that layer, which can then be used many times to package different applications with Docker.

The major downside to this type of JeAS runtime is that it isn't possible to remove additional pieces. For instance, if your application requires only servlets, there's no way to remove parts such as JAX-RS. The advantages of this approach might outweigh such a downside, but that's a decision for an enterprise to make based on its situation. We'll cover a more flexible approach to JeAS a bit later.

What does Payara Micro provide? Figure 3.6 compares the Payara Micro distribution with the Web Profile.

Let's take a look at how your JAX-RS, CDI, JMS microservice uses Payara Micro; see figure 3.7.

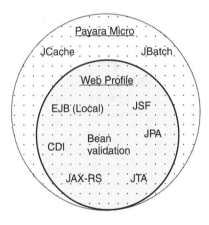

Figure 3.6   Payara Micro compared to Web Profile

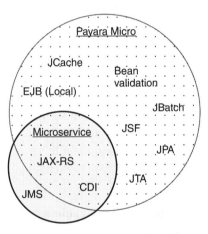

Figure 3.7   Microservice usage in Payara Micro

Because Payara Micro doesn't include the JMS specification, you need to add an implementation to your microservice yourself. This isn't a major issue, but needing to include additional implementations is easier if they're already provided in a distribution. But then you're back to the problem of application server pieces being present but not used.

To create your Payara Micro project, you create a regular Maven WAR project as if you were developing a Java EE application that was being deployed to an application server. You can add a Maven dependency

```
<dependency>
  <groupId>javax</groupId>
  <artifactId>javaee-web-api</artifactId>
  <version>7.0</version>
  <scope>provided</scope>
</dependency>
```

and gain access to all the APIs that your application may require.

Because you also want to use JAXB, with Jackson, you need to add the following dependency:

```
<dependency>
  <groupId>org.glassfish.jersey.media</groupId>
  <artifactId>jersey-media-json-jackson</artifactId>
  <version>2.23.1</version>
</dependency>
```

Now that you have your project, let's modify the basic code so it can be used with Payara Micro. For the `CartItem` bean, you need to identify it as being mappable to JAXB, create a default constructor, and use properly named setter methods.

Listing 3.7 `CartItem` with JAXB mappings

```
@XmlRootElement                              ◁──┐ Enables Java class as
public class CartItem {                          │ JAXB mapping element
    public CartItem() {
    }
    ...
    public CartItem setItemName(String itemName) {
        this.itemName = itemName;
        return this;
    }                                                        Method changed
    ...                                                      from itemQuantity()
    public CartItem setItemQuantity(Integer itemQuantity) { ◁──┘ to setItemQuantity()
        this.itemQuantity = itemQuantity;
        return this;
    }
}
```

NOTE Payara Micro requires that a bean use proper setter methods, as you have in listing 3.7. A bean that contains Builder pattern–type named setter methods won't correctly marshal to JSON.

Your `CartController`, as shown in listing 3.8, needs the same modifications to make it RESTful as you made for Dropwizard. Both use the JAX-RS APIs for RESTful endpoints.

Listing 3.8 CartController with Payara

```
@Path("/")
public class CartController {
    @GET
    @Produces(MediaType.APPLICATION_JSON)
    public List<CartItem> all() throws Exception {}

    @GET
    @Path("/add")
    public String addOrUpdateItem(
        @QueryParam("item") String itemName,
        @QueryParam("qty") Integer qty) throws Exception {
    }

    @GET
    @Produces(MediaType.APPLICATION_JSON)
    @Path("/get/{itemName}")
    public CartItem getItem(
        @PathParam("itemName") String itemName) throws Exception {
    }
}
```

Endpoint is accessible as /add.

Method parameters that will be passed on the URL, such as /add?item=hat&qty=2

Parameter defined as part of the URL path, /get/hat.

Now that your RESTful endpoint is defined, you need to tell the runtime that you want to make it available. With Payara Micro, you do that with a custom JAX-RS `Application` class that registers your resource.

Listing 3.9 JaxrsApplication with Payara

```
@ApplicationPath("/")
public class JaxrsApplication extends Application {
    @Override
    public Set<Class<?>> getClasses() {
        Set<Class<?>> resources = new HashSet<>();
        resources.add(CartController.class);
        return resources;
    }
}
```

You specify a URL path for the whole application and then add your `CartController` class to a set of classes that the application makes available to the JAX-RS runtime for instantiation.

Now that you've developed the application, let's run it. Before you can run it, you need to download the Payara Micro runtime from www.payara.fish/downloads.

NOTE After downloading the runtime, it's worth renaming the file to payara-micro.jar and removing the version information. You don't need this information for running the file locally, and the omission makes the command line easier to read.

Because it's a regular Maven WAR project, you build it as usual:

```
mvn clean package
```

and run the application:

```
java -jar payara-micro.jar --deploy target/chapter3.war
```

It's now possible to access the application at http://localhost:8080/chapter3/ in a browser. This returns the list of current items in the cart. You can look at the details of hat in your cart by navigating to http://localhost:8080/chapter3/get/hat. Update the quantity of an existing item with http://localhost:8080/chapter3/add?item=towel&qty=1 or add a new item to your cart with http://localhost:8080/chapter3/add?item =kite&qty=2.

3.2.4 *Spring Boot—opinionated Spring microservices*

Spring Boot came about from a desire to remove the need for boilerplate configuration by following conventions instead. Annotations were also introduced to provide a means of enabling various parts of Spring Boot without needing configuration to do so.

Spring Boot provides many starters as dependencies for your project that combine related libraries and frameworks and configuration for many features that you may require when developing a microservice. For example, the `spring-boot-starter-data-jpa` dependency brings in all that's required to use Spring and JPA for accessing a database. A full list of all the available starters can be found in the GitHub repository: http://mng.bz/cuQ3. Or take a look at http://start.spring.io, where you can create a Maven project based on the starters that you need for your application.

Figure 3.8 shows how your JAX-RS, CDI, JMS microservice uses Spring Boot. The biggest challenge with this microservice would be rewriting existing code that uses CDI to use Spring dependency injection instead. Options are available to make CDI work inside Spring, but if you're looking for the project to remain as a Spring-based project, rewriting it to use Spring injection makes better sense.

With *starters,* Spring Boot is able to provide a flexible JeAS runtime that can be expanded or contracted as required based on the evolving requirements of the application. Modifying the application's functionality is only a matter of adding or removing Spring Starter dependencies and rebuilding the application.

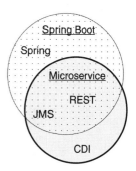

Figure 3.8 Microservice usage in Spring Boot

If you're not sure what specific starters you might need, head over to http://start.spring.io to look at the options. The website contains a project generator that's a great place to see the entire landscape of available starters and the types of functionality they provide, or the use cases they might solve. Starters are available for regular development tasks such as database access, but also for microservice programming patterns such as circuit breaking and service discovery.

NOTE Spring Boot started in October 2012, and it has surpassed version 1.5.10.

You can use http://start.spring.io to create a project that includes the Web starter. This should give you a pom.xml that contains the following dependency:

```
<dependency>
  <groupId>org.springframework.boot</groupId>
  <artifactId>spring-boot-starter-web</artifactId>
</dependency>
```

Now that you have your project, let's modify the basic code so it can be used with Spring Boot. For the CartItem bean, you need to add only the @XmlRootElement to it. With your CartController, you need to add the necessary annotations to make it a RESTful endpoint. This is similar to your JAX-RS-based annotations, but the names are slightly different.

Listing 3.10 CartController with Spring Boot

```
@RestController                                        ◁─── Indicates to Spring that the
public class CartController {                               class will provide RESTful
    @RequestMapping(                                        endpoint methods
        method = RequestMethod.GET,
        path = "/",
        produces = "application/json")
    public List<CartItem> all() throws Exception {}

    @RequestMapping(
        method = RequestMethod.GET,
        path = "/add",
        produces = "application/json")
    public String addOrUpdateItem(
        @RequestParam("item") String itemName,          ◁───
        @RequestParam("qty") Integer qty) throws Exception {
    }

    @RequestMapping(
        method = RequestMethod.GET,
        path = "/get/{itemName}",
        produces = "application/json")
    public CartItem getItem(
        @PathVariable("itemName") String itemName)      ◁───
        throws Exception {
    }
}
```

Method will be available on a URL path of / for HTTP GET requests.

A URL query parameter called item will be mapped into this method parameter.

URL path variable is expected after /get/ for this endpoint.

URL path variable will be mapped to this method parameter.

Each of the methods on your controller provide the same details as your other JAX-RS examples but in a single annotation. @RequestMapping holds all the information of your JAX-RS examples that used `@GET`, `@Produces`, and `@Path`. The other difference is that `@QueryParam` from JAX-RS is `@RequestParam` with Spring, and `@PathParam` from JAX-RS is `@PathVariable` with Spring.

> **NOTE** Spring offers shortcuts for `@RequestMapping` as well. Instead of `@Request-Mapping(method = RequestMethod.GET, path = "/", produces = "application/json")`, you could use `@GetMapping(path = "/", produces = "application/json")`.

Your RESTful endpoint has now been defined, so last of all you create your Spring Boot application class.

Listing 3.11 Chapter3SpringBootApplication

```
@SpringBootApplication
public class Chapter3SpringBootApplication {

    public static void main(String[] args) {
            SpringApplication.run(Chapter3SpringBootApplication.class, args);
    }
}
```

All you're doing here is saying that `main()` should activate `@SpringBootApplication`. It's in this class that you'd add additional annotations for various parts of Spring Boot that you want to activate.

Now that you've developed the application, let's run it. With Spring Boot, you have a couple of options for running your application:

- Running from the command line
- Building the project and running an uber jar

Providing multiple execution options allows developers to choose what's best for their situation. For instance, when doing lots of iterative development, running from the command line may be faster because it doesn't require the project to be built on every change. But when a developer wants to verify production-like behavior, running the uber jar will provide a more accurate reflection of production. Not that there's anything broken with one method as opposed to another, but it's always preferable to verify applications prior to production deployment in an environment and manner that reflects the way it'll be executed in production.

To run from the command line without having built your application with Maven, you can start the Spring Boot server with the following:

```
mvn spring-boot:run
```

This uses the Maven plugin from Spring Boot to execute the application as if it had been packaged into an uber jar.

The alternative approach is to construct an uber jar. You build the Maven project as usual:

```
mvn clean package
```

and run the application:

```
java -jar target/chapter3-spring-boot-1.0-SNAPSHOT.jar
```

It's now possible to access the application at http://localhost:8080/ in a browser. This will return the list of current items in the cart. You can look at the details of hat in your cart by navigating to http://localhost:8080/get/hat. Update the quantity of an existing item with http://localhost:8080/add?item=towel&qty=1 or add a new item to your cart with http://localhost:8080/add?item=kite&qty=2.

3.2.5   *Thorntail—the most flexible JeAS runtime*

Thorntail was born out of the desire to take advantage of the modularization within the WildFly application server. That effort enables different groups of modules to be gathered and installed into the server for use. This also enables Thorntail to be the most flexible JeAS runtime available for Java EE. Choosing a single piece of Java EE functionality to use with your application is now super simple.

Thorntail defines each dependency that can be included by your application, such as JPA, JAX-RS, and most parts of Java EE. In addition to Java EE dependencies, Thorntail provides dependencies for libraries that can assist with developing Enterprise Java microservices such as Swagger, Keycloak, and other frameworks and libraries.

If you're unsure of what Thorntail dependencies might be needed by your application, you have a couple of options. You can generate a skeleton project by visiting http://wildfly-swarm.io/generator and selecting the types of functionality that you need for your microservice. There are options for Java EE features and non-Java EE features such as Eclipse MicroProfile, Hibernate Search, fault tolerance, and security, to name a few.

The other option for developing your Thorntail application, if you're unsure of what dependencies you need, is to add the Maven plugin to your pom.xml and allow the plugin to autodetect dependencies. *Auto Detect* inspects your application code to determine which APIs are being used, and therefore which dependencies are required. This is usually the simplest means of using Thorntail, especially when converting from an existing Java EE application; it allows the rest of the application to remain the same because you added only a new plugin into pom.xml.

> **NOTE** Though *Auto Detect* is easy for getting started, it does mean the plugin is a bit slower to package an application than specifying dependencies directly.

After a developer is more familiar with the available dependencies or requires dependencies that can't be detected by the plugin, switching to using direct Maven dependencies is easy. An easy way to see what dependencies are detected by the plugin is to look at the log output from building the project. It's then possible to use that list as a set of Maven dependencies that need to be added.

> **NOTE**   Thorntail was founded in February 2015, and has now surpassed version 2.2.0.Final. The project was renamed from WildFly Swarm to Thorntail in May 2018.

Figure 3.9 illustrates how your JAX-RS, CDI, JMS microservice uses specifications within Thorntail. Here you can see that Thorntail provides exactly what your microservice needs—no more and no less. Thorntail provides the ideal JeAS runtime because it always gives you just enough for your microservice. No other JeAS runtime can match your application's requirements so closely. The other runtimes have unused portions or require you to include additional libraries in your application.

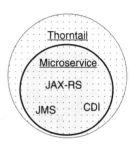

Figure 3.9   Microservice usage in Thorntail

To create your project, you'll use a basic Maven WAR project and add the following plugin definition.

Listing 3.12   Plugin configuration

```
<plugin>
  <groupId>io.thorntail</groupId>
  <artifactId>thorntail-maven-plugin</artifactId>        <--  Artifact ID for the
  <version>2.2.0.Final</version>        <--                   Thorntail plugin
  <executions>                            Version of Thorntail
    <execution>
      <goals>
        <goal>package</goal>        <--  Execute plugin during
      </goals>                           package phase.
    </execution>
  </executions>
</plugin>
```

And then you add the Java EE Web APIs in the provided scope:

```
<dependency>
  <groupId>javax</groupId>
  <artifactId>javaee-web-api</artifactId>
  <version>7.0</version>
  <scope>provided</scope>
</dependency>
```

Now that you have your project, let's modify the basic code so it can be run with the Thorntail JeAS runtime.

For the `CartItem` bean, you need to add only the `@XmlRootElement` to it. The `CartController` needs the same JAX-RS annotations as you added for Payara Micro and Dropwizard. Finally, you need an `Application` class to activate JAX-RS.

Listing 3.13 `JaxrsApplication` with Thorntail

```
@ApplicationPath("/")
public class JaxrsApplication extends Application {
}
```

Now that you've developed the application, let's run it. With Thorntail, you have a couple of options for running your application:

- Running from the command line
- Building the project and running an uber jar

As with Spring Boot, Thorntail provides flexibility as to how a developer might prefer to run an application based on their requirements. Without having built your application with Maven, you can start the Thorntail JeAS runtime with this:

```
mvn thorntail:run
```

This uses the Maven plugin from Thorntail to execute the application as if it had been packaged into an uber jar.

The other approach is to construct an uber jar. You build the Maven project as usual:

```
mvn clean package
```

and run the application:

```
java -jar target/chapter3-thorntail.jar
```

It's now possible to access the application at http://localhost:8080/ in a browser. This returns the list of current items in the cart. You can look at the details of hat in your cart by navigating to http://localhost:8080/get/hat. Update the quantity of an existing item with http://localhost:8080/add?item=towel&qty=1 or add a new item to your cart with http://localhost:8080/add?item=kite&qty=2.

3.2.6 *How do they compare?*

You've taken a look at some JeAS runtimes and the way the code for each differs for a simple application that exposes a few RESTful endpoints. Let's compare some of the features of the JeAS runtimes in table 3.2.

Table 3.2 JeAS runtime comparison

Feature	Dropwizard	Payara Micro	Spring Boot	Thorntail
Dependency injection (DI)		✔	✔	✔
Uber jar packaging	✔		✔	✔
WAR deployment		✔	✔	✔
Maven plugin run			✔	✔
Project generator	✔		✔	✔
Auto Detect dependencies				✔
Java EE APIs		✔		✔

When it comes to choosing the best JeAS runtime for your application or enterprise, many factors play a role. Some of the more critical factors are as follows:

- Is there experience and knowledge of either Java EE or Spring?
- What's the preferred packaging method for production?
- Is there prior experience of either of the non-JeAS runtimes of the frameworks?

These are just some of the factors that will influence which is the preferred JeAS framework for an application. It may be that Thorntail is the preferred choice for developers with previous Java EE experience, but developers looking for a simple stack that doesn't require many Java EE APIs may choose Dropwizard instead.

Summary

- JeAS enables the packaging of just enough runtime along with a microservice. Of the runtimes covered in this chapter, Thorntail is the most customizable JeAS runtime.
- You choose pieces of an Enterprise Java application server by using a JeAS runtime, selecting only what you need.
- JeAS runtimes are the perfect deployment method for RESTful microservices.
- MicroProfile offers critical features for cloud native microservice development.

Microservices testing

This chapter covers

- What types of testing do you need to consider?
- Which tools are appropriate for microservices?
- Implementing unit testing for microservices
- Implementing integration testing for microservices
- Using consumer-driven contract testing

Where to start! So many types and levels of testing can be implemented for anything. Complicating things further is that different people will likely have different points of view, specifically in regard to what the various types of testing should accomplish.

Let's get on the same page with respect to the types of testing and create a common understanding of their meaning for us all! In this chapter, you'll focus only on the types of testing that are relevant for our purposes. There are too many types of testing to cover them all; it'd become overwhelming.

Then you'll use the admin service you created in chapter 2 to show the types of testing that can be performed with a microservice.

4.1 *What type of testing do you need?*

Three types of testing are covered in this chapter:

- *Unit testing* is focused on testing the internals of your microservice.
- *Integration testing* covers the entirety of your service, in addition to the way it interacts with external services, such as a database.
- *Consumer-driven contract testing* deals with the boundary between a consumer of your microservice and the microservice itself, via a Pact document that defines the contract.

It's important to note that unit and integration testing are far from new concepts. They've been part of software development for decades. The application of integration testing to microservices may increase its complexity, through more external integration points, but the way we develop them hasn't greatly changed.

Why did I choose these three types of testing to focus on, given that dozens of types are available? I'm not saying that these three are the only types you need to worry about, but these are certainly crucial to your goal of ensuring that a microservice is as robust as possible. Unit and integration testing are focused on ensuring that what you, as a developer of a microservice, have written meets the requirements that have been outlined for a microservice. Consumer-driven contract testing changes perspectives to look from outside a microservice, to ensure that a microservice can correctly process whatever clients are passing to you. Though it may not be part of the requirements of a microservice, it's possible that a client expects slightly different behavior than has been developed. Figure 4.1 shows how the three types of testing fit in terms of your code.

The key point with respect to testing of any type is that you're not writing tests for fun or for one-off execution. The purpose, and benefit, of writing any test is the ability to continually execute it against code as it changes and is modified, typically as part of a continuous integration process that regularly builds your code. And why do you want these tests running all the time on old and updated code? For the simple reason that it reduces the number of errors, or bugs, that make it into production code. As I mentioned in chapter 1, anything you can do to reduce the number of times you're called about production bugs, the better you are for it.

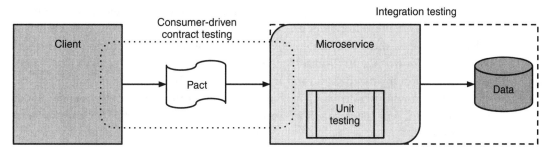

Figure 4.1 Types of testing

4.2   *Unit testing*

Typically created by developers as part of writing code, *unit testing* tests the internal behavior of classes and their methods. Doing so often requires mocks or stubs to *mimic* the behavior of external systems.

> **NOTE** Stubs and mocks are tools you can employ to make it possible to unit test code that interacts with external services, such as a database, without needing a database. Though serving the same purpose, they operate in different ways. *Stubs* are handcrafted implementations of a service that a developer has written to return precanned responses to each method. *Mocks* offer greater flexibility, as each test can set up whatever you expect the method to return for that particular test, and then verify that the mock acted in the way you anticipated. Testing with mocks requires each test to set the expectations for the service being called and then verify it afterward, but it saves you from writing every test situation possible into a stub.

Why do you need unit testing at all? You need to ensure that a method on a class performs the function as it's intended. If a method has parameters passed to it, these should be validated to ensure they're appropriate. This can be as simple as ensuring that the value is non-null, or as complex as validating an email address format. Likewise, you need to verify that passing particular inputs as parameters returns the result you expect from those inputs. Unit testing is the lowest level of testing, but is often the most crucial to get right. If your smallest unit of code, a method, doesn't perform as you expect, then your entire service could function incorrectly.

The two most popular and widely used frameworks for this level of testing are JUnit (http://junit.org/) and TestNG (http://testng.org/doc/). JUnit has been around the longest and was the inspiration for TestNG being created. There aren't many differences between their features, or even the names of annotations in some cases!

The biggest difference is in their goals. JUnit's focus is purely on unit testing, and was a huge driver for the adoption of test-driven development. TestNG aims to support wider testing use cases than just unit testing.

Whichever a developer chooses is purely a personal choice. At any time, JUnit or TestNG may have more features than the other, but it's highly likely that the other will soon catch up. Such back and forth has happened over the years many times.

The code as it stood from chapter 2 has been copied to /chapter4/admin, to enable you to see the differences in the code after you've added tests. This is particularly important to show relevant code changes that were required to fix any dreaded bugs found. For writing our unit tests, I use JUnit, simply because I've used that framework the most in my career and I'm the most familiar with it.

The admin microservice is focused on CRUD operations for the `Category` model at the moment, and has a JAX-RS resource for providing the RESTful endpoints to interact with it.

As you're dealing with unit testing, `Category` is the only viable code you can test with unit tests without mocking databases. It's certainly possible to mock out `Entity-Manager` to test the JAX-RS resource as well, but it's preferable to test it fully with a database as part of integration testing.

The first thing you need to do is add dependencies to your pom.xml for testing:

```xml
<dependency>
  <groupId>junit</groupId>
  <artifactId>junit</artifactId>
  <scope>test</scope>
</dependency>
<dependency>
  <groupId>org.easytesting</groupId>
  <artifactId>fest-assert</artifactId>
  <scope>test</scope>
</dependency>
```

Now let's take a look at some unit tests for `Category`, as it's the lowest level in any method execution stack at runtime.

> **Listing 4.1 `CategoryTest`**

```java
public class CategoryTest {
  @Test
  public void categoriesAreEqual() throws Exception {    ⟵  Test for verifying that two Category instances are identified as equal in all ways.
    LocalDateTime now = LocalDateTime.now();
    Category cat1 = createCategory(1, "Top", Boolean.TRUE, now);    ⟵  Uses a helper method on the test to create any Category instances you need for testing
    Category cat2 = createCategory(1, "Top", Boolean.TRUE, now);

    assertThat(cat1).isEqualTo(cat2);    ⟵  Uses fluent methods from Fest Assertions to simplify test code
    assertThat(cat1.equals(cat2)).isTrue();
    assertThat(cat1.hashCode()).isEqualTo(cat2.hashCode());
  }

  @Test
  public void categoryModification() throws Exception {
    LocalDateTime now = LocalDateTime.now();
    Category cat1 = createCategory(1, "Top", Boolean.TRUE, now);
    Category cat2 = createCategory(1, "Top", Boolean.TRUE, now);

    assertThat(cat1).isEqualTo(cat2);
    assertThat(cat1.equals(cat2)).isTrue();
    assertThat(cat1.hashCode()).isEqualTo(cat2.hashCode());

    cat1.setVisible(Boolean.FALSE);    ⟵  Test for ensuring that a Category is different after calling a setter on it.

    assertThat(cat1).isNotEqualTo(cat2);
    assertThat(cat1.equals(cat2)).isFalse();
    assertThat(cat1.hashCode()).isNotEqualTo(cat2.hashCode());
  }
```

Test of whether a parent with
the same ID on a Category is
considered equal.

```
@Test
public void categoriesWithIdenticalParentIdAreEqual() throws Exception { ◁──┘
    LocalDateTime now = LocalDateTime.now();
    Category parent1 = createParentCategory(1, "Top", now);
    Category parent2 = createParentCategory(1, "Tops", now);
    Category cat1 = createCategory(5, "Top", Boolean.TRUE, now, parent1);
    Category cat2 = createCategory(5, "Top", Boolean.TRUE, now, parent2);

    assertThat(cat1).isEqualTo(cat2);
    assertThat(cat1.equals(cat2)).isTrue();
    assertThat(cat1.hashCode()).isEqualTo(cat2.hashCode());
}

private Category createCategory(Integer id, String name, Boolean visible,
        LocalDateTime created, Category parent) {    ◁──┐  Helper method to
                                                          │  create a Category
    return new TestCategoryObject(id, name, null,         │  instance for testing.
        visible, null, parent, created, null, 1);
}
}
```

You may have noticed that in the createCategory() method of the test class, you instantiated a TestCategoryObject class. Where did that come from? TestCategoryObject has an important purpose for our testing. Because it extends Category, you can directly set fields such as id and version that have only getter methods on Category. This allows you to retain the important immutability parts of Category, while still being able to set and change the properties of Category that you need for testing. TestCategoryObject provides two constructors that allow you to set the ID of a Category, which is extremely useful for testing. Take a look at the chapter code (on GitHub or downloaded from www.manning.com/books/enterprise-java-microservices) for the full code listing.

4.3   *What is immutability?*

Immutability is a concept from object-oriented programming for identifying whether an object's state can be altered. An object's state is considered immutable if it can't be altered after its creation.

In our case, Category isn't entirely immutable, but id, created, and version are fields that you want to be immutable. For that reason, Category has only getter methods defined for them, no setter methods.

To run the tests with Maven from inside /chapter4/admin, you run this:

```
mvn test -Dtest=CategoryTest
```

When running CategoryTest with the existing code from chapter 2, you see a failure! The categoriesWithIdenticalParentIdAreEqual() test fails, because it doesn't consider the two categories to be equal.

With any test failure, two possibilities exist for what happened. Did you make incorrect assertions in your test, or is there a bug in your code?

In this case, do you expect a Category with the same ID but different names to be equal? A first instinct might be to say no, they shouldn't be equal. But for this situation, you need to remember that the ID is a unique identifier for Category, so you'd expect there to be only a single Category with any particular ID present. So here it's apparent that your test assertions are correct, as the name of a Category could've been modified in subsequent requests, but there's a bug in your code in how it determines whether a Category is equal.

Let's take a look at the equals() implementation you currently have on Category, which was autogenerated by an IDE:

```java
public boolean equals(Object o) {
    if (this == o) return true;
    if (o == null || getClass() != o.getClass()) return false;
    Category category = (Category) o;
    return Objects.equals(id, category.id) &&
            Objects.equals(name, category.name) &&
            Objects.equals(header, category.header) &&
            Objects.equals(visible, category.visible) &&
            Objects.equals(imagePath, category.imagePath) &&
            Objects.equals(parent, category.parent) &&
            Objects.equals(created, category.created) &&
            Objects.equals(updated, category.updated) &&
            Objects.equals(version, category.version);
}
```

You can see that you're comparing the entirety of the parent of each Category instance. As you saw in your test, a parent Category with the same ID but different names will fail an equality test.

From what we discussed earlier, it doesn't make sense to compare the entire state of one parent category with another. There's always a chance that one category instance might be retrieved after another, and in between those retrievals the parent category could be updated with a different name. Although the ID is the same, other state differs between the two instances.

You can resolve this conflict by concerning yourself with only the ID of the parent category, and not the entire object state:

```java
public boolean equals(Object o) {
    if (this == o) return true;
    if (o == null || getClass() != o.getClass()) return false;
    Category category = (Category) o;
    return Objects.equals(id, category.id) &&
            Objects.equals(name, category.name) &&
            Objects.equals(header, category.header) &&
            Objects.equals(visible, category.visible) &&
            Objects.equals(imagePath, category.imagePath) &&
            (parent == null ? category.parent == null
```

```
            : Objects.equals(parent.getId(), category.parent.getId())) &&
        Objects.equals(created, category.created) &&
        Objects.equals(updated, category.updated) &&
        Objects.equals(version, category.version);
}
```

Here you've modified the parent equality check to verify whether either parent is null, before comparing whether the ID value is equal. This change makes your code more robust and less error prone.

A similar change is required to `Category.hashCode()` to ensure that you include the parent category ID only when generating a hash for a `Category` instance.

You've just seen how some short unit tests can assist in improving your internal code by reducing the potential for bugs. Let's take the next step and write some integration tests!

4.4   *Integration testing*

Integration testing is similar to unit testing, and uses the same frameworks, but it's also used to test a microservice interaction with external systems. This could include databases, messaging systems, other microservices, or pretty much anything it needs to talk to that isn't internal code to the microservice. If you had unit tests that used mocks or stubs to integrate with external systems, as part of integration testing the mocks and stubs are replaced with calls to the actual systems instead. Removing mocks or stubs opens your code to execution paths that haven't been tested before, as well as introducing more test scenarios as you need to test handling of errors in those external systems.

Depending on the type of systems a microservice integrates with, it may not be possible to execute these tests on a local developer's machine. Integration testing is perfectly suited to continuous improvement environments, where resources are more plentiful and any systems that are required can be installed.

With integration testing, you can expand the scope of what you're intending to test and verify that it works as you expect. It also allows you to use external systems as part of your testing as opposed to mocking anything external. Testing with the actual services and systems that a microservice will rely on in production greatly improves your confidence that going to production won't result in errors from your code changes. You aren't going to be running your integration tests against production systems, but you can run them against systems that closely mirror production setup and data.

To assist in developing integration tests, you'll be using Arquillian. *Arquillian* is a highly extensible testing platform for the JVM that allows the easy creation of integration, functional, and acceptance tests. Many extensions to the core of Arquillian exist to handle specific frameworks, such as JSF, or for browser testing integration with Selenium. Full details of all the extensions available for Arquillian can be found at http://arquillian.org/.

I've chosen Arquillian to help with integration testing because it assists in replicating a production environment as closely as possible without being in production. Your services are started in the same runtime container as would be the case in production, so your service has access to CDI injection, persistence, or whatever runtime pieces your service needs.

To be able to use Arquillian for integration testing, you need to add the necessary dependencies into your pom.xml:

```
<dependency>
  <groupId>io.thorntail</groupId>
  <artifactId>arquillian</artifactId>
  <scope>test</scope>
</dependency>
<dependency>
  <groupId>org.jboss.arquillian.junit</groupId>
  <artifactId>arquillian-junit-container</artifactId>
  <scope>test</scope>
</dependency>
```

The first dependency adds the runtime container for Thorntail to be used within Arquillian tests, and the second adds the integration you require between Arquillian and JUnit. For Arquillian to be able to *deploy* anything, it needs access to a runtime container. The `arquillian` dependency of Thorntail registers itself with Arquillian as being a runtime container, enabling Arquillian to deploy to it. Without either of these, you couldn't execute your integration tests within a runtime container.

To simplify the code required in your tests to execute HTTP requests, you'll use REST Assured, which also needs to be added to your pom.xml:

```
<dependency>
  <groupId>io.rest-assured</groupId>
  <artifactId>rest-assured</artifactId>
  <scope>test</scope>
</dependency>
```

The focus of your integration testing will be on the JAX-RS `Resource` class, as it defines the RESTful endpoints a consumer will interact with, as well as persisting changes to the database. With integration testing we focus on the provider side of microservice interactions—you're only validating that your service API works as you've designed. This doesn't take into account what a consumer expects of your API; that's dealt with in consumer-driven contract testing.

To begin, as shown in listing 4.2, you'll create a test to verify that all categories from the database are correctly retrieved. This single integration test will verify that your external-facing API returns information that's expected, as well as validate that your persistence code is properly reading database entries to return. Either of those aspects not working as you expect will result in the test failing.

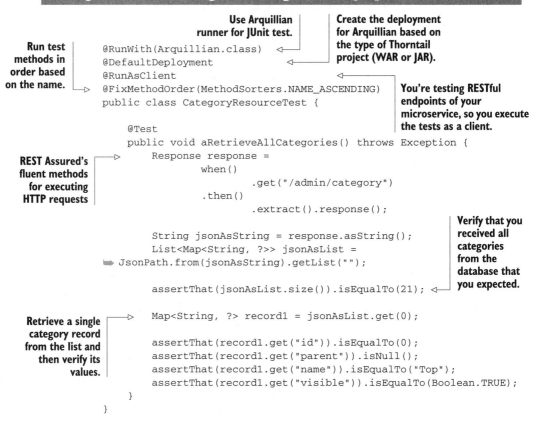

Listing 4.2   Retrieve all categories in listing 4.1's `CategoryResourceTest`

Run test methods in order based on the name.

Use Arquillian runner for JUnit test.

Create the deployment for Arquillian based on the type of Thorntail project (WAR or JAR).

You're testing RESTful endpoints of your microservice, so you execute the tests as a client.

REST Assured's fluent methods for executing HTTP requests

Verify that you received all categories from the database that you expected.

Retrieve a single category record from the list and then verify its values.

```java
@RunWith(Arquillian.class)
@DefaultDeployment
@RunAsClient
@FixMethodOrder(MethodSorters.NAME_ASCENDING)
public class CategoryResourceTest {

    @Test
    public void aRetrieveAllCategories() throws Exception {
        Response response =
                when()
                        .get("/admin/category")
                .then()
                        .extract().response();

        String jsonAsString = response.asString();
        List<Map<String, ?>> jsonAsList =
    JsonPath.from(jsonAsString).getList("");

        assertThat(jsonAsList.size()).isEqualTo(21);

        Map<String, ?> record1 = jsonAsList.get(0);

        assertThat(record1.get("id")).isEqualTo(0);
        assertThat(record1.get("parent")).isNull();
        assertThat(record1.get("name")).isEqualTo("Top");
        assertThat(record1.get("visible")).isEqualTo(Boolean.TRUE);
    }

}
```

The first line in your test is to tell JUnit, via `@RunWith`, that you want to use an Arquillian test runner. `@DefaultDeployment` informs the Thorntail integration with Arquillian to create an Arquillian deployment to execute the tests against, which will use the type of Maven project to create a WAR or JAR for deployment.

The other key annotation on the test class is `@RunAsClient`. This annotation tells Arquillian that you want to treat the deployment as a black box and execute the tests from outside the container. Not including the annotation would indicate to Arquillian that the tests are intended to be executed within the container. It's also possible to mix the use of `@RunAsClient` on individual test methods, but in this case you're testing entirely from outside the container.

The test itself executes an HTTP GET request on `"/admin/category"` and converts the response JSON into a list of maps with key/value pairs. You verify that the size of the list you get back matches the number of `Category` records you know are present in the database, and then you retrieve the first map from the list and assert that the details on the `Category` match the root-level category in the database.

As with the unit test, you execute your integration test with this:

```
mvn test
```

As the test executes, you'll see the Thorntail container starting and the SQL being executed to insert the initial category records into the database, as was discussed in chapter 2. With this first test run, you have one successful test with `Category-ResourceTest`, in addition to the existing `CategoryTest` unit tests.

Let's add a test for retrieving a single category directly, but also map the JSON you receive onto a `Category` object to verify that deserialization is working. This test differs from the previous one in that it uses a different method on the `EntityManager` from JPA to retrieve a single `Category` instead of all of them. There's the double bonus that you're testing additional methods on your JAX-RS resource, but also validating that your persistence and database entities are properly defined.

Listing 4.3 Retrieve category in `CategoryResourceTest`

```
@Test
public void bRetrieveCategory() throws Exception {
    Response response =
            given()
                    .pathParam("categoryId", 1014)
            .when()
                    .get("/admin/category/{categoryId}")
            .then()
                    .extract().response();

    String jsonAsString = response.asString();

    Category category = JsonPath.from(jsonAsString).getObject("",
        Category.class);

    assertThat(category.getId()).isEqualTo(1014);
    assertThat(category.getParent().getId()).isEqualTo(1011);
    assertThat(category.getName()).isEqualTo("Ford SUVs");
    assertThat(category.isVisible()).isEqualTo(Boolean.TRUE);
}
```

Set a parameter into the request for categoryId.

Convert the JSON, via deserialization, you received into the Category instance.

Specify where in the URL path the categoryId should be added.

If you now execute the test again, your new test fails with this error:

```
com.fasterxml.jackson.databind.JsonMappingException: Unexpected token
➥ (START_OBJECT), expected VALUE_STRING: Expected array or string.
```

Following that error in the log is the JSON message you received, but at the end it references the piece of data that caused the issue, `ejm.chapter4.admin.model.Category ["created"]`. From this, you know that the test had an issue deserializing the `created` field on `Category` into a `LocalDateTime` instance.

To resolve the problem, you need to give the JSON serialization library, in this case Jackson, help to convert your `LocalDateTime` instance into JSON that the library knows how to deserialize. To give Jackson help, you need to register a JAX-RS provider to add configuration to Jackson with the `JavaTimeModule`. First, though, you need to add a dependency to the pom.xml, making that available:

```
<dependency>
  <groupId>com.fasterxml.jackson.datatype</groupId>
  <artifactId>jackson-datatype-jsr310</artifactId>
</dependency>
```

Now let's look at the provider:

Listing 4.4 `ConfigureJacksonProvider`

Specify that this provider is used for resolving ObjectMapper instances.

Identify the class as a JAX-RS provider.

Register JavaTimeModule with the Jackson mapper to correctly serialize LocalDateTime.

```
@Provider
public class ConfigureJacksonProvider implements
    ContextResolver<ObjectMapper> {

    private final ObjectMapper mapper = new ObjectMapper()
            .registerModule(new JavaTimeModule());

    @Override
    public ObjectMapper getContext(Class<?> type) {
        return mapper;
    }
}
```

Rerunning `mvn test`, you see the test pass. Another bug resolved by a test!

You've now covered two cases of retrieving categories from your RESTful endpoints. Let's see whether your JAX-RS resource can store data as well.

Listing 4.5 Create category in `CategoryResourceTest`

Indicate you're sending JSON in the HTTP request.

Set the Category instance you created as the body of the request.

Verify you received a response of 201, and the category was created.

Location will be the URL of the Category that was created for you.

```
@Test
public void cCreateCategory() throws Exception {
    Category bmwCategory = new Category();
    bmwCategory.setName("BMW");
    bmwCategory.setVisible(Boolean.TRUE);
    bmwCategory.setHeader("header");
    bmwCategory.setImagePath("n/a");
    bmwCategory.setParent(new TestCategoryObject(1009));

    Response response =
            given()
                    .contentType(ContentType.JSON)
                    .body(bmwCategory)
            .when()
                    .post("/admin/category");

    assertThat(response).isNotNull();
    assertThat(response.getStatusCode()).isEqualTo(201);
    String locationUrl = response.getHeader("Location");
```

```
                    Integer categoryId = Integer.valueOf(
                        locationUrl.substring(locationUrl.lastIndexOf('/') + 1)
                    );
```

Extract the ID of the Category you created from the Location.

```
                    response =
                            when()
```

Assert that the total number of categories retrieved is now 22 and not 21.

```
                                .get("/admin/category")
                            .then()
                                .extract().response();

                    String jsonAsString = response.asString();
                    List<Map<String, ?>> jsonAsList =
                        JsonPath.from(jsonAsString).getList("");
```

Set a path parameter to be the category ID you retrieved from Location for a new GET request.

```
                    assertThat(jsonAsList.size()).isEqualTo(22);

                    response =
                            given()
                                .pathParam("categoryId", categoryId)
```

Deserialize the JSON you received into a Category instance.

```
                            .when()
                                .get("/admin/category/{categoryId}")
                            .then()
                                .extract().response();
```

Set the path for the request, defining where the parameter for the category ID needs to be replaced.

```
                    jsonAsString = response.asString();

                    Category category =
                        JsonPath.from(jsonAsString).getObject("", Category.class);

                    assertThat(category.getId()).isEqualTo(categoryId);
                    ...
                }
```

Validate that the ID on the category matches what you extracted from Location.

The preceding test starts by creating a new Category instance and setting appropriate values on it, including setting a parent with id of 1009. Next you submit a POST request to the RESTful endpoint for Category to create a new record. You validate that the response you received was correct and extract the new id for the category. Then you retrieve all the categories and validate that you now have 22 records instead of 21, and finally retrieve the new record and validate that its information is the same as what you submitted when you created it.

Let's run mvn test again to see whether your code has any bugs! This time, your test fails because it expected to receive an HTTP status code of 201, but you received 500 instead. What went wrong? If you trace back through the terminal output, you can see the microservice experienced an error:

```
Caused by: org.hibernate.TransientPropertyValueException:
  object references an unsaved transient instance
    - save the transient instance before flushing:
      ejm.chapter4.admin.model.Category.parent ->
    ejm.chapter4.admin.model.Category
```

You can see it's not able to save the link to the parent category that you specified. That's because the instance you provided to POST doesn't have any data on it that helps the persistence layer understand that this instance is already saved.

To resolve this, you need to have your RESTful method for creation retrieve the persistence object for the parent category before you attempt to save your new one.

Listing 4.6   `CategoryResource`

```
@POST
@Consumes(MediaType.APPLICATION_JSON)
@Produces(MediaType.APPLICATION_JSON)
@Transactional
public Response create(Category category) throws Exception {
    if (category.getId() != null) {
        return Response
                .status(Response.Status.CONFLICT)
                .entity("Unable to create Category, id was already set.")
                .build();
    }

    Category parent;
    if ((parent = category.getParent()) != null && parent.getId() != null) {
        category.setParent(get(parent.getId()));
    }

    try {
        em.persist(category);
    } catch (Exception e) {
        return Response
                .serverError()
                .entity(e.getMessage())
                .build();
    }
    return Response
            .created(new URI("category/" + category.getId().toString()))
            .build();
}
```

Check that you have a parent category and ID before trying to retrieve it.

Get the parent category and set it on the new category instance.

All you've done is add into `create()` the ability to retrieve a valid parent category from the persistence layer, and then set it onto your new category instance. Everything else in the method is as it was from chapter 2.

Rerunning `mvn test`, you now see all tests pass! Let's add one more test, to see whether your error handling can properly reject a bad request.

Listing 4.7   Fail to create category in `CategoryResourceTest`

Create a Category instance with no name set.

```
@Test
public void dFailToCreateCategoryFromNullName() throws Exception {
    Category badCategory = new Category();
    badCategory.setVisible(Boolean.TRUE);
```

```
badCategory.setHeader("header");
badCategory.setImagePath("n/a");
badCategory.setParent(new TestCategoryObject(1009));

Response response =
        given()
                .contentType(ContentType.JSON)
                .body(badCategory)
        .when()
                .post("/admin/category");

assertThat(response).isNotNull();
assertThat(response.getStatusCode()).isEqualTo(400);   ◁──┐ Should receive
                                                           HTTP status
...                                                        code 400.

response =
        when()
                .get("/admin/category")
        .then()
                .extract().response();

String jsonAsString = response.asString();
List<Map<String, ?>> jsonAsList =
JsonPath.from(jsonAsString).getList("");        │ Validate you still have
                                                │ only 22 categories in
assertThat(jsonAsList.size()).isEqualTo(22);  ◁─┘ the database.
}
```

Running `mvn test` with this new test method results in a failure. Your test is expecting a response code of 400, but you receive 500 instead.

Scrolling through the terminal output, you see this:

```
Caused by: javax.validation.ConstraintViolationException:
    Validation failed for classes [ejm.chapter4.admin.model.Category]
        during persist time for groups [javax.validation.groups.Default, ]
List of constraint violations:[
    ConstraintViolationImpl{
        interpolatedMessage='may not be null', propertyPath=name,
        rootBeanClass=class ejm.chapter4.admin.model.Category,
        messageTemplate='{javax.validation.constraints.NotNull.message}'
    }
]
```

Though that's the correct error you'd expect to see in the logs, your microservice isn't handling the error properly. On completion of the RESTful method, the transaction was trying to commit the database changes, but that failed because you didn't have a valid `Category` instance.

You need to bring forward the point at which the validation occurs, so that your method can properly handle it and return the response code you desire (listing 4.8).

Listing 4.8   `CategoryResource.create()`

<table>
<tr>
<td>

Catch any
constraint-
specific
exceptions.

</td>
<td>

```
try {
    em.persist(category);
    em.flush();
} catch (ConstraintViolationException cve) {
    return Response
              .status(Response.Status.BAD_REQUEST)
              .entity(cve.getMessage())
              .build();
} catch (Exception e) {
    return Response
              .serverError()
              .entity(e.getMessage())
              .build();
}
```

</td>
<td>

Flush the changes present
in the entity manager.

</td>
</tr>
</table>

Return the
response with
400 status
code and error
messages.

All you've done here is modify `create()` to flush the changes in the entity manager, which causes the validation to be triggered, and then catch any constraint violations to return a response. Running `mvn test` with this change now allows the test to pass, because it's now returning the correct response code.

Integration testing is a crucial piece that all microservices need. As you've just seen, it'll quickly identify potential failure points in integrating with external systems, such as a database, caused by situations that the existing code wasn't written to handle. Integrating with databases and transferring data via HTTP requests are two common uses for which problems with your existing code can be exposed.

Developers are human; we make mistakes. Proper integration testing is a key way to ensure that you've developed code that matches what's expected. It's often a good idea to have a different developer create these types of tests, because another developer won't have any preconceived notions about how the code works and will be concerned only with testing the required functionality of the microservice.

4.5   *Consumer-driven contract testing*

When developing a microservice, you don't necessarily have real consumers of your service available to test against. But if a service can be provided with details of what a consumer will pass on a request, and what the expected response is, then you can execute those expectations against your real service to ensure that you meet them. What better way to validate that your service's API works than a consumer specifying what it's expecting for you to test with!

Consumer-driven contract testing uses this approach, as you're testing both a consumer and a provider to ensure that proper information is passed between them. How do you do that? Figure 4.2 shows how to use a *mock server* to capture requests from a consumer, and return the response that was defined for that request.

Bear in mind, the response being returned is what the developer of the consumer thinks should be returned. This expectation can easily differ from the service's

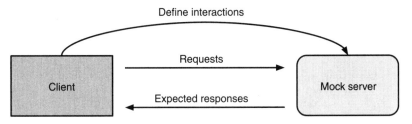

Figure 4.2　Mock responses to a client request

response, but then again, finding those types of problems is the benefit of this type of testing.

By executing what's shown in figure 4.2, a *contract* of what the consumer is expecting to send and receive when communicating with the provider microservice can be created. Figure 4.3 shows how it's then possible to replay those requests on your service, with the service returning a response based on its actual code. Then each response received from the service can be compared against what's expected, to ensure that both consumer and provider are in agreement about what should occur.

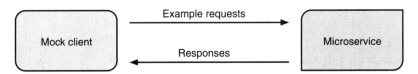

Figure 4.3　Requests sent to the microservice

A popular tool for testing these concepts is Pact (https://docs.pact.io/), which you'll use in listing 4.10. The process sounds tricky, but it's not too bad when using Pact. Pact is a family of frameworks that makes it easy to create and use tests for consumer-driven contracts.

The first thing you need to do is create a consumer that's trying to integrate with the admin microservice, shown next. In chapter4/admin-client, you have the following consumer.

Listing 4.9　`AdminClient`

```
public class AdminClient {
    private String url;

    public AdminClient(String url) {          ◁──── Constructor for AdminClient that
        this.url = url;                              takes the URL representing the
    }                                                admin microservice

    public Category getCategory(final Integer categoryId) throws IOException {  ◁─┐
        URIBuilder uriBuilder;                  Method to retrieve a single Category by its ID
        try {
            uriBuilder = new URIBuilder(url).setPath("/admin/category/" +
```

```
⇒ categoryId);
        } catch (URISyntaxException e) {
            throw new RuntimeException(e);
        }

        String jsonResponse =
                Request
                    .Get(uriBuilder.toString())
                    .execute()
                        .returnContent().asString();

        if (jsonResponse.isEmpty()) {
            return null;
        }

        return new ObjectMapper()
                .registerModule(new JavaTimeModule())
                .readValue(jsonResponse, Category.class);   ◁──┐
    }
}
```

Use Jackson to map the response JSON into Category, registering the JavaTimeModule as well.

You now have a basic client for interacting with the admin microservice. To have Pact create the necessary contract for it, you need to add it as a dependency in pom.xml:

```
<dependency>
  <groupId>au.com.dius</groupId>
  <artifactId>pact-jvm-consumer-junit_2.12</artifactId>
  <scope>test</scope>
</dependency>
```

This dependency specifies that you'll be using JUnit to generate the contract. Let's create a JUnit test to generate the contract.

Listing 4.10   ConsumerPactTest

Extend ConsumerPactTestMk2 to have the required integration hooks for Pact and JUnit.

```
public class ConsumerPactTest extends ConsumerPactTestMk2 {   ◁──┐
    private Category createCategory(Integer id, String name) {   ◁──┐
        Category cat = new TestCategoryObject(id,
⇒ LocalDateTime.parse("2002-01-01T00:00:00"), 1);
        cat.setName(name);
        cat.setVisible(Boolean.TRUE);
        cat.setHeader("header");
        cat.setImagePath("n/a");

        return cat;
    }

    @Override
    protected RequestResponsePact createPact(PactDslWithProvider builder) {
        Category top = createCategory(0, "Top");
```

Helper method for creating categories with the required creation date

Return the Pact that the consumer expects.

```
        Category transport = createCategory(1000, "Transportation");
        transport.setParent(top);

        Category autos = createCategory(1002, "Automobiles");
        autos.setParent(transport);

        Category cars = createCategory(1009, "Cars");
        cars.setParent(autos);

        Category toyotas = createCategory(1015, "Toyota Cars");
        toyotas.setParent(cars);

        ObjectMapper mapper = new ObjectMapper()
                .registerModule(new JavaTimeModule());

        try {
            return builder
                    .uponReceiving("Retrieve a category")
                        .path("/admin/category/1015")
                        .method("GET")
                    .willRespondWith()
                        .status(200)
                        .body(mapper.writeValueAsString(toyotas))
                    .toPact();
        } catch (JsonProcessingException e) {
            e.printStackTrace();
        }

        return null;
    }

    @Override
    protected String providerName() {
        return "admin_service_provider";
    }

    @Override
    protected String consumerName() {
        return "admin_client_consumer";
    }

    @Override
    protected PactSpecVersion getSpecificationVersion() {
        return PactSpecVersion.V3;
    }

    @Override
    protected void runTest(MockServer mockServer) throws IOException {
        Category cat = new
 AdminClient(mockServer.getUrl()).getCategory(1015);

        assertThat(cat).isNotNull();
        assertThat(cat.getId()).isEqualTo(1015);
        assertThat(cat.getName()).isEqualTo("Toyota Cars");
        assertThat(cat.getHeader()).isEqualTo("header");
```

Define what should be received as a response based on the request that's received.

⟵— **Set a unique name for the provider.**

⟵— **Set a unique name for the consumer.**

Which version of the Pact specification you should use for the contract

Run the AdminClient against the Pact mock server and verify the expected results.

```
        assertThat(cat.getImagePath()).isEqualTo("n/a");
        assertThat(cat.isVisible()).isTrue();
        assertThat(cat.getParent()).isNotNull();
        assertThat(cat.getParent().getId()).isEqualTo(1009);
    }
}
```

Though there's a lot here, the listing boils down to the following:

- A method that identifies what should be returned from a request to the admin microservice, given a particular response it receives. This is what Pact uses to mock the provider side of the contract creation process.
- A method to use your client code that interacts with the mock server from Pact, and verifies that the response object you receive has the appropriate values.

Running mvn test will then execute the JUnit Pact test and produce a JSON file in /chapter4/admin-client/target/pacts.

Listing 4.11 Pact JSON output

```
{
    "provider": {
        "name": "admin_service_provider"
    },
    "consumer": {
        "name": "admin_client_consumer"
    },
    "interactions": [
        {
            "description": "Retrieve a category",
            "request": {
                "method": "GET",
                "path": "/admin/category/1015"
            },
            "response": {
                "status": 200,
                "body": {
                    "id": 1015,
                    "name": "Toyota Cars",
                    "header": "header",
                    "visible": true,
                    "imagePath": "n/a",
                    "parent": {
                        "id": 1009,
                        "name": "Cars",
                        "header": "header",
                        "visible": true,
                        "imagePath": "n/a",
    ...

    ],
    "metadata": {
        "pact-specification": {
```

```json
        "version": "3.0.0"
    },
    "pact-jvm": {
        "version": "3.5.8"
    }
}
}
```

NOTE For brevity, I've included only the start of the JSON that's generated, because all the response data is lengthy.

With this JSON file generated, you can now set up the other side of consumer-driven contract testing: verifying that the provider works as the consumer expects it to.

For simplicity, I've manually copied the generated JSON across to /chapter4/admin/src/test/resources/pacts. For serious testing with continuous integration, Pact has other ways to store the JSON so that it can be automatically retrieved when running the provider test.

For verifying the provider, because you require an instance of the admin microservice to be running, you'll use Maven to execute the Pact verification. The verification will take place in the integration test phase of Maven. First you modify your pom.xml to start and stop the Thorntail container around the integration test phase.

Listing 4.12 Thorntail Maven plugin execution for integration tests

```xml
<plugin>
  <groupId>io.thorntail</groupId>
  <artifactId>thorntail-maven-plugin</artifactId>
  <executions>
    <execution>
      <id>start</id>
      <phase>pre-integration-test</phase>          Start the microservice during
      <goals>                                       the pre-integration-test phase
        <goal>start</goal>         ◁──────────      of Maven.
      </goals>
      <configuration>
        <stdoutFile>target/stdout.log</stdoutFile>
        <stderrFile>target/stderr.log</stderrFile>
      </configuration>
    </execution>
    <execution>
      <id>stop</id>
      <phase>post-integration-test</phase>
      <goals>
        <goal>stop</goal>          ◁───── Stop the microservice in the
      </goals>                            post-integration-test phase.
    </execution>
  </executions>
</plugin>
```

Define locations for the logs of the microservice.

Next you add the Pact plugin to execute the contract against your provider.

Listing 4.13   Pact Maven plugin execution

```xml
<plugin>
  <groupId>au.com.dius</groupId>
  <artifactId>pact-jvm-provider-maven_2.12</artifactId>
  <configuration>
    <serviceProviders>                              Define the location of the
      <serviceProvider>                     ◁────── admin microservice provider.
        <name>admin_service_provider</name>
        <protocol>http</protocol>
        <host>localhost</host>
        <port>8081</port>
        <path>/</path>
        <pactFileDirectory>src/test/resources/pacts</pactFileDirectory> ◁──┐
      </serviceProvider>
    </serviceProviders>                         Set the directory where the Pact
  </configuration>                               contract files can be found.
  <executions>
    <execution>
      <id>verify-pacts</id>
      <phase>integration-test</phase>        ◁──┐ Pact verification runs during the
      <goals>                                     integration-test phase of Maven.
        <goal>verify</goal>         ◁─────┐
      </goals>
    </execution>                      Use the verify goal of the Pact plugin.
  </executions>
</plugin>
```

Running `mvn verify` will execute all the tests you'd defined previously, but also run the Pact verification as the last step. You should see output in the terminal to indicate it succeeded:

```
returns a response which
  has status code 200 (OK)
  has a matching body (OK)
```

Well, that was smooth, but what does it look like if it doesn't work? To try that out, you can add the following code into the `CategoryResource.get()` method, before the current `return` statement, so that you return a different category for your Pact test:

```
if (categoryId.equals(1015)) {
    return em.find(Category.class, 1010);
}
```

If you now run the test with `mvn verify` again, you'll see a test failure with output containing the following:

```
returns a response which
  has status code 200 (OK)
  has a matching body (FAILED)
```

```
Failures:

0) Verifying a pact between admin_client_consumer and admin_service_provider
     - Retrieve a category returns a response which has a matching body
       $.parent.parent.parent.parent -> Type mismatch: Expected Map Map(parent
     -> null, name -> Top, visible -> true, imagePath -> n/a, version -> 1,
     id -> 0, updated -> null, header -> header, created -> List(2002, 1, 1,
     0, 0)) but received Null null

         Diff:

         -{
         -     "parent": null,
         -     "name": "Top",
         -     "visible": true,
         -     "imagePath": "n/a",
         -     "version": 1,
         -     "id": 0,
         -     "updated": null,
         -     "header": "header",
         -     "created": [
         -         2002,
         -         1,
         -         1,
         -         0,
         -         0
         -     ]
         -}
         +

         $.parent.parent.parent.name -> Expected 'Transportation' but received
         'Top'

         $.parent.parent.parent.id -> Expected 1000 but received 0

         $.parent.parent.name -> Expected 'Automobiles' but received
         'Transportation'

         $.parent.parent.id -> Expected 1002 but received 1000

         $.parent.name -> Expected 'Cars' but received 'Automobiles'

         $.parent.id -> Expected 1009 but received 1002

         $.name -> Expected 'Toyota Cars' but received 'Trucks'

         $.id -> Expected 1015 but received 1010
```

This log message provides detailed information about what crucial data, such as ID
and name, it found for each category in the hierarchy, and how that differs from what
the Pact contract had defined.

As mentioned previously, such a discrepancy could be a result of an invalid assumption on the part of the consumer, or a bug in the provider. What such a failure really indicates is that developers from the consumer and provider sides need to discuss how the API needs to operate.

4.6   Additional reading

As I mentioned earlier, there are many other types of testing I won't be covering. A couple of the critical ones are user acceptance testing and end-to-end testing. Though they are both crucial to ensuring that adequate testing is performed, they're beyond the scope of this book because they deal with a higher level of testing. For additional information on testing with microservices, I recommend *Testing Java Microservices* by Alex Soto Bueno, Jason Porter, and Andy Gumbrecht (Manning, 2018).

4.7   Additional exercises

Here are some additional tests that you could write to experiment with the different testing methods, and also help improve the code for the example!

- Add a method to `CategoryResourceTest` that verifies the ability to update `Category`.
- Add a method to `CategoryResourceTest` to verify that `Category` can be removed from the database successfully.
- Add methods to `AdminClient` for retrieving all categories, adding a category, updating a category, and removing a category. Then add the request/response pairs in `ConsumerPactTest.createPact()` for the new methods, and update `ConsumerPactTest.runTest()` to execute and verify each of them.

If you take on any of these exercises and would like to see them included in the code for the book, please submit a pull request to the project on GitHub.

Summary

- Unit testing is important, but the need to test doesn't end there. You need to test all aspects of a service as realistically as possible.
- Arquillian is a great framework for simplifying more-complex testing that requires a runtime container to interact with and provide near-production execution.
- The key to microservice testing is ensuring that the contract that a microservice defines, the API it exposes, is tested against not only what the microservice intends to expose, but also what a client is expecting to pass and receive.

Cloud native development

This chapter covers

- Why is the cloud important?
- What is cloud native development?
- What do you need to deploy your microservice to the cloud?
- How does your application scale in the cloud?
- Can you test your application in the cloud before production?

In this chapter, you'll extend the admin service from chapter 4, giving it the ability to be deployed to a local cloud environment, and then run tests against the service deployed to that environment.

First, you'll learn what *cloud* means and about the cloud providers you have to choose from. You'll also explore your options for running the cloud on your local machine. After you've chosen a type of cloud, you'll modify the admin service from chapter 4 to deploy into the cloud. After completing deployment, you'll scale the application to show how it can handle the additional load, and finish up by running tests with your application deployed in the cloud.

5.1   What is the cloud anyway?

The cloud, and cloud computing, have been present in software engineering for decades. These terms are usually used in reference to a platform for distributed computing. It wasn't until the early to mid-1990s that their use became more prevalent.

Some of the key benefits of the cloud are as follows:

- *Cost efficiencies*—Most cloud providers charge enterprises to use their services as a measure of CPU time that's spent. This significantly reduces the overall cost of running the environments compared to physical machines.
- *Ability to scale*—Cloud providers provide ways to scale up and down individual services as required, ensuring that you never have too much or too little capacity. The spread of information can occur quickly, thanks to social media, so being able to immediately scale up identical instances to handle immediate short-term load is crucial. How quickly can an enterprise scale up when it takes months to purchase and provision just one machine? In such a situation, the cloud provider will provide scale by replicating instances with identical configuration of memory, CPU, and so forth.
- *Freedom of choice*—If you work for an enterprise that develops only in Java, because that's what its operations team knows how to manage, how do you experiment with new programming languages such as Node.js or Go? Cloud brings additional languages to your fingertips like never before. You don't need to have internal experience maintaining environments for new languages; that's what a cloud provider is for!

5.2   Service models

Figure 5.1 shows the multiple types of service models for the cloud, along with where an application fits within that. In this illustration, an application has code on the server. If you have an application that's purely mobile or is browser based that interacts with one or more services via Software as a Service (SaaS), it's still an application, but not an application as depicted here. In this context, an application could be an executable JAR, or a WAR or EAR deployed to an application server.

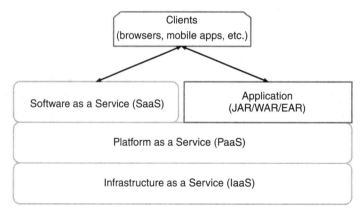

Figure 5.1   Service models in the cloud

Let's briefly describe each of these layers:

- *Infrastructure as a Service* (IaaS)—Provides an abstraction over network infrastructure that includes computing resources, data partitioning, scaling, security, and backup. IaaS usually involves a hypervisor that runs virtual machines as guests. To use an IaaS requires constructing a virtual machine that could be deployed to the environment. Some well-known IaaS providers are Amazon Web Services, OpenStack, Google Compute Engine, and Microsoft Azure.

- *Platform as a Service* (PaaS)—Forms the layer above IaaS to provide a development environment that includes an operating system, an execution environment for various programming languages, databases, and web servers. A PaaS saves a developer from needing to purchase, install, and configure hardware and software to have an environment for deploying an application. Popular PaaS providers include Red Hat OpenShift, Amazon Web Services, Google App Engine, IBM Bluemix, Cloud Foundry, Microsoft Azure, and Heroku.

- *Software as a Service* (SaaS)—Provides common pieces of applications, or sometimes entire applications, on an as-needed or on-demand basis. SaaS is usually charged on a pay per use basis. What's offered as a SaaS can vary from a niche service, such as everything related to marketing, to an entire suite of SaaS to manage a business from beginning to end. Many SaaS providers exist, and more are cropping up every day. Some of the well-known ones are Salesforce.com, Eloqua, NetSuite, and Cloud9.

Over the last couple of years—with the rise of containers, and in particular the growth and popularity of Docker as a container solution—a new layer has been created in cloud service models.

Figure 5.2 introduces *Containers as a Service* (CaaS) as a new foundation for PaaS providers. CaaS takes advantage of container technology, such as Docker, to simplify the deployment, scaling, and management of multiple applications or services.

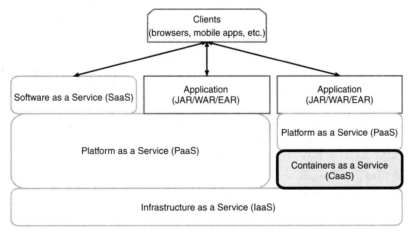

Figure 5.2 Service models in the cloud with containers

Containers allow you to package any application or service into its own operating system environment, with whatever custom software or configuration might be required, while also being able to reduce the size of the image that's generated when compared to traditional virtual machines.

The other major advantage to CaaS, and containers in general, is their immutable nature. Because a container image is derived from a specific version of that container, updating that container in any way requires a new container image and version to be built. Mutable deployments have long been an issue with deploying to internally managed servers, because operations could update something on the system and potentially break an application. Immutable container images can then be sent through CI/CD processes to verify that the container performs as expected before being released in production.

Currently, the most popular CaaS provider is Kubernetes. Kubernetes was created by Google and was heavily influenced by the way it managed containerized applications internally. Previous PaaS providers already have shifted to be built on top of a CaaS, and in particular Kubernetes. Red Hat OpenShift is one such PaaS that now takes advantage of Kubernetes as its CaaS.

CaaS is the best way to manage deployments, but you don't always want something that low level. Generally, our ideal environment is a PaaS that's built on top of a CaaS, such as with Red Hat OpenShift.

5.3   *Cloud native development*

You may have heard the term *cloud native development* before, but new terms are always cropping up, so it doesn't hurt to clarify the definition. *Cloud native development* is the process of developing an application or service for deployment to cloud environments, where it can take advantage of loosely coupled cloud services.

Shifting to this type of development requires an alteration in mindset when developing, as you're no longer concerned with the details of external services that an application requires. All you need to know is that there will be a service, such as a database, available to your application in the cloud, and which environment variables you might require to connect with it.

You can also look at cloud native development from another angle, in that it abstracts away much of what your application or service requires to function correctly. Cloud native development allows the developer to expend effort on things that add business value, by focusing on developing business logic and not plumbing code.

Though not present with most cloud providers, the idea of a service catalog is being introduced into Kubernetes for just this purpose. A *service catalog* provides a definition of services that can be connected to within the cloud, along with the environment variables that are required to connect with them. It's then possible for a service to specify criteria about an external service it needs to connect to. Criteria could include `database` and `postgresql`, which would translate into a PostgreSQL database instance from the service catalog.

This concept isn't that much different from providing environment-specific configuration for databases, as we've done for many years. But as work on the service catalog continues, we may reach a point where an application connecting to an external service through specific environment variables is no longer needed. A database client may be injected into a service, with configuration already set by the service catalog.

Cloud native development sounds great, but how can you quickly test and debug your service if you have to deploy it to the cloud every time? Won't that slow your development speed? Yes, deploying to the cloud for every code change to see the impact would likely slow development speed, if only marginally, and possibly more.

But what if you can bring the cloud, or something as near as identical to the cloud used for production, onto your local development machines? That would certainly speed up the round-trip time from code change to seeing it in action. Do cloud providers offer such a thing? Some of them do!

Minikube was the first to offer a single-node Kubernetes cluster that could be run on your local machine. All that's required is a virtual environment, such as VirtualBox, Hyper-V, or xhyve driver, installed on your machine that can be used by Minikube to create a virtual cluster on your machine.

Since Minikube formed, Minishift was founded to extend Minikube with a built-in PaaS of a single-node OpenShift cluster. Minishift uses the upstream of OpenShift, OpenShift Origin, as the PaaS. Revisiting where a CaaS fits into service models, figure 5.3 shows what Minishift provides.

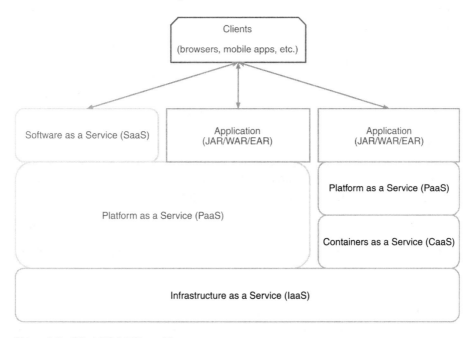

Figure 5.3 What Minishift provides

There's nothing wrong with using a CaaS directly, such as Kubernetes, but there are benefits of using a PaaS on top. One main benefit is a nice UI to visualize what's deployed. Because of its simplicity in setting up, and wanting to use a PaaS over a CaaS, we'll use Minishift to create our local cloud environment.

5.4 Deploying to the cloud

Quite separate from the service model that the cloud might offer, there are also three main deployment models that the cloud could use:

- *Private cloud*—A cloud that's solely for the use of a single enterprise, which is usually hosted internally.
- *Public cloud*—Services within the cloud are available over a public network. The main difference between this and a private cloud relates to security. Whether a microservice or database, they need to have more stringent security because these services are accessible on a public network.
- *Hybrid cloud*—A combination of public and private clouds. It's also possible that each of these clouds could use different providers. The hybrid cloud deployment model is quickly becoming the most common, as it provides the best of both worlds, especially when wanting to quickly ramp up capacity and scale.

Minishift, in essence, gives you your own private cloud instance running on your local machine. But the PaaS within Minishift, OpenShift, is the same PaaS that would be used in a public cloud or hybrid cloud deployment. The only difference is it's running locally.

Whether you're using a cloud for microservices, a monolith, or anything else, the way a deployment is pushed to the cloud is no different. The only difference might be that a microservice is more likely to have a CI/CD process that automatically pushes releases into production. It's more likely that a deployment of a monolith will require greater coordination than an automatic deployment.

5.5 Starting Minishift

The first thing you need to do is install Minishift on your local machine. Head over to http://mng.bz/w6g8 and follow the instructions to install the necessary prerequisites, if they aren't already installed, and then install Minishift.

> **NOTE** The examples have been tested with Minishift 1.12.0 and OpenShift 3.6.1.

After Minishift is installed, open a terminal window and start it with the default settings:

```
minishift start
```

By default, this gives you a virtual machine with two virtual CPUs, 2 GB of RAM, and 20 GB of hard drive space for it. The terminal provides details of what Minishift is doing as it starts, including which version of OpenShift Origin is being installed. After the installation is finished, the last output will provide details for the web console URL, and login credentials for developer and administrator accounts:

```
OpenShift server started.

The server is accessible via web console at:
    https://192.168.64.11:8443

You are logged in as:
    User:     developer
    Password: <any value>

To login as administrator:
    oc login -u system:admin
```

For most things you need to do, either through the web console or via the OpenShift command-line interface (CLI), you need only the developer credentials. There's also a handy way to launch the OpenShift web console without having to remember the URL and port:

```
minishift console
```

This command opens a browser window directly at the login page of the web console. After logging in, the console looks like figure 5.4.

Figure 5.4 OpenShift web console

By default, a fresh instance of OpenShift sets up an empty project called My Project for you. You can then choose to delete it and create your own, or use it; the choice doesn't really matter.

You now have a cloud that you can deploy your services into, but you first need to make your service deployable to it.

5.6 *Microservice cloud deployment*

You'll take the admin service that you updated in chapter 4, and add the necessary configuration to support deploying to the cloud.

By far, the easiest way to deploy your application is the fabric8 Maven plugin (https://maven.fabric8.io/). A huge benefit to the plugin is it can bring Java applications to OpenShift or Kubernetes! You can go from no configuration deployments to adding as much configuration as you might require.

Let's start by modifying your pom.xml to include the plugin in a profile called openshift.

Listing 5.1   Maven profile for OpenShift deployment

```
<profile>
  <id>openshift</id>
  <build>
    <plugins>
      <plugin>
        <groupId>io.fabric8</groupId>
        <artifactId>fabric8-maven-plugin</artifactId>      ◁── Name of the fabric8
        <version>3.5.33</version>                              Maven plugin
        <executions>
          <execution>
            <goals>
              <goal>resource</goal>      ◁── Creates Kubernetes or
              <goal>build</goal>            OpenShift resource descriptors
            </goals>
          </execution>
        </executions>
      </plugin>
    </plugins>
  </build>
</profile>
```

Generates a Docker image of the application in a container

The goals that are defined in the plugin inform it of what you want it to do. With this configuration, the plugin will create the necessary resource descriptors for OpenShift and then use Docker to build a container image with your deployment inside it. What the code does is no different than if you created an image with Docker directly, but without the hassle of having to remember the correct command each time you need it!

I mentioned that the plugin generates resource descriptors for you, but what are they? Take a look at this listing.

Listing 5.2   service-chapter5-admin.json

```
{
  "apiVersion":"v1",
  "kind":"Service",
  "metadata": {
    "annotations": {
      "fabric8.io/git-branch":"master",
      "fabric8.io/git-commit":"377ac684babee220885246de1700d76e3d11a8ab",
      "fabric8.io/iconUrl":"img/icons/wildfly.svg",
      "fabric8.io/scm-con-url":"scm:git:git@github.com:kenfinnigan/ejm-
  ➥ samples.git/chapter5/chapter5-admin",
      "fabric8.io/scm-devcon-url":"scm:git:git@github.com:kenfinnigan/ejm-
  ➥ samples.git/chapter5/chapter5-admin",
      "fabric8.io/scm-tag":"HEAD",
      "fabric8.io/scm-url":"https://github.com/kenfinnigan/ejm-
  ➥ samples/chapter5/chapter5-admin",
```

```
        "prometheus.io/port":"9779",
        "prometheus.io/scrape":"true"
      },
      "creationTimestamp":"2017-11-21T01:47:02Z",
      "finalizers":[],
      "labels": {
        "app":"chapter5-admin",
        "expose":"true",
        "group":"ejm",
        "provider":"fabric8",
        "version":"1.0-SNAPSHOT"
      },
      "name":"chapter5-admin",
      "namespace":"myproject",
      "ownerReferences":[],
      "resourceVersion":"3074",
      "selfLink":"/api/v1/namespaces/myproject/services/chapter5-admin",
      "uid":"decf5db7-ce5d-11e7-994e-0afca351eb6b"
    },
    "spec": {
      "clusterIP":"172.30.221.166",
      "deprecatedPublicIPs":[],
      "externalIPs":[],
      "loadBalancerSourceRanges":[],
      "ports": [
        {
          "name":"http",
          "port":8080,
          "protocol":"TCP",
          "targetPort":8080
        }
      ],
      "selector": {
        "app":"chapter5-admin",
        "group":"ejm",
        "provider":"fabric8"
      },
      "sessionAffinity":"None",
      "type":"ClusterIP"
    },
    "status": {
      "loadBalancer": {
        "ingress":[]
      }
    }
  }
}
```

This is just one of the many resource descriptors that could be created by the plugin, depending on which options are specified. You don't want to be handcrafting files this long for every microservice you deploy! The beauty of the fabric8 Maven plugin is that it hides all that boilerplate configuration you don't need to know about unless you want to.

If finer control over service configuration is needed, it can be achieved with custom YAML files that are used by the plugin to generate the necessary JSON. That's beyond the scope of this book, but further information is available at the fabric8 website, https://maven.fabric8.io/.

Though Minishift is already started, you need to do one more thing before you can deploy your service with the fabric8 Maven plugin. You need to log in to OpenShift in the terminal, because the fabric8 Maven plugin uses the credentials to create resources within OpenShift. This is necessary only once, or until your authenticated session expires and you need to log in again.

To log in, you need the OpenShift CLI installed. There are two ways to do that:

- Add the .minishift/cache/oc/v3.6.0 directory onto your path, because the `oc` binary is retrieved by Minishift for you.
- Download the CLI directly from www.openshift.org/download.html.

After the CLI is installed, you can authenticate in the terminal:

```
oc login
```

You'll be prompted to enter the user ID, `developer`, and any value for a password.

You're going to use the default My Project for now, so you can deploy the admin service into OpenShift with the following:

```
mvn clean fabric8:deploy -Popenshift
```

You invoke the fabric8 `deploy` goal, which will be executed after the `resource` and `build` goals you defined in pom.xml. You also specified the `openshift` profile so that the fabric8 Maven plugin is available.

In the terminal, you'll see the usual Maven build logging, mixed in with messages from the fabric8 plugin telling you what it's generating for deployment to OpenShift. After it's finished deploying the service, you can open My Project in the console and see all the details of your deployed service, as shown in figure 5.5.

Here you can easily see at a glance the various pieces of information in your service:

- Name of the deployment
- Which Docker image is used for the deployment
- Which build created the Docker image
- The ports that are exposed from the container
- How many pods are running and whether they're healthy
- The external route pointing at your deployment

NOTE A *pod* is a grouping of container(s), such as Docker containers, that use shared storage and network infrastructure. A pod is equivalent to a physical or virtual machine with collocated applications.

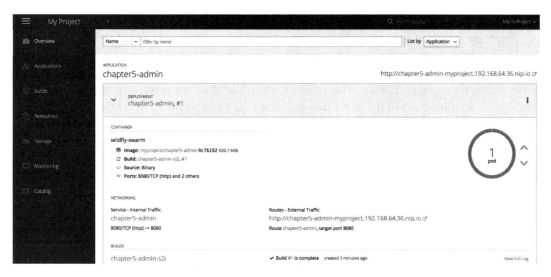

Figure 5.5   OpenShift web console, showing the admin service

Clicking the route URL for external traffic opens a new browser window at the root URL of the service. Because the admin service doesn't serve anything at /, you need to modify the URL in the browser to include /admin/category before you can see the JSON data that was retrieved from the database.

With the admin service functioning, can you scale the number of instances you have of that service running? Within the OpenShift console, scaling is super easy. All you do is expand the section for the chapter5-admin deployment, if it's not already expanded, as shown in figure 5.6. Then click the arrowheads next to the blue circle, which denotes the number of current pods. As noted previously, *pod* is the Kubernetes

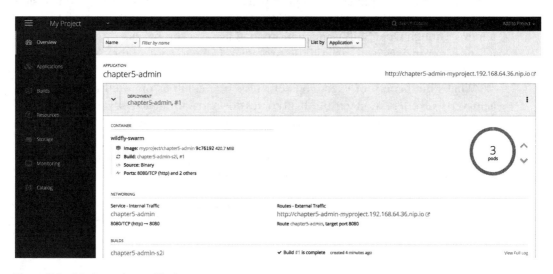

Figure 5.6   Admin service pod instances

term for the containerized deployment, but essentially it's the number of instances of a given service.

Here you can see that the number of pods has increased from the default of 1, up to 3. Open several private browser windows and click the endpoint for /admin/category a few times in each. Then head back to the OpenShift console and take a look at the logs for each of the pods that are running. You should see the SQL calls that were made against the different pods.

If you want to remove the admin service, you can just as easily remove it from OpenShift with the following:

```
mvn fabric8:undeploy -Popenshift
```

> **WARNING**   To undeploy your service, you didn't use the Maven clean goal. As part of deploy, fabric8 stores files in /target that contain details of all the resources that were deployed to OpenShift. If you clean them out before undeploy can run, fabric8 has absolutely no idea what it's trying to undeploy and is unable to do anything.

You can now deploy and undeploy the admin service to OpenShift locally running inside Minishift, but can you execute tests in the same way? That's what the next section is all about!

5.7   *Testing in the cloud*

Because you're able to deploy the admin service to a local cloud with Minishift, can you also use that local cloud to test it as well? You most certainly can!

To help develop tests that integrate with OpenShift you're going to use an extension from the Arquillian ecosystem called *Arquillian Cube* (http://arquillian.org/arquillian-cube/). Arquillian Cube gives you the ability to run tests against code inside Docker containers, by providing hooks for controlling the execution of Docker containers. Though OpenShift is much more than just Docker, because it uses Docker for its container images, you can still use Arquillian Cube to control the deployment and run tests against it.

What's the benefit of executing your tests in a cloud as opposed to what can be achieved with integration testing? It all comes down to wanting to test your microservice in an environment that, as closely as possible, resembles production. If you're deploying your microservice into production in a cloud, your best chance of finding out problems with such a deployment is being able to deploy your tests to a cloud as well. To be able to do that, you need to add the following to pom.xml.

Listing 5.3   Arquillian Cube dependencies

```
<dependencyManagement>
  <dependencies>
    <dependency>
      <groupId>org.arquillian.cube</groupId>
```

```
            <artifactId>arquillian-cube-bom</artifactId>      ◁──┐ Import all Arquillian
            <version>1.12.0</version>                              Cube dependencies so
            <type>pom</type>                                       they're available.
            <scope>import</scope>
        </dependency>
    </dependencies>
</dependencyManagement>

<dependencies>
    <dependency>
        <groupId>org.arquillian.cube</groupId>
        <artifactId>arquillian-cube-openshift</artifactId>   ◁──┐ Add the main Arquillian
        <scope>test</scope>                                       Cube artifact as a test
        <exclusions>                                              dependency to the project.
            <exclusion>
                <groupId>io.undertow</groupId>
                <artifactId>undertow-core</artifactId>   ◁──┐ Exclude Undertow as a transitive
            </exclusion>                                       dependency from Arquillian Cube.
        </exclusions>                                          It interferes with Thorntail.
    </dependency>
    <dependency>
        <groupId>org.awaitility</groupId>
        <artifactId>awaitility</artifactId>          ◁──┐ Add a test dependency for
        <version>3.0.0</version>                           Awaitility to help with waiting
        <scope>test</scope>                                for endpoints to be available.
    </dependency>
</dependencies>
```

Because you want to be able to run tests outside the cloud as well, though the code for chapter 5 has them currently removed, you need a separate profile to activate the tests you have for your cloud, OpenShift:

```
<profile>
    <id>openshift-it</id>
    <build>
        <plugins>
            <plugin>
                <groupId>org.apache.maven.plugins</groupId>
                <artifactId>maven-failsafe-plugin</artifactId>
                <executions>
                    <execution>
                        <goals>
                            <goal>integration-test</goal>
                            <goal>verify</goal>
                        </goals>
                    </execution>
                </executions>
            </plugin>
        </plugins>
    </build>
</profile>
```

Here you tell Maven that you want the `maven-failsafe-plugin` to execute your test, `integration-test` goal, and then `verify` the results.

Now it's time to create your test! You're going to create a test similar to one of your integration tests from chapter 4, but it'll be executed against your cloud, OpenShift, instead of a local instance. As the fail-safe plugin requires IT in the test class name to activate it, you'll name it CategoryResourceIT.

Listing 5.4   `CategoryResourceIT`

```
@RunWith(Arquillian.class)
public class CategoryResourceIT {        Inject a URL pointing at
                                         the OpenShift Route for
    @RouteURL("chapter5-admin")    ◁──── chapter5-admin.
    private URL url;
                                   Execute the method before a test to
                                   ensure you're ready for testing.
    @Before
    public void verifyRunning() {  ◁──
        await()
                .atMost(2, TimeUnit.MINUTES)    ◁──  Wait no more than 2 minutes
                .until(() -> {                       for /admin/category to respond
                    try {                            with a 200 response.
                        return get(url + "admin/category").statusCode() ==
➥ 200;
                    } catch (Exception e) {
                        return false;
                    }
                });
                                                              Set the root URL for
                                                              use with RestAssured.
        RestAssured.baseURI = url + "/admin/category";  ◁──
    }

    @Test
    public void testGetCategory() throws Exception {
        Response response =
                given()
                        .pathParam("categoryId", 1014)
                .when()
                        .get("{categoryId}")
                .then()                               Retrieve the category
                        .statusCode(200)              with ID 1014, ensuring you
                        .extract().response();   ◁──  received a 200 response.

        String jsonAsString = response.asString();

        Category category = JsonPath.from(jsonAsString).getObject("",
➥ Category.class);

        assertThat(category.getId()).isEqualTo(1014);        ◁──────
        assertThat(category.getParent().getId()).isEqualTo(1011);
        assertThat(category.getName()).isEqualTo("Ford SUVs");
        assertThat(category.isVisible()).isEqualTo(Boolean.TRUE);
    }
}                              Verify that the details of the Category you
                               received match what you expected.
```

It's time to test it out!

First you need to ensure that you have Minishift running, and that you've recently logged in with `oc login`. Authentications do expire! If all that's done, you run the following:

```
mvn clean install -Popenshift,openshift-it
```

Here you activate the profiles for `openshift` and `openshift-it`. The `openshift-it` profile will execute your test, but without the `openshift` profile being present, the admin service won't be deployed to OpenShift! If the service successfully deploys and the tests pass, the terminal should show a Maven build that completed without error.

You've only just scratched the surface of what's possible with the fabric8 Maven plugin and Minishift, but you have a solid footing to begin exploring further on your own. Because it'll be a while before you use Minishift again, let's stop it for now:

```
minishift stop
```

5.8   Additional exercises

Here are additional exercises for you to grow your understanding of OpenShift and to help improve the code for the example:

- Modify the deployment of the admin service to use PostgreSQL or MySQL when running on OpenShift.
- Add test methods for `CategoryResourceIT` for creating a `Category`, and another that fails the name validation.

If you take on these exercises and would like to see them included into the code for the book, please submit a pull request to the project on GitHub.

Summary

- You can take advantage of immutable container images by choosing a PaaS that uses a CaaS internally.
- Minishift provides a cloud environment with OpenShift on your local machine, to simplify both the execution and testing of microservices without needing to provision lots of machines.
- The fabric8 Maven plugin removes all the boilerplate needed to define resources and services within OpenShift or Kubernetes to reduce the configuration hurdles before seeing a microservice running in the cloud.

Part 2

Implementing Enterprise Java microservices

In part 2, we delve deeper into microservice development by covering topics such as consuming other microservices, service registration and discovery, fault tolerance, and security.

These six chapters also cover the development of a microservice hybrid from the Cayambe monolith, using the microservices that you've developed throughout the book. Finally, you'll add data streaming with Kafka as you learn about sharing data among microservices and with hybrids.

Consuming microservices

6

This chapter covers

- How to consume a microservice
- Your choices when consuming a microservice

Consuming a microservice can mean many things to many people. Clients of a microservice could be scripts, web pages, other microservices, or pretty much anything that can make HTTP requests. If we covered them all, this chapter would be a whole book by itself!

Developing a microservice is interesting, but it doesn't get you far until you introduce many microservices interacting with each other. To enable two services to interact with each other, you need a method by which one service can call another.

This chapter provides examples focused on one microservice consuming another with Java-based libraries, but the methods shown can be equally applied to any generic Java client consuming a microservice.

With Enterprise Java, two services would interact with a direct service call, as shown in figure 6.1.

Runtime

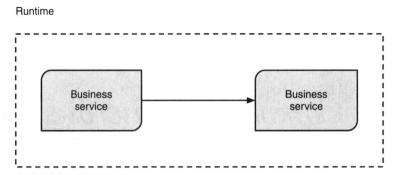

Figure 6.1   Enterprise Java business service calls

The service call could be accomplished by the following:

- `@EJB` injection when using EJBs
- `@Inject` with CDI
- Retrieving an instance of a service via a `static` method or variable
- Spring dependency injection, either XML or annotation based

All these options require that your two services reside in the same JVM and runtime, as shown in figure 6.1.

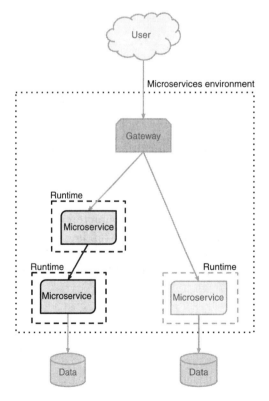

Figure 6.2   Consuming microservices

In the figure one microservice is calling another microservice. In the diagram, they're within the same microservices environment, but they don't have to be. Revisiting figure 1.4, figure 6.2 highlights the focus of this chapter, solving the means by which two microservices in separate runtimes are able to communicate.

In our particular case, you'll be taking the new Cayambe administration microservice from chapter 2 and developing clients for it with different libraries. Figure 6.3 illustrates where the microservice client fits; you use a short-term way of retrieving category data until such time as the final solution is in place.

You'll start with a look at consuming a microservice by using low-level libraries that deal directly with HTTP requests. Because they deal with HTTP requests, they can be used with microservices that don't expose RESTful endpoints. Then you'll learn about client libraries that are specifically designed to simplify the code required to call RESTful endpoints. They offer a higher level of abstraction over HTTP requests, which simplifies the client code significantly, as you'll see in our examples. The code for this section can be found in the /chapter6 directory of the book's example code.

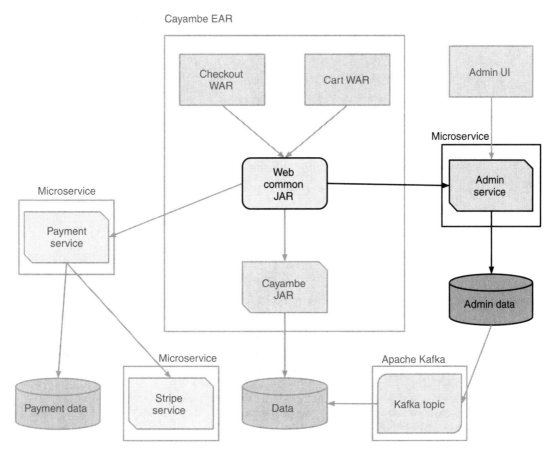

Figure 6.3 Cayambe administration microservice client

For each client library, a service will be implemented that calls the `CategoryResource` RESTful endpoint, which you created in chapter 2, and then returns the received data as the response to the caller.

> **TIP** You can set the port that the `CategoryResource` starts on to prevent port clashes with the other microservices. You set the `swarm.port.offset` property in the Maven plugin to 1.

Each of these services needs an object to represent the category JSON that you'll receive from the administration service. To facilitate that, each client library Maven module will have its own `Category` object, which will be used when deserializing the response from the administration service.

Listing 6.1   Category model class

```
@JsonIdentityInfo(generator = ObjectIdGenerators.PropertyGenerator.class,
  property = "id")                          ⬅  Defines the key as the ID for Category,
public class Category {                         which is used for deserializing the
                                                collection of children received as JSON
    protected Integer id;

    protected String name;

    protected String header;

    protected Boolean visible;

    protected String imagePath;                 Initializes the collection of children to
                                                ensure that you always have a valid
    protected Category parent;                     collection, even if it's empty

    private Collection<Category> children = new HashSet<>();    ⬅

    protected LocalDateTime created = LocalDateTime.now();

    protected LocalDateTime updated;

    protected Integer version;

    ...
}
```

The getter and setter methods are omitted for brevity, but the full source of `Category` is available in the book's source code.

In addition, each of these services needs access to `ExecutorService` to submit work for processing on a new thread. You want to use one provided by Java EE so the services all retrieve one the same way:

```
private ManagedExecutorService executorService() throws Exception {
    InitialContext ctx = new InitialContext();
    return (ManagedExecutorService)
      ctx.lookup("java:jboss/ee/concurrency/executor/default");
}
```

This does a simple JNDI lookup of the service by name and returns the instance you can use for submitting work.

> **NOTE**   The `ExecutorService` is defined for you by WildFly. You don't need to do anything to make it available in order to retrieve it from JNDI.

Your services could just as easily have created a new `Thread` directly to perform any required work, but then your new thread would be outside the Java EE thread pool management. Is this a problem? Not always, but you could have problems if the thread pool size of the runtime is almost as large as the available JVM threads. In that case, you could exhaust all available JVM threads when creating threads outside the Java EE thread pool. As a general rule, it's best not to create threads directly, but instead use the `ExecutorService`.

Because you want to show how synchronous and asynchronous usage scenarios result in different client code for consuming a microservice, each resource that uses a client library will contain two endpoints:

- `/sync`—Synchronously processes a request from the caller
- `/async`—Asynchronously processes a request from the caller

Traditionally, services were developed to communicate synchronously with any other resources required to complete a response. With increasing demands from the enterprise to deliver greater performance and scalability, we've moved toward greater asynchronous behavior in our services. In this chapter and the remainder of the book, you'll learn about both synchronous and asynchronous usage patterns. Enhancing the benefits of microservices also requires some level of asynchronous behavior; otherwise, you minimize the benefits of their distributed nature. If you take that route, you may as well stick with a monolith!

> **NOTE**   Each of your microservices defines a field called `categoryUrl`, which is hardcoded to http://localhost:8081/admin/categorytree. This isn't what you'd go into production doing, but it serves our purpose to simplify the examples. In a later chapter, you'll see how service discovery can be used for connecting to other services.

6.1   *Consuming a microservice with a Java client library*

In this section, you'll see examples of consuming a microservice that uses lower-level libraries to deal with HTTP requests directly. Though that results in more verbose and extra handling of data, it does provide the greatest flexibility as to how a call can be made. For instance, using these libraries may be a better choice if a microservice needs to communicate with many types of HTTP resources, because it doesn't make sense to add another library just for RESTful endpoint interaction.

6.1.1 java.net

The classes in the java.net package have been part of the JDK from the beginning. Though they've been enhanced and updated over the years, they focus on low-level HTTP interactions. They're in no way designed for RESTful endpoint consumption, so some level of cumbersome code is required.

Let's take a look at our first method for the `DisplayResource`.

Listing 6.2 `DisplayResource` with java.net

```java
@GET
@Path("/sync")
@Produces(MediaType.APPLICATION_JSON)
public Category getCategoryTreeSync() throws Exception {
    HttpURLConnection connection = null;

    try {
        URL url = new URL(this.categoryUrl);
        connection = (HttpURLConnection) url.openConnection();
        connection.setRequestMethod("GET");
        connection.setRequestProperty("Accept", MediaType.APPLICATION_JSON);

        if (connection.getResponseCode() != HttpURLConnection.HTTP_OK) {
            throw new RuntimeException("Request Failed: HTTP Error code: " +
                connection.getResponseCode());
        }

        return new ObjectMapper()
                .registerModule(new JavaTimeModule())
                .readValue(connection.getInputStream(), Category.class);

    } finally {
        assert connection != null;
        connection.disconnect();
    }
}
```

- Set HTTP GET as the request method for your connection.
- Create a URL pointing to your CategoryResource.
- Set "application/json" as the media type that you'll accept in a response.
- Check for a non-OK response code.
- Create a new ObjectMapper to perform the JSON deserialization.
- Register the JavaTimeModule to handle conversion of JSON to LocalDateTime instances.
- Pass the InputStream you received in the response to the ObjectMapper for deserialization, into an instance of Category.
- Close the connection to CategoryResource.

Though you're dealing with a simple RESTful endpoint, the client code to communicate with it certainly isn't, and this is only synchronous!

The next listing shows how the preceding code changes if you want to handle the client request to your microservice asynchronously.

Listing 6.3 `DisplayResource` with java.net asynchronously

```java
@GET
@Path("/async")
@Produces(MediaType.APPLICATION_JSON)
public void getCategoryTreeAsync(
    @Suspended final AsyncResponse asyncResponse)
    throws Exception {
```

- Request processing will be handled asynchronously.

```
executorService().execute(() -> {                          Pass the lambda expression to
    HttpURLConnection connection = null;                   an executor for processing.

    try {
        // The code to open the connection, check the status code,
        // and process the response is identical to the synchronous
        // example and has been removed.

        asyncResponse.resume(category);          Resume the AsyncResponse with the
    } catch (IOException e) {                     deserialized Category instance.
        asyncResponse.resume(e);
    } finally {                                  Resume the AsyncResponse
        assert connection != null;              with an exception.
        connection.disconnect();
    }
});
}
```

The listing introduced concepts you haven't seen before—namely, @Suspended and AsyncResponse. These two pieces are the core of how JAX-RS handles client requests asynchronously. @Suspended informs the JAX-RS runtime that the HTTP request from the client should be suspended until a response is ready. AsyncResponse indicates how the developer informs the runtime that a response is ready or has failed to complete.

What does that look like? Take a look at figure 6.4.

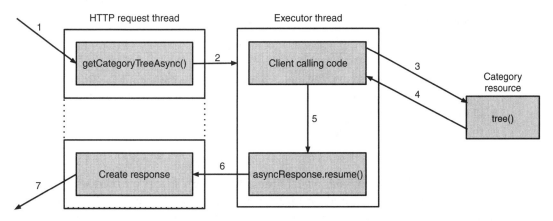

Figure 6.4 JAX-RS AsyncResponse handling

Here's what is happening at each step within figure 6.4:

1 An HTTP request arrives from a browser or another client.

2 getCategoryTreeAsync() triggers code to be executed in a separate thread. On completion of getCategoryTreeAsync(), the client request is suspended and the HTTP request thread that was handling it is made available to handle additional requests.

3   An HTTP request is made to an external microservice.

4   An HTTP response is received from the external microservice.

5   The response data is passed to `asyncResponse.resume()`.

6   The client request is reactivated in the HTTP request thread and a response is constructed.

7   The response is returned to the browser, or to whatever client made the request.

WARNING   Using `@Suspended` in a RESTful endpoint doesn't prevent the client that's calling the endpoint from blocking. It benefits only the server side of the request by allowing greater request throughput. Without the use of `@Suspended`, a JAX-RS resource can handle only as many requests as there are available threads, because each request blocks the thread until the method completes.

Now that you have your services built, you can start them.

Change into the /chapter6/admin directory of the book's example code and run this:

```
mvn thorntail:run
```

`CategoryResource` will be started and available at http://localhost:8081/admin/categorytree in a browser.

Now you start your `DisplayResource`. Change into the /chapter6/java-net directory and run this:

```
mvn thorntail:run
```

It's now possible to access the microservices by accessing them in a browser: http://localhost:8080/sync and http://localhost:8080/async. Either of the preceding URLs opened in the browser will show the tree of categories that are currently present within the administration microservice.

6.1.2   *Apache HttpClient*

With Apache HttpClient, you get an abstraction over classes you used with java.net, minimizing the code required for interacting with the underlying HTTP connection. The code in `DisplayResource` isn't vastly different from your previous code, but it does improve the code's readability.

For instance, let's look at your first method for `DisplayResource`.

Listing 6.4   DisplayResource with HttpClient

```
@GET
@Path("/sync")
@Produces(MediaType.APPLICATION_JSON)
public Category getCategoryTreeSync() throws Exception {
    try (CloseableHttpClient httpclient = HttpClients.createDefault()) {  ◁──┐
```

Create an HTTP client inside the try-with-resources statement.

Execute HttpGet, passing a handler for the Response.

Create an HttpGet instance with the CategoryResource URL endpoint.

Specify that you'll accept JSON responses.

Verify that the response code is OK.

Extract HttpEntity from Response. Convert the entity to a Category instance using an ObjectMapper.

```java
        HttpGet get = new HttpGet(this.categoryUrl);
        get.addHeader("Accept", MediaType.APPLICATION_JSON);

        return httpclient.execute(get, response -> {
            int status = response.getStatusLine().getStatusCode();
            if (status >= 200 && status < 300) {
                return new ObjectMapper()
                        .registerModule(new JavaTimeModule())
                        .readValue(response.getEntity().getContent(),
    Category.class);
            } else {
                throw new ClientProtocolException("Unexpected response
    status: " + status);
            }
        });
    }
}
```

Even with this short example, you can see how much simpler your client code is when making an HTTP request. Now let's see how much simpler your code becomes when you use @Suspended.

Listing 6.5 DisplayResource with HttpClient and @Suspended

Execute your calling code in a separate thread.

Resume the AsyncResponse with the received category.

```java
@GET
@Path("/async")
@Produces(MediaType.APPLICATION_JSON)
public void getCategoryTreeAsync(@Suspended final AsyncResponse
    asyncResponse) throws Exception {
    executorService().execute(() -> {
        try (CloseableHttpClient httpclient = HttpClients.createDefault()) {
            HttpGet get = new HttpGet(this.categoryUrl);

            // The code to initiate the HTTP GET request and convert the
    HttpEntity
            // is identical to the synchronous example and has been removed.

            asyncResponse.resume(category);
        } catch (IOException e) {
            asyncResponse.resume(e);
        }
    });
}
```

Once again, this approach is similar to our synchronous example, but you use @Suspended and AsyncResponse to indicate to JAX-RS that you want the HTTP request to be suspended while you make your call to an external microservice.

If you already have your CategoryResource microservice running at http://localhost:8081, you can now start your new microservice by using Apache HttpClient.

> **WARNING**   You need to stop any previously running microservices before you
> can run this one, because they use the same port.

Change into the /chapter6/apache-httpclient directory and run this:

```
mvn thorntail:run
```

It's now possible to access the microservices by accessing them in a browser:
http://localhost:8080/sync and http://localhost:8080/async. As with your previous
microservice, you'll see a tree of categories that are currently present within the
administration microservice.

In this section, you looked at client libraries that focus on using URLs and HTTP
request methods directly. They're great for interacting with HTTP resources, but
they're verbose when dealing with RESTful endpoints. Can you find client libraries
that simplify your client code even further?

6.2   *Consuming a microservice with a JAX-RS client library*

This section introduces client libraries that bring your abstraction level even higher
than HTTP. Both libraries provide APIs that are designed specifically for use in communicating with JAX-RS endpoints.

6.2.1   *JAX-RS client*

JAX-RS has been defined over the years as part of the JSR 311 and JSR 339 specifications of Java EE. As part of these specifications, JAX-RS has a client API that provides a
developer with a cleaner means of calling RESTful endpoints from a JAX-RS resource.

So what are the benefits of using the JAX-RS client library? It allows you to forget
about the low-level HTTP connection you need for connecting to a RESTful microservice, and focus on the required metadata such as the following:

- HTTP method
- Parameters to be passed
- MediaType format of parameters and return type
- Required cookies
- Any other piece of metadata required to consume a RESTful microservice

When using the JAX-RS client library, you need to register a provider to handle the
deserialization of JSON into `LocalDateTime` instances when processing a response.
For that, you need the following listing, which you'll use in our subsequent examples.

Listing 6.6   `ClientJacksonProvider`

Create a new ObjectMapper instance.   **Provide ContextResolver for**
                                                                       ObjectMapper instances.

```
public class ClientJacksonProvider implements ContextResolver<ObjectMapper> {  ⟵

    private final ObjectMapper mapper = new ObjectMapper()
```

```
                    .registerModule(new JavaTimeModule());
    @Override
    public ObjectMapper getContext(Class<?> type) {
        return mapper;
    }
}
```

Register the JavaTimeModule for handling LocalDateTime conversion.

Return the instance of ObjectMapper that you created when it's requested.

Once again, you start with your synchronous example endpoint.

Listing 6.7 DisplayResource with JAX-RS client

```
@GET
@Path("/sync")
@Produces(MediaType.APPLICATION_JSON)
public Category getCategoryTreeSync() {
    Client client = ClientBuilder.newClient();

    return client
            .register(ClientJacksonProvider.class)
            .target(this.categoryUrl)
            .request(MediaType.APPLICATION_JSON)
            .get(Category.class);
}
```

Create a JAX-RS client.

Specify that your response should return JSON.

Register the provider you defined in listing 6.6.

Set the target of the client to be the CategoryResource URL.

Make an HTTP GET request and convert the response body to Category.

When comparing the preceding listing to either of the pure Java client libraries, you have a significantly simplified and more coherent piece of code for calling an external microservice.

Is that important? In terms of the functionality required to execute a request and process the response, not at all. But that isn't anywhere near as critical as how easily a developer can understand existing or develop new code. I'll leave it up to you to judge, but I know I'd prefer to see the preceding example than anything else we've seen so far.

Can the JAX-RS client library likewise improve the readability of your code for asynchronous use? See the next listing.

Listing 6.8 DisplayResource with JAX-RS client and @Suspended

```
@GET
@Path("/async")
@Produces(MediaType.APPLICATION_JSON)
public void getCategoryTreeAsync(@Suspended final AsyncResponse
➥ asyncResponse) throws Exception {
    executorService().execute(() -> {
        Client client = ClientBuilder.newClient();

        try {
            Category category = client.target(this.categoryUrl)
```

```
            .register(ClientJacksonProvider.class)
            .request(MediaType.APPLICATION_JSON)
            .get(Category.class);

        asyncResponse.resume(category);
    } catch (Exception e) {
        asyncResponse.resume(Response
                    .serverError()
                    .entity(e.getMessage())
                    .build());
    }
  });
}
```

> **Return a response you construct, including the exception message, instead of just passing the exception along.**

As with all asynchronous usage, you specify @Suspended and AsyncResponse. You also use ManagedExecutorService to provide a new thread for processing your call, and you set the response with asyncResponse.resume().

You also could've used the asynchronous functionality of the JAX-RS client library itself.

Listing 6.9   DisplayResource with JAX-RS client and InvocationCallback

```
@GET
@Path("/asyncAlt")
@Produces(MediaType.APPLICATION_JSON)
public void getCategoryTreeAsyncAlt(@Suspended final AsyncResponse
➥ asyncResponse) {
    Client client = ClientBuilder.newClient();
    WebTarget target = client.target(this.categoryUrl)
            .register(ClientJacksonProvider.class);
    target.request(MediaType.APPLICATION_JSON)
            .async()
            .get(new InvocationCallback<Category>() {
                @Override
                public void completed(Category result) {
                    asyncResponse.resume(result);
                }

                @Override
                public void failed(Throwable throwable) {
                    throwable.printStackTrace();
                    asyncResponse.resume(Response
                        .serverError()
                        .entity(throwable.getMessage())
                        .build());
                }
            });
}
```

> **Indicate you want the call to be asynchronous.**

> **Pass InvocationCallback with methods for completed and failed handling.**

This second asynchronous version alters which pieces of your code execute in a new thread, but it doesn't alter the end result. In getCategoryTreeAsync(), you pass all your RESTful endpoint code into a new thread so that the HTTP request thread can be unblocked almost as quickly as it was processed. `getCategoryTreeAsyncAlt()` differs by executing only the HTTP request to your external microservice in a new thread. All the setup code required to make your HTTP request occurs in the same thread as the client request.

As `getCategoryTreeAsyncAlt()` uses the HTTP request thread opened for the client the longest, it reduces the throughput of the RESTful endpoints by causing each client to block on a thread for longer than necessary. Though the impact may be minimal, given a large enough number of requests, the impact exists.

So why show an *inferior* method that negatively affects throughput? First, as a way to show that there can be many means to achieve a similar goal. Second, many microservices may not have a large enough number of concurrent client requests for such a performance impact to be noticeable and cause problems. In such a case, a developer may prefer callbacks over any alternative—because when an option doesn't impact performance, that's a reasonable choice to make.

In switching to using the JAX-RS client library, you've simplified your calling code and made it clearer to understand. That certainly makes it more pleasurable to develop with than the lower-level libraries, but it does come at a cost in terms of how flexibly it can be used.

What kind of flexibility is lost? For most use cases, the JAX-RS client library wouldn't cause any impact, but calling a microservice that uses a binary protocol would be more difficult. Depending on the protocol, it may require developing custom handlers and providers or incorporating additional third-party libraries that provide such features.

Change into the /chapter6/jaxrs-client directory and run this:

```
mvn thorntail:run
```

It's now possible to access the microservices by accessing them in a browser: http://localhost:8080/sync and http://localhost:8080/async. As with our previous examples, you'll see a tree of categories that are currently present within the administration microservice.

6.2.2 *RESTEasy client*

RESTEasy is an implementation of the JAX-RS specification that's made available within WildFly as well as separately. Though many parts of its client library are identical to those provided by the JAX-RS client API, RESTEasy provides a particularly interesting feature that's worthwhile.

With the JAX-RS client library, you specify what RESTful endpoint you want to call by chaining methods together to build up a picture of the endpoints, URL path, parameters, return type, media types, and so forth. There's nothing wrong with that, but it's not overly natural for developers who are more familiar with creating RESTful endpoints with JAX-RS.

With RESTEasy, you can re-create the RESTful endpoint that you want to communicate with as an interface and have a proxy of that interface generated for you. This process allows you to use an interface of the external microservice as if it were present within your own codebase.

For your external `CategoryResource` microservice, you'd create an interface like the following.

Listing 6.10 `CategoryService`

```
@Path("/admin/categorytree")
public interface CategoryService {
    @GET
    @Produces(MediaType.APPLICATION_JSON)
    Category getCategoryTree();
}
```

There's nothing special about the code here. It looks like any other JAX-RS endpoint class, except that it's an interface and there's no method implementation. Another benefit is needing to define only the methods on the interface that your microservice requires. For instance, if an external microservice has five endpoints and your microservice needs to use only one, your interface defining that external microservice requires only a single method. You don't need to define the entire external microservice.

Is there an advantage to this? Definitely! It allows you to have a focused definition of an external microservice that you need to consume. If methods are updated on that microservice that you don't consume, there's no need to update your interface because you don't use those endpoints.

NOTE Taking this approach, it'd be possible to share the same interface between service and client. The service would provide an implementation of the interface for the actual endpoint code.

WARNING Such an approach, though possible, isn't recommended practice for microservices because it becomes a separate library that both microservices depend on, introducing release timing and sequencing issues. This is a dangerous road to head down and will result in only continual pain for an enterprise. It's therefore preferable to replicate the methods that you need to call.

Now that you've defined an interface that maps onto your external microservice, how can it be used?

Listing 6.11 `DisplayResource` with RESTEasy

```
@GET
@Path("/sync")
@Produces(MediaType.APPLICATION_JSON)          Create the client with RESTEasy.
public Category getCategoryTreeSync() {
    ResteasyClient client = new ResteasyClientBuilder().build();   ◄───┘
```

Set the target URL base path for your request.

```
ResteasyWebTarget target = client.target(this.categoryUrl)
            .register(ClientJacksonProvider.class);

CategoryService categoryService = target.proxy(CategoryService.class);
return categoryService.getCategoryTree();
}
```

Call CategoryResource via your proxy.

Generate a proxy implementation of your CategoryService.

With this approach, you shift setting all the request parameters such as URL path, media types, and return types into your CategoryService interface. Now your client code interacting with the proxy behaves just like a local method call. You've gained a further simplification in your code by separating common request parameter values into a single place. This is particularly important when a microservice may require calling the same external microservice in different RESTful endpoints, because you don't want to repeat information that isn't going to change wherever it might be called from.

Let's see some asynchronous examples with your proxy interface.

Listing 6.12 DisplayResource with RESTEasy and @Suspended

```
@GET
@Path("/async")
@Produces(MediaType.APPLICATION_JSON)
public void getCategoryTreeAsync(@Suspended final AsyncResponse
  asyncResponse) throws Exception {
    executorService().execute(() -> {
        ResteasyClient client = new ResteasyClientBuilder().build();

        try {
            ResteasyWebTarget target = client.target(this.categoryUrl)
                    .register(ClientJacksonProvider.class);

            CategoryService categoryService =
        target.proxy(CategoryService.class);
            Category category = categoryService.getCategoryTree();
            asyncResponse.resume(category);
        } catch (Exception e) {
            asyncResponse.resume(Response
                                .serverError()
                                .entity(e.getMessage())
                                .build());
        }
    });
}
```

The only changes you need between synchronous and asynchronous RESTful endpoints are the JAX-RS asynchronous requirements of @Suspended and @AsyncResponse, submitting the client code for processing in a separate thread, and setting either success or failure on asyncResponse.resume().

The one drawback with the proxy approach you've been using with the RESTEasy client library is that it doesn't support invoking a callback when executing the call to your external microservice. As such, your `getCategoryTreeAsyncAlt()` with RESTEasy would be identical to when you used the JAX-RS client library.

Change into the /chapter6/resteasy-client directory and run this:

```
mvn thorntail:run
```

It's now possible to access the microservices at http://localhost:8080/sync and http://localhost:8080/async. Each URL will return a tree of categories that are currently present within the administration microservice, as the result.

Now we've covered a couple of client libraries that provide a higher level of abstraction for interacting with RESTful endpoints. The examples show the benefits to the client code in reducing complexity and improving readability.

Summary

- Java-based client libraries, such as java.net and Apache HttpClient, provide low-level access to networking in Java but create more verbose code than necessary.
- JAX-RS-based client libraries provide an abstraction that makes consuming microservices easier.

Discovering microservices for consumption

This chapter covers

- Why service discovery is important
- How to register a microservice so it can be discovered by clients
- Which service registries are supported by Thorntail
- How to look up a microservice within a client

As part of decomposing pieces of the Cayambe monolith into separate microservices, you've decided that you need a service for processing order payments. This new microservice will then be used within the Cayambe monolith in chapter 10.

Dozens, if not hundreds, of providers offer payment processing services. Initially, you'll develop basic integration with Stripe (https://stripe.com/docs/quickstart). To facilitate future expansion of payment providers, you'll integrate with Stripe in its own microservice. The new payment microservice will then use the Stripe microservice to process and record the payment with the Stripe online service.

In previous chapters, you've seen how to access separate microservices directly by referring to the URL where a microservice is running. In this chapter, you'll take calling microservices a step further by decoupling your client from the microservice it's consuming, making it easier to scale.

Unless you're developing a microservice for your own use, it's virtually guaranteed that you'll need the ability to scale the number of instances of your microservice in production. Without the ability to scale, your application will always have problems coping with the load placed upon it by users.

7.1   Why does a microservice need to be discovered?

Taking the approach to microservices from chapter 6, the new Payment microservice would locate Stripe via a hardcoded URL, as shown in figure 7.1.

Figure 7.1   Microservice direct lookup

This approach is perfectly fine for local testing of microservices, to make sure they do what you want, but you don't want to be relying on locating microservices with hardcoded strings in production! The operational nightmare of moving a single instance of a microservice from one environment to another would require any of its clients being rebuilt to use the new URL location of the microservice! That's not conducive to delivering business value in a timely manner. That's not even taking into account the desire to have more than one instance of a microservice available for handling requests to better scale an application.

If you kept relying on hardcoded URLs, your Payment microservice would contain an ever-growing list of possible instances for Stripe to distribute its requests across, as shown in figure 7.2.

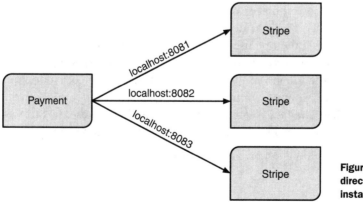

Figure 7.2   Microservice direct lookup with multiple instances

This architecture also requires the client, Payment, to have code designed to spread the load across the instances of Stripe. When the client is responsible for determining which instance of a microservice to consume, this process is known as c*lient-side load balancing.* The client is making a determination about which instance to consume.

Developing load-balancing techniques for the microservices you need to consume isn't where you want to be spending your precious development time. Ideally, you want a framework or library to handle that complexity for you, allowing your code to request a single instance to operate on.

What can be done to reduce some of the pain of your situation? Enter service discovery!

7.1.1 *What is service discovery?*

Service discovery is the means by which one microservice retrieves the physical location of another microservice, at runtime, for the purpose of consuming it. Service discovery requires the use of a *service registry*. Otherwise, there's no place from which the discovery process can retrieve the URL.

How does adding service discovery into the flow of consuming a microservice affect the way your consuming microservice operates? See figure 7.3.

Here's how your Payment microservice makes a call to the Stripe microservice by discovering it through a service registry:

1 The Payment microservice requests the locations for the Stripe microservice from a known service registry.
2 The service registry returns all the available Stripe instances.
3 The Payment microservice sends a request to the Stripe microservice instance retrieved from the service registry.
4 The Payment microservice receives a response from the Stripe microservice.

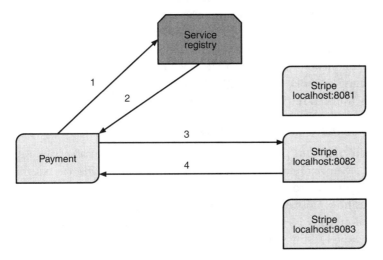

Figure 7.3 Service discovery

The process seems simple enough, but how does service discovery work? First, you need to have a place to look to find the microservices you need. That's the role of the service registry.

You now have a place to look for the microservices you need, but that doesn't mean a lot if it's empty! Anytime an instance of a microservice is started, it needs to contact the service registry to provide it with a name and a URL location where it can be accessed. The name doesn't need to be unique, but all microservice instances registered under an identical name do need to expose the same API. If they don't, any client of those microservices is going to see very different and unexpected results!

After a service registry is populated with data, your client microservice can ask it to provide the URL locations of all instances for a specified service name. At this point, it's up to your client as to how it determines which location to use when consuming the microservice.

Depending on whether you're using a framework or consuming microservices without one, several algorithms can be used to choose a specific location. The algorithm could be as simple as cycling through each location in order, known as a *round-robin*. Or the algorithm can increase in complexity by taking into account factors such as current load and response times.

As we discussed earlier, your microservice shouldn't be developing custom load-balancing algorithms. If a microservice needs anything more complicated than a basic round-robin, or a random choice from a list, you should consider including a library to provide those algorithms for you.

Whether your microservice uses a simple load-balancing algorithm internally, or you use a library for it, there is the question of how long to retain the instance URL you've been given. In an ideal world, you wouldn't retain the instance URL for any length of time, allowing instances of microservices to come and go without affecting clients. If at all possible, you're in a better place if you can start with this approach.

If an environment isn't suited to real-time service discovery every time, your microservice shouldn't hold onto any physical URLs for more than 10 to 15 seconds. That may not seem like much, but a microservice instance can quickly go from functioning to failing. An extra burden with caching URLs is that your code needs to be more vigilant about catching network failure and microservice errors, either with retries or by using service discovery to retrieve a fresh instance.

7.1.2 *What are the benefits of service discovery and a registry?*

Why do you want the extra infrastructure and management of a service registry for your microservices environment? Can't you use a properties file to externalize the URL of anything your microservice needs to consume?

Sure, this was how most external services were integrated into applications in the past. This technique provided an easy way to change the URL of external services when moving between testing and production environments.

But this approach doesn't allow for easy scaling of an application or microservice, either up or down. With a shift toward cloud deployments, one of the biggest changes is the way such an environment is charged to an enterprise.

In the past, enterprises would have internal infrastructure to host all their applications, whether for internal or public use. The main cost with internal infrastructure is in the initial setup. When that's complete, the ongoing hardware cost is minimal, though it does result in a larger operations cost from managing an internal infrastructure.

A migration to the cloud for most enterprises means not hosting applications on their own infrastructure but instead deploying to external hosting providers. Examples of these are Red Hat OpenShift, Google Cloud, and Amazon Web Services. These providers shift the cost away from large up-front hardware installations to regular infrastructure usage charges, usually on a monthly basis. This shift in the cost mechanism opens the door to reducing cost by scaling down an application when it's less used.

Another upside to a scalable environment is being able to scale up when load increases without the often long hardware provision process of an enterprise. This is particularly beneficial to an enterprise that experiences extremely high load during holidays. November and December are big for most retail stores, and a scalable environment provides enterprises the ability to scale their available servers without those servers sitting idle for the remainder of the year.

The ability to quickly and easily scale up or down a particular microservice, or even a group of them, when operating in a cloud environment is a tremendous advantage to enterprise developers. It allows them to shift from the past, where they needed to anticipate increased demand to allow the time required for provisioning new hardware (which often takes months). Enterprise developers deploying to the cloud can move to a future where a new instance, or series of them, can be running and processing user load within minutes.

Being able to scale an application is tightly linked to how loosely coupled it is. As I mentioned earlier, separating URLs that an application must use into an external registry greatly decreases the amount of coupling between components, when compared to the coupling through properties files that I also mentioned earlier.

Failover of external services is a concern for all distributed architectures. Maintaining loose coupling, through a service registry, allows failover of a microservice to happen without bringing down the entire application, provided the microservice is scaled to more than a single instance!

Using a service registry in conjunction with service discovery opens the door to enabling you to handle failovers gracefully, but in their own right they aren't the complete solution. You also need frameworks and libraries that can assist with providing fault tolerance, as you don't want to be writing it yourself! Chapter 8 shows how fault tolerance can be incorporated into your microservices.

As in figure 7.3, here are the steps for your Payment microservice to make a call to the Stripe microservice by discovering it through a service registry; see figure 7.4:

1 The Payment microservice requests the locations for the Stripe microservice from a known service registry.

2 The service registry returns all the available Stripe instances.

3 The Payment microservice sends a request to the Stripe microservice instance retrieved from the service registry.

4 The Payment microservice receives a response from the Stripe microservice.

In figure 7.3, Payment consumed the Stripe instance running on port 8082. But in figure 7.4, you can see that the Stripe instance on port 8082 is no longer functioning when another request is processed. How it failed, we don't know, but it's no longer available in the service registry. That's okay; Payment will contact the service registry for instances of Stripe and will choose the one running on port 8083 from the two that are available.

This sounds fantastic! You can scale microservices up or down as you please, within the limits of how the environment performs scaling, without worrying about how clients can find them.

Without a service registry providing metadata about Stripe to Payment, your microservice wouldn't have any way to insulate itself from failovers or migrations, or a way to recover from them. A service registry is good for more than just getting a new live instance if one has failed. It also handles migrating a microservice to a different environment by hiding from Payment where Stripe is actually running until Payment needs that information.

You can easily create new instances for Stripe in a completely different environment from the existing ones, but still have them available within the same service registry.

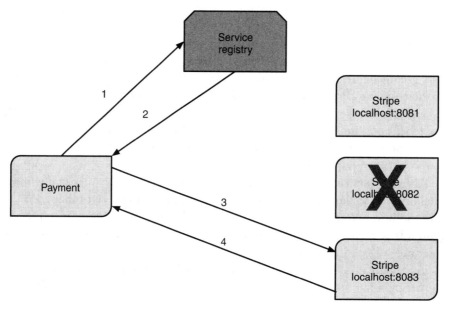

Figure 7.4 Service discovery with failed microservice

After the new instances are active, if you were migrating, you could scale down the old instances to shut them down—all without any impact to Payment needing to consume Stripe.

7.1.3 Stateless vs. stateful microservices

Being able to scale microservices at will is most certainly fantastic, but there's a catch. So far, you've been implicitly dealing with stateless microservices, in that the microservice doesn't retain any data within itself between requests.

What about your state? Microservice development is heavily focused on statelessness. This is a key ability for microservices to be scaled up and down without any concern for user state from previous requests.

To support scaling of microservices, it's not possible for them to be stateful—at least not in the same way that stateful session beans were in Java EE. As the often used saying goes, we want our microservices to be more like cattle and less like pets. Better to have many that can come or go without impact (cattle), instead of a few from which one disappearing can cause major issues (pets). You can still use user data from a previous request in your microservice, but it has to have been stored somewhere for you to retrieve it.

The shift to more stateless services has already begun in Enterprise Java over the last five years, but the push toward microservices has made it even more prominent than before. For developers and architects, it's no simple feat to switch from thinking in terms of state to stateless. The change requires additional thought up front, and during development, to prevent state from creeping into a microservice.

If there's a service you already have that's stateful, and there's simply no way to break it down into stateless microservices, or the challenge in doing so poses a risk that's too great, then microservices might not be the best approach. Stick with a more traditional Java EE application server to handle the stateful service and scaling of that service across a small cluster.

7.1.4 What is Netflix Ribbon?

Earlier we talked about load balancing across multiple instances of a single service, and how it wasn't a good idea to create complicated load balancers in your own code. What do you do if you want load balancing in your client that's not random or round-robin?

Thorntail provides integration with Netflix Ribbon just for that purpose, saving you from having to develop the algorithms yourself. Ribbon is a client-side software load-balancing framework developed by Netflix for its internal services. It was open sourced in January 2013 as part of a suite of projects that Netflix heavily relies on for its interprocess communication of services. The primary usage for Ribbon is calling RESTful endpoints, which is why it's a good fit for what you need when consuming Enterprise Java microservices.

Later in the chapter, I'll show how Ribbon can use a service registry to retrieve instances. Right now, let's focus on the load-balancing options it provides:

- *Round Robin*—Chooses an available server from all those present in sequential order, regardless of whatever load each server may be experiencing.
- *Availability Filtering*—Skips any servers that are deemed to have had their "circuit tripped," connection failures the last three times, or a high number of concurrent connections.
- *Weighted Response Time*—Each server is given a weighting based on average response times, which is used to generate a range of random values representing the server. For instance, if servers A and B have a weighting of 5 and 25, respectively, the range would be 1–5 (A) and 6–30 (B). A random number is generated between 1 and the sum of all the server weights, which determines the server based on the ranges. A server with a higher weighting, or shorter response time, has a greater chance of being selected.
- *Zone Aware Round Robin*—Particularly useful for deployments to Amazon Web Services, where servers are distributed across availability zones. This rule chooses servers based on whether they're in the same zone as the client, and that are available.
- *Random*—Purely random distribution across available servers.

The default choice is Round Robin. If performance is critical to your microservice, Weighted Response Time would be the best choice for load balancing. It's similar to Round Robin in its behavior, while also favoring those servers that are performing better.

This option is particularly beneficial if a server instance is performing badly to the point that the microservice environment deems it needs to be restarted. You don't want to continue sending lots of traffic to a microservice that could be restarted at any time.

It might be unclear from what we've discussed so far where Ribbon fits with respect to figure 7.3. You can see in figure 7.5 that Ribbon is part of your microservice, in this case Payment, that wants to consume another microservice, Stripe. Ribbon is then responsible for interacting with a service registry, choosing which server instance from those available to use, and finally executing a request against that instance.

For Ribbon to know where the service registry is located, you need to specify a class that's responsible for retrieving the list of available instances for a service. Which class is required depends on the service registry being used. For instance, `com.netflix` `.niws.loadbalancer.DiscoveryEnabledNIWSServerList` is the class to be used when accessing a service registry provided by Eureka through its custom client code. Eureka is a service registry developed by Netflix, but integration with Eureka isn't available in Thorntail.

> **WARNING** Last year, Netflix announced that it was no longer actively maintaining Ribbon. Its GitHub site (https://github.com/Netflix/ribbon) details which parts Netflix still uses and which it doesn't. Although Ribbon isn't actively maintained, it's stable and production ready for most use cases. As Thorntail makes Ribbon available for consuming microservices, the Thorntail team is actively investigating alternatives to Ribbon for the long term.

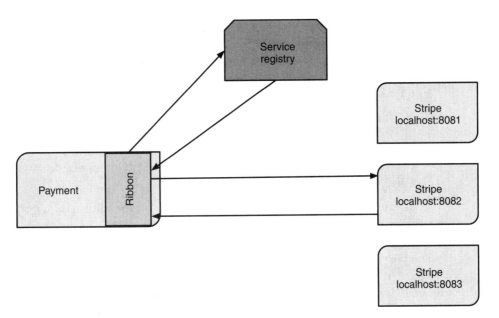

Figure 7.5   Service discovery with Netflix Ribbon

7.2   *Registering a microservice with Thorntail*

You've seen how a service registry can benefit your microservices by decoupling you from the URL locations of anything you need to consume. That's the theory. Now it's time to see service registration and discovery in action! You'll take a look at your options for a service registry with Thorntail, which are known as topologies, before seeing how to register a microservice so it can be discovered by others.

7.2.1   *Thorntail's topologies*

Thorntail provides an abstraction over a service registry that's referred to as a *topology*. What benefit does the abstraction provide? It means your client code doesn't need to change if your microservice is moved into an environment with a different service registry implementation. The most likely use case for this is developing and testing locally against one type of service registry and then using a different one in test and production environments.

In an ideal world, you could run a like-for-like production environment on your local machine for testing, but that's not always possible with enterprises today. Moving toward a more cloud-based infrastructure, like Kubernetes and OpenShift, combined with Linux containers, does make it easier to replicate those environments with fewer resources. But not all enterprises may ever reach such a point.

What service registry implementations, or topology types, does Thorntail offer? It offers these:

- *JGroups*—JGroups is a toolkit for reliable messaging in which clusters of nodes can be created for the purpose of sending messages to each other. Thorntail is able to create a pseudo service registry by creating a cluster from every microservice and notifying each one of new services that are available as they register themselves.
- *OpenShift*—Red Hat OpenShift is a container platform using Kubernetes to manage containers. You can use an online version, install it locally into your own environment, or use it within Minishift, as you saw earlier.
- *Consul*—Consul, developed by HashiCorp, is a popular service discovery framework.

How do you choose which one to use? In some cases, the choice is determined by where your microservice is being deployed. If it's being deployed to Red Hat OpenShift, using the OpenShift topology is logical.

The JGroups topology is best used for local development on a laptop, or in CI environments for which a full-fledged service discovery implementation may not be installed. As you saw in chapter 5, you also can use Minishift to ensure that your local development environment is as close as possible to production if you're deploying to Red Hat OpenShift.

Beyond those natural alignments, your choice depends on the requirements around service discovery and which particular implementation best fits the needs of the environment. Such a decision is usually not in the hands of developers, unless they're part of a DevOps culture that allows each team to build its own preferred stack of technologies.

Where does a topology implementation, using Consul as an example, fit in relation to figure 7.3? Take a look at figure 7.6.

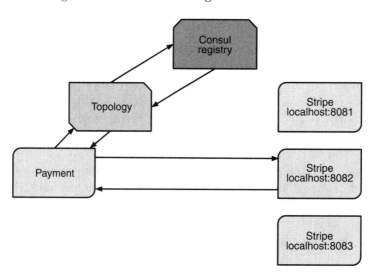

Figure 7.6 Thorntail topology integration

The topology sits between the microservice and the service registry implementation. This enables your microservice code to remain unchanged, whether you're deployed in an environment that uses JGroups, OpenShift, or Consul!

To select one of these topology implementations for use in your microservice, you need to add a dependency of one of the following:

- topology-jgroups
- topology-openshift
- topology-consul

Thorntail also provides a topology servlet, through the `topology-webapp` dependency, that sends server-sent events (SSEs) whenever services are registered or removed from the topology. The topology servlet works alongside any of the topology implementations from the preceding list. To see these events, add the following dependency to pom.xml:

```
<dependency>
  <groupId>io.thorntail</groupId>
  <artifactId>topology-webapp</artifactId>
</dependency>
```

After the microservice is running, either locally or in the cloud, open a browser to http://host:port/topology/system/stream to see the events showing the available instances. This allows a UI to visually represent the instances of each service that are present in the topology, as well as maintain a current list of which service instances are available for use.

7.2.2 *Registering a microservice with a topology*

In our example, you have the Payment and Stripe microservices. Because Payment needs to "discover" Stripe, it first must be registered.

With Thorntail, you have options for registering a microservice. Any of the approaches require only that the topology dependency you've chosen from the previous section be added to your application's pom.xml.

Before you delve into the options for registering your microservices, let's see the code for the Stripe microservice. This will aid in your understanding of what's going on later in the chapter. For the pom.xml, you'll focus on what dependencies you need. There are plenty more there, but it's not necessary for understanding what's going on:

```
<dependency>
  <groupId>io.thorntail</groupId>
  <artifactId>jaxrs</artifactId>
</dependency>
<dependency>
  <groupId>io.thorntail</groupId>
  <artifactId>cdi</artifactId>
</dependency>
```

```
<dependency>
  <groupId>com.stripe</groupId>
  <artifactId>stripe-java</artifactId>
  <version>5.27.0</version>
</dependency>
```

The first two dependencies add `jaxrs` and `cdi` capabilities and are familiar from previous examples. The last dependency provides access to the payment APIs from *Stripe*.

> **NOTE** *Stripe* (https://stripe.com) is a service offering card transaction processing for merchants and websites. A nice aspect of Stripe is the ability to use test API keys, as you'll use in your examples, and test credit card tokens to generate particular responses from its APIs. If you'd like to set up your own Stripe account to see the data appearing in its test dashboard, replace the `stripe.key` value in project-defaults.yml, and the transactions will reach your own test account.

To define the Stripe microservice, first you create the `Application` class to provide the JAX-RS root endpoint.

Listing 7.1   StripeApplication

```
@ApplicationPath("/stripe")
public class StripeApplication extends Application {
}
```

`StripeApplication` is similar to the previous examples. The only point to note is that you're setting the JAX-RS root path to be /stripe.

For deploying to OpenShift and using Thorntail topologies for service discovery, you need to create a service account that gives the topology access to OpenShift services. A service account is like a user account for services: a service can be granted or denied permissions to perform certain actions. With the fabric8 Maven plugin, this is easy enough to do with YAML files.

Listing 7.2   service-sa.yml

```
metadata:
  name: service          ⟵── Name of service account
```

For the topology to see the services within OpenShift, you need the `view` role for your microservice. Now you need to define a role binding to match the service account with that role.

Listing 7.3   service-rb.yml

```
metadata:
  name: view-service     ⟵── Name of the role binding
```

```
subjects:
- kind: ServiceAccount          ◁─┐ Service account to use
  name: service              ◁──┘ for the role binding
roleRef:
  name: view        ◁──┐ Role name from OpenShift to
                      └ give access to service names
```

Now you need to associate the service account with your microservice.

Listing 7.4   deployment.yml

```
apiVersion: v1
kind: Deployment
metadata:
  name: ${project.artifactId}    ◁── OpenShift deployment name
spec:
  template:
    spec:                               ┌ Service account to associate
      serviceAccountName: service  ◁──┘ with the deployment
```

Without settings to the contrary, the deployment name would usually be set to
${project.artifactId}. The custom deployment.yml is solely required to associate
the service account with it.

@ADVERTISE

Now let's take a look at the JAX-RS resource that will interact with the Stripe APIs.

Listing 7.5   StripeResource

```
@Path("/")
@ApplicationScoped                          ┌ Defines the name under
@Advertise("chapter7-stripe")        ◁──┤ which you want to advertise a
public class StripeResource {               └ microservice via the topology

  @Inject
  @ConfigurationValue("stripe.key")    ◁──┐ Inject the configuration value
  private String stripeKey;               │ defined by stripe.key in
                                          └ project-defaults.yml.
  @POST
  @Path("/charge")
  @Consumes(MediaType.APPLICATION_JSON)
  @Produces(MediaType.APPLICATION_JSON)
  public ChargeResponse submitCharge(ChargeRequest chargeRequest) {
▷ Stripe.apiKey = this.stripeKey;
                                              ┌ Create a Map of all the
    Map<String, Object> chargeParams = new HashMap<>();   request parameters,
    chargeParams.put("amount", chargeRequest.getAmount());  ◁ taking them from
    chargeParams.put("currency", "usd");                    └ ChargeRequest.
    chargeParams.put("description", chargeRequest.getDescription());
    chargeParams.put("source", chargeRequest.getCardToken());
                                              ┌ Call the Stripe API
    Charge charge = Charge.create(chargeParams);  ◁── to initiate a charge.
```

Set the
Stripe API
key onto
the Stripe
API main
class.

```
    return new ChargeResponse()
        .chargeId(charge.getId())
        .amount(charge.getAmount());
  }
}
```
> Return a ChargeResponse
> containing the amount and charge
> ID that was received from Stripe.

So you've added @Advertise to your Stripe microservice, but how does that relate to the topology?

The Thorntail topology will find all the @Advertise annotations you've added to RESTful endpoints in your microservice code, and store each name into a file within your deployment that's created at runtime. The topology has runtime code that's added to your microservice deployment that will advertise those names, with appropriate host and port information indicating where the microservice is located, to whichever implementation you've chosen (JGroups, OpenShift, Consul) when the deployment is started. @Advertise abstracts away the need for your microservice code to know the details of how to register a microservice. You simply provide a name for it.

> **NOTE** When using `Topology` and deploying to OpenShift, the advertising function is essentially a NoOp because OpenShift registers all microservices with its internal DNS. The main advantage to using @Advertise on the producing microservice is that you can easily switch your topology environment without altering your code.

TOPOLOGY.LOOKUP()

You also can register services in a way that provides greater control over the timing of when a service is available, by using `Topology.lookup()`. `Topology` provides the main abstraction over each service registry implementation by offering methods for static `lookup()`, adding and removing listeners to be notified as services are added or removed, registering a microservice through `advertise()`, and retrieving all the current registry entries with `asMap()`.

Whichever topology implementation you've chosen for your microservice—JGroups, OpenShift, or Consul—`Topology` is always available for a microservice to use directly.

Let's say you want to use `Topology` to manually advertise and unadvertise a microservice. One advantage to this approach is restricting the microservice from being added into the service registry until the RESTful endpoint is active and available to handle requests.

Listing 7.6 Topology

```
AdvertisementHandle handle = Topology.lookup().advertise("allevents");
...
handle.unadvertise();
```
> Look up the Topology instance and
> advertise your service, retaining a handle.

> When your service is finishing, use
> the handle to unadvertise yourself.

7.3   *Consuming a registered microservice with Thorntail*

Now that you've registered your Stripe microservice, it's time to develop Payment to be able to discover it so you can consume it. This section covers two approaches for service discovery. Each uses a different client library, Netflix Ribbon and RESTEasy, for different implementations of Payment.

7.3.1   *Service lookup with Netflix Ribbon*

To use Netflix Ribbon as your client framework, the first thing you need to do is add it as a dependency to your Maven module:

```
<dependency>
  <groupId>io.thorntail</groupId>
  <artifactId>ribbon</artifactId>
</dependency>
```

This dependency gives your microservice access to the Netflix Ribbon libraries. In addition, it integrates with whichever topology implementation you've chosen for your registry. This enables Netflix Ribbon to use your topology implementation for retrieving service instances for load balancing. Next you need to create an interface to represent the external microservice, Stripe, that you want to call.

Listing 7.7   StripeService

```
                        Name of the service in the
                        Service Registry you want to call
@ResourceGroup(name = "chapter7-stripe")   ◁──┘         Creates a proxy of
public interface StripeService {                        your interface you
  StripeService INSTANCE = Ribbon.from(StripeService.class);  ◁── can use

    @TemplateName("charge")
    @Http(                                          Defines the HTTP parameters to execute
          method = Http.HttpMethod.POST,            the external request for charge() including
          uri = "/stripe/charge",                   HTTP Method, URI path, and HTTP header
          headers = {                               for content type
  Identifies the   @Http.Header(
  method name for         name = "Content-Type",
  which Ribbon            value = "application/json"
  creates a template  )
          }                                         Defines a transformer to
    )                                                convert ChargeRequest
    @ContentTransformerClass(ChargeTransformer.class)  ◁──┘  into ByteBuf
    RibbonRequest<ByteBuf> charge(@Content ChargeRequest chargeRequest);  ◁──┐
}                                                  Method must return a RibbonRequest
```

If Stripe had more than a single RESTful endpoint that you wanted to make requests against, each method definition in the interface would require its own `@TemplateName` and `@Http` annotations to define them.

Listing 7.7 uses the annotation-based approach of Netflix Ribbon, but if you prefer a fluent API, you can use `HttpResourceGroup` and `HttpRequestTemplate` to build up an equivalent HTTP request.

Now let's take a look at `ChargeTransformer`, which is responsible for converting `ChargeRequest` into `ByteBuf`.

Listing 7.8 ChargeTransformer

Use an ObjectMapper to convert ChargeRequest into JSON format.

```
public class ChargeTransformer implements ContentTransformer<ChargeRequest> {
  @Override
  public ByteBuf call(ChargeRequest chargeRequest, ByteBufAllocator
    byteBufAllocator) {
    try {
      byte[] bytes = new ObjectMapper().writeValueAsBytes(chargeRequest);
      ByteBuf byteBuf = byteBufAllocator.buffer(bytes.length);
      byteBuf.writeBytes(bytes);
      return byteBuf;
    } catch (JsonProcessingException e) {
      e.printStackTrace();
    }
    return null;
  }
}
```

Write the JSON as bytes into the ByteBuf.

Allocate a new ByteBuf instance with the appropriate length.

`ChargeTransformer` handles the conversion only when making the request. You need to handle converting `ByteBuf` into a meaningful response within your calling code.

Let's see what your Payment resource looks like when using Netflix Ribbon.

Listing 7.9 PaymentResource

```
@Path("/")
public class PaymentServiceResource {

  @POST
  @Path("/sync")
  @Consumes(MediaType.APPLICATION_JSON)
  @Produces(MediaType.APPLICATION_JSON)
  public ChargeResponse chargeSync(ChargeRequest chargeRequest) {
    ByteBuf buf = StripeService.INSTANCE.charge(chargeRequest).execute();
    return extractResult(buf);
  }

  @POST
  @Path("/async")
  @Consumes(MediaType.APPLICATION_JSON)
  @Produces(MediaType.APPLICATION_JSON)
  public void chargeAsync(@Suspended final AsyncResponse asyncResponse,
    ChargeRequest chargeRequest)
      throws Exception {
```

Call Stripe synchronously.

Extract the result and return it.

```
executorService().submit(() -> {                Create an Observable to call Stripe asynchronously.
    Observable<ByteBuf> obs =
        StripeService.INSTANCE.charge(chargeRequest).toObservable();    <──
    obs.subscribe(
        (result) -> {
            asyncResponse.resume(extractResult(result));    <──
        },
        asyncResponse::resume
    );                                          Extract the ChargeResponse
});                                             from the result and set it on
}                                               the AsyncResponse.

private ChargeResponse extractResult(ByteBuf result) {    <──  Convert a ByteBuf into
    byte[] bytes = new byte[result.readableBytes()];            a ChargeResponse.
    result.readBytes(bytes);
    try {
        return new ObjectMapper()                <──      Use an ObjectMapper to
                .readValue(bytes, ChargeResponse.class);      convert bytes of JSON
    } catch (IOException e) {                              into a ChargeResponse
        e.printStackTrace();                              instance.
    }

    return null;
}
}
```

Subscribe to the Observable, passing success and failure methods.

Let's see how this all works!

First you need to have Minishift running (see chapter 5 for details) and be logged into the OpenShift client. Next you need to run the Stripe microservice; to do that, change into the /chapter7/stripe directory and run this:

```
mvn clean fabric8:deploy -Popenshift -DskipTests
```

With the Stripe microservice now running, change into the /chapter7/ribbon-client directory and run this:

```
mvn clean fabric8:deploy -Popenshift -DskipTests
```

The URL of the service is the URL in the OpenShift console for the chapter7-ribbon-client service, with /sync or /async added to the end.

Because you need to issue an HTTP POST request on either of these URLs, the process is a bit more complicated than just opening a browser and entering the URL. Many tools can be used for issuing the request you need, including `curl` on the command line, but you'll use Postman, shown in figure 7.7.

> **NOTE** Postman has a lot of functionality, across a few versions, but at its core it provides the ability to test API endpoints. Most important, for me, it offers the ability to save requests, including headers and body content, so that the same request can be repeated whenever you need it. For further details, take a look at www.getpostman.com.

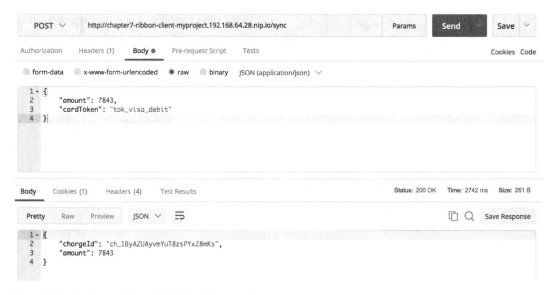

Figure 7.7   Postman calling the Ribbon client service

Here you can see the request details—including the body of the HTTP POST in the top half, and the response you received from the service at the bottom.

The most important header to set is `Content-Type` with a value of `application/json`. If you don't set that header, JAX-RS doesn't believe it's receiving JSON and will reject the request. You would receive an HTTP response code of 415, indicating an unsupported media type.

To see the topology, you can install the `topology-webapp` dependency into `ribbon-client` to see all the registration events. Modify the pom.xml to include the following:

```
<dependency>
  <groupId>io.thorntail</groupId>
  <artifactId>topology-webapp</artifactId>
</dependency>
```

Then from the /chapter7/ribbon-client directory, run this:

```
mvn clean fabric8:deploy -Popenshift -DskipTests
```

In the OpenShift console, click the URL for the ribbon-client microservice. Then add /topology/system/stream to the end of the URL in the browser window. The browser will immediately show the event that registered both your microservices, chapter7-stripe and chapter7-ribbon-client, with the topology:

```
event: topologyChange
data: {
  "chapter7-stripe": [
```

```
      {
        "endpoint": "http://chapter7-stripe:8080",
        "tags":["http"]
      }
    ],
    "chapter7-ribbon-client": [
      {
        "endpoint": "http://chapter7-ribbon-client:8080",
        "tags":["http"]
      }
    ]
}
```

One thing you'll notice about the URLs for each of the microservices is that they don't include the usual IP address and nip.io suffix of OpenShift URLs. These URLs are internal OpenShift URLs; they won't work when used outside the OpenShift environment.

7.3.2   *Service lookup with the RESTEasy client*

Apart from using different client frameworks for calling the Stripe microservice, with RESTEasy you're going to use the Topology.lookup method for retrieving information from Topology. You need to do that because RESTEasy doesn't have a way to perform the lookup for you as Ribbon does.

To use RESTEasy as your client framework, the first thing you need to do is add it as a dependency to your Maven module:

```
<dependency>
  <groupId>org.jboss.resteasy</groupId>
  <artifactId>resteasy-client</artifactId>
  <version>3.0.24.Final</version>
  <scope>provided</scope>
</dependency>
```

You mark it as provided because it's on the classpath from Thorntail but you need it defined for local compilation. Next you need to create an interface to represent the external microservice, Stripe, that you want to call.

Listing 7.10   StripeService

```
@Path("/stripe")
public interface StripeService {

    @POST
    @Path("/charge")
    @Consumes(MediaType.APPLICATION_JSON)
    @Produces(MediaType.APPLICATION_JSON)
    ChargeResponse charge(ChargeRequest chargeRequest);

}
```

As you can see, this code is a lot simpler and easier to comprehend than the Ribbon equivalent. Let's see what your Payment resource looks like when using RESTEasy.

Listing 7.11   `MessageResource`

```
@Path("/")
public class PaymentServiceResource {
  private Topology topology;

  public PaymentServiceResource() {
    try {
      topology = Topology.lookup();
    } catch (NamingException e) {
      e.printStackTrace();
    }
  }

  @POST
  @Path("/sync")
  @Consumes(MediaType.APPLICATION_JSON)
  @Produces(MediaType.APPLICATION_JSON)
  public ChargeResponse chargeSync(ChargeRequest chargeRequest) throws
  Exception {
    ResteasyClient client = new ResteasyClientBuilder().build();
    URI url = getService("chapter7-stripe");
    ResteasyWebTarget target = client.target(url);
    StripeService stripe = target.proxy(StripeService.class);
    return stripe.charge(chargeRequest);
  }

  ...

  private URI getService(String name) throws Exception {
    Map<String, List<Topology.Entry>> map = this.topology.asMap();

    if (map.isEmpty()) {
      throw new Exception("Service not found for '" + name + "'");
    }

    Optional<Topology.Entry> seOptional = map
            .get(name)
            .stream()
            .findFirst();
    Topology.Entry serviceEntry =
        seOptional.orElseThrow(
          () -> new Exception("Service not found for '" + name + "'")
        );

    return new URI("http", null, serviceEntry.getAddress(),
  serviceEntry.getPort(), null, null, null);
  }
}
```

On creation of **PaymentServiceResource**, retrieve the Topology instance.

Retrieve a URI for the chapter7-stripe service.

Get the Service Registry to find the service you need.

For a list of registrations for the chapter7-stripe service, find the first one.

If the Optional is empty, throw an exception that a service couldn't be found.

You likely noticed the extra work you had to do with looking up `Topology` by calling `Topology.lookup()`, which wasn't required when using Netflix Ribbon as a client. Netflix Ribbon performs the service lookup based on the `@ResourceGroup` name, directly interacting with `Topology` to retrieve the information it needs.

As you can see when retrieving a topology entry from the map, you're finding only the first URI for a given service, because you're not load balancing across possibly multiple instances. With OpenShift, it's not necessary to load balance on the client side, because DNS in OpenShift will perform this task for you on the server.

If you're deploying to a different environment, it's likely that for a production situation you'd want to use an algorithm, or a variety of algorithm options, to choose which service instance to consume. With the Stripe microservice running from earlier, change into the /chapter7/resteasy-client directory and run this:

```
mvn clean fabric8:deploy -Popenshift -DskipTests
```

As with the Ribbon example, the URL of the service is the URL in the OpenShift console for the chapter7-resteasy-clientservice, with /sync or /async added to the end. Once again, to test the endpoints, you need a tool (either Postman or whatever you prefer) to execute the POST request. If all has gone well, you should receive a similar response to the Ribbon example when executing the requests.

Summary

- Code that includes locations of microservices to consume is prone to failures as instances come up and down. Failures can also occur when requiring updates to code or configuration when microservices move locations, and redeploying those changes across any impacted environment. Service discovery provides the separation you need for your microservices to scale without relying on IP addresses directly.

- To be able to discover services to consume, you need them to be registered in a central place so your microservice can retrieve them. A service registry fulfills that role in a microservice environment.

- Thorntail allows you to use JGroups, OpenShift, or Consul as a service registry implementation in your microservice environments.

- Using a Netflix Ribbon client in your microservice removes lookups from your client code while allowing you to take advantage of Thorntail topology implementations for service discovery.

Strategies for fault
tolerance and monitoring

8

This chapter covers

- What is latency?
- Why do microservices need to be fault tolerant?
- How do circuit breakers work?
- What tools can mitigate against distributed failure?

You'll use the example from the previous chapters to expand the functionality of Stripe and Payment to include fault mitigation as you explore the concepts of fault tolerance and monitoring. Fault tolerance is especially important when your Payment microservice is communicating over a network to external systems. You need to expect failures and time-outs when communicating across networks.

8.1 Microservice failures in a distributed architecture

Figure 8.1 revisits what your distributed architecture for microservices looks like.

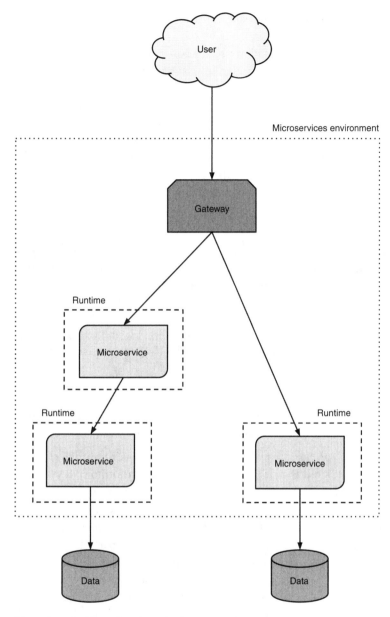

Figure 8.1   Microservices in a distributed architecture

How is this distributed architecture relevant to failures? By virtue of your microservices containing smaller chunks of business logic, as opposed to a monolith that contains everything, you end up with a significantly larger number of services to maintain. You're no longer dealing with a UI that might communicate with a single backend service that handles all its needs. More likely, that same UI is now integrating with dozens of microservices, or more, that need to be just as reliable as your previous monolith.

But your microservices won't fail in production, right? Nothing fails in production! We've all likely made statements similar to that at some point, usually before we've been bitten by a major failure in production! Once bitten, twice fault tolerant!

Why is it that, without previous experiences of production failures, we tend toward grandiose statements about the reliability of our production systems? Some of it's because we can be optimistic in nature, but mostly it's a lack of experience. If you've never had to deal with fixing production issues for your application, especially in the middle of the night, it's hard to appreciate the valid concerns around the reliability of systems.

Pager nightmares

I remember in the late '90s—yes, I was in IT back then—that the most dreaded experience of the novice was to be handed the pager for *on-call* duty. There's no worse feeling than getting a page around 2 a.m. about failed jobs that need to be fixed, and then trying to complete them before the staff arrives in the office at 8 a.m.! These were only nightly batch jobs, but the anxiety over being paged was terrible.

I can only imagine what it's like to receive a page (if pagers are still around today) for a production failure on a live application that needs to be resolved because it's affecting the 24/7 running of the business!

Here are some of the statements you might falsely believe regarding production systems, and distributed architectures in particular:

- *The network of computing devices is reliable.* Without taking into account the possibility of network failures, it's possible for an application to stall while waiting for a response that won't arrive. Worse, the application would be unable to retry any failed operations when the network is available again.

- *There's no delay in making a request and having it acted upon (known as zero latency).* Ignoring network latency, and associated network packet loss, can result in wasted bandwidth and an increase in dropped network packets as the amount of traffic on the network grows without limitation.

- *There's no limitation to the available bandwidth on the network.* If clients are sending too much data, or too many requests, the available network bandwidth could shrink to the point that bottlenecks appear and application throughput is reduced. The impact of latency on network throughput can last for a few seconds or be constantly present.

- *The entire network is secure from possible attack, external or internal.* It's naive to ignore the possibility that a malicious user, such as a disgruntled employee, could attempt to cause damage to an application. Likewise, a once-internal application can be easily exposed to external threats by making it available publicly without proper security vetting. Even an innocuous change in firewall rules for a port could make it unintentionally accessible externally.
- *Location and arrangement of computing devices on a network never changes.* When networks are altered, and devices moved to different locations, the available bandwidth and latency can be diminished.
- *There's a single administrator for everything.* With multiple administrators for different networks within an enterprise, conflicting security policies could be implemented. In this case, a client who needs to communicate across differently secured networks needs to be aware of the requirements of both to successfully communicate.
- *Zero transport cost.* Though the transport of physical data through a network may cost zero, it's a nonzero cost to maintain a network after it's built.
- *The entire network is homogeneous.* In a homogeneous network, every device on the network uses similar configurations and protocols. A nonhomogeneous network can lead to the problems described in the first three points of this list.

All these statements are known as the Fallacies of Distributed Computing (www.rgoarchitects.com/Files/fallacies.pdf).

8.2 Network failures

Though there are many ways a network can fail, in this section you'll focus on network latency and time-outs. Previously, I mentioned zero latency as being part of the Fallacies of Distributed Computing, which equates to no delay in making a request and having it acted upon.

Why is *latency* important for your microservice? It affects almost anything your microservice might want to do:

- Calling another microservice
- Waiting for an asynchronous message
- Reading from a database
- Writing to a database

Without being mindful of the existence of latency in your network, you'd presume that all communication of messages and data is near instantaneous, assuming the network devices involved in the communication are sufficiently close.

Time-outs are another crucial source of network failure you need to be mindful of when developing microservices. Time-outs can be linked to high latency; requests aren't responded to in a timely manner not only because of network delays, but also because of issues with the consuming microservice. If the microservice you're calling has gone down, is experiencing high load, or failing for any other number of reasons, you'll notice problems when you try to consume it, most often in the form of a time-out. There's no way to predict when a time-out will occur, so your code needs to be aware that time-outs happen, and of how you want to handle the situation when you receive one.

Do you try again, either immediately or after a short delay? Do you presume a standard response and proceed anyway?

It's these network failures that you want to especially mitigate against. Otherwise, you leave your microservices, and entire application, open to unexpected network failure with no means of recovering other than restarting services. Because you can't afford to be restarting services every time a network problem occurs, you need to develop your code to prevent restarting from being your only option.

8.3 *Mitigating against failures*

In looking at how to mitigate against failure, you could certainly implement the features you need yourself. But you might not be an expert in all the best ways to implement the features you need. Even if you were, accomplishing that implementation requires more than a short development lifecycle. You'd rather be developing more applications! Though you might be able to use many different libraries, in this case you're going to be using Hystrix from Netflix Open Source Software.

8.3.1 *What is Hystrix?*

Hystrix is a latency and fault-tolerance library intended to isolate access points with remote systems, services, and libraries; halt cascading failure; and enable resilience in distributed systems. Wherever failure is inevitable, as with distributed systems, the Hystrix library improves the resiliency of microservices in these environments.

A lot of things are going on with Hystrix, so how does this library do it? We can't cover the entirety of Hystrix within this single chapter; that would require an entire book in its own right. But this section provides a high-level view of how Hystrix performs its segregation.

Figure 8.2 shows a view of a microservice handling the load of many user requests. This microservice needs to communicate with an external service. In this situation, it's easy for the microservice you've developed to become blocked as it's waiting for external service 2 to respond. Worse, you could overload the external service to the point it stops functioning completely.

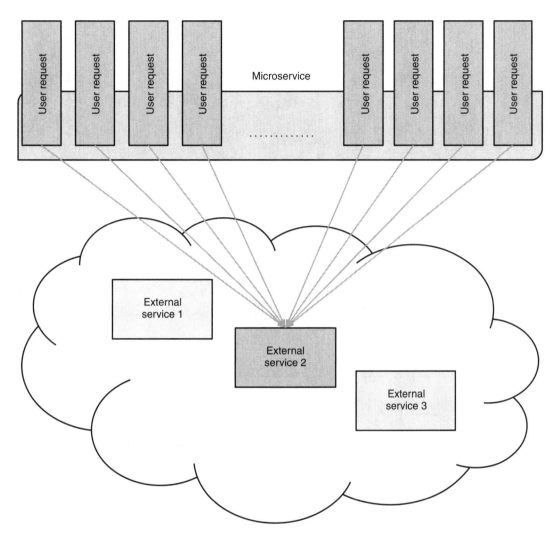

Figure 8.2 Microservice processing user requests without Hystrix

This is where Hystrix comes in, to be the middleman and mediate your external communication in order to mitigate against various failures. Figure 8.3 adds Hystrix into the picture, by wrapping your external service calls inside HystrixCommand instances that use configuration to define its behavior, such as the number of available threads.

In figure 8.3, each external service has a different number of threads available to the respective HystrixCommand. This is an indication that some services might be easier to overload than others, and you need to restrict the number of concurrent requests that you send.

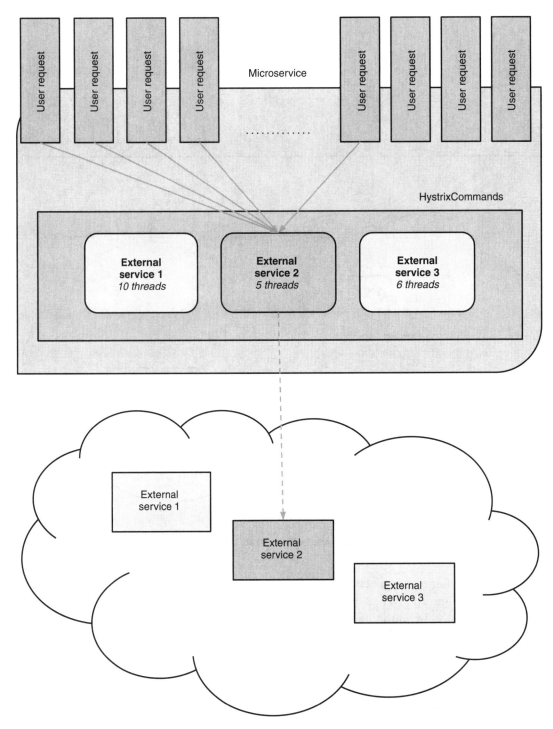

Figure 8.3   Microservice processing user requests with Hystrix

By wrapping external service 2 into a `HystrixCommand`, you're limiting the number of requests that call it from your microservice concurrently. Though you've added mitigation for interacting with that particular external service, you've just increased the likelihood of requests failing in your microservice because you're rejecting additional requests out to the external service! Such a situation may be fine, or it may not; the outcome depends on the speed with which the external request can process your requests.

This does raise an important point. Adding failure mitigation to a single microservice within an entire ecosystem isn't that beneficial. Making your microservice a better citizen within the distributed network is great, but if everyone else in the network doesn't have the same mitigation for interacting with your microservice, you've simply moved where the bottleneck and failure point reside. For this reason, it's critical that failure mitigation is an enterprise-wide concern, or at least within a grouping of microservices that all communicate with each other.

Another advantage to Hystrix that you can see in figure 8.3 is the isolation it provides between external services. If calls to external service 2 weren't limited, there's a good chance it could consume all available threads within the JVM, preventing your microservice from handling requests that don't need to interact with external service 2!

For the remainder of the chapter, our approach will be to outline the theory behind a mitigation strategy for failures, and then show how that strategy is implemented within Hystrix. You know you need to mitigate against network failures in your code, so what strategies do you have at your disposal?

8.3.2 *Circuit breakers*

If you're in any way familiar with the way fuses work in your home's electrical panel, you'll understand the principles of a circuit breaker. Figure 8.4 shows that electricity flows through a fuse unhindered unless it's tripped open, causing the flow to be interrupted.

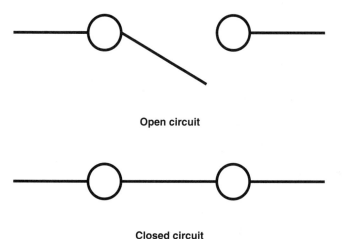

Open circuit

Closed circuit

Figure 8.4   Electrical circuit-breaker states

The one difference between an electrical panel and software is that a software circuit breaker will automatically close itself without manual intervention, based on thresholds that have been defined to indicate the level at which it becomes unhealthy.

Figure 8.5 shows the initial part of a larger flow to mitigate against failures when calling external services. As you progress through this chapter, additional parts will be added to the flow, providing additional functionality to assist with mitigation. This first part focuses on providing a circuit breaker.

When the circuit breaker is Closed, all requests continue through the flow. When the circuit breaker is Open, the requests

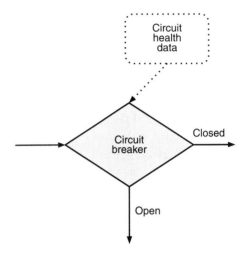

Figure 8.5   Failure mitigation flow with basic circuit

exit the flow early. You can see in figure 8.5 that your circuit breaker requires Circuit Health Data, which is used in determining whether the circuit should be open or closed. In addition to the states in figure 8.5, a circuit breaker can be in a Half Open state. See figure 8.6.

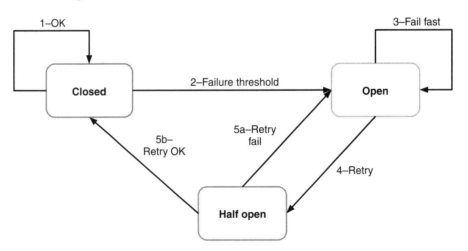

Figure 8.6   Circuit-breaker states

Here are the transitions between states of a circuit breaker:

1   All requests pass through unhindered, as the circuit is Closed.
2   When a failure threshold is reached, the circuit becomes Open.
3   While the circuit is Open, all requests are rejected, failing fast.

4 The circuit's Open time-out expires. The circuit moves to Half Open to allow a single request to pass.
5 The request fails or succeeds:
   a The single request fails, returning the circuit to Open.
   b The single request succeeds, returning the circuit to Closed.

In the Half Open state, the circuit breaker is officially still Closed. But after a sleep time-out is reached, a single request will be allowed to pass through. The success or failure of this single request then determines whether the state shifts back to Closed (a single request was successful), or whether it remains Open until making another attempt when the next time-out interval is reached.

A circuit breaker is only a way to allow or prevent requests from passing through. The key piece to it behaving the way you want is the Circuit Health Data. Without capturing any Circuit Health Data, the circuit breaker would always remain Closed, regardless of how many requests might fail or for what reasons.

Hystrix provides sensible defaults for a circuit breaker to handle time-outs, network congestion, and latency with any request you make. Let's take a look at a simple Hystrix circuit breaker.

Listing 8.1 `StockCommand`

```
public class StockCommand extends HystrixCommand<String> {    ◁─┐ Specify String as the
    private final String stockCode;                                 HystrixCommand Type.

    public StockCommand(String stockCode) {
        super(HystrixCommandGroupKey.Factory.asKey("StockGroup"));   ◁─┐
        this.stockCode = stockCode;                          Unique key for grouping data
    }                                                        in the Hystrix dashboard

    @Override
    protected String run() throws Exception {              ◁─┐ Execution of
        // Execute HTTP request to retrieve current stock price    call to external
    }                                                             service
}
```

You can then call this command synchronously with code such as the following:

```
String result = new StockCommand("AAPL").execute();
```

If you prefer asynchronous execution, you use this:

```
Future<String> fr = new StockCommand("AAPL").queue();
String result = fr.get();
```

In each of the examples, you're expecting only a single result from executing the request, whether you're calling it synchronously or asynchronously. For that reason, you choose to extend `HystrixCommand`, which caters to single-response executions.

What happens if you expect multiple responses instead of one? Stock prices change extremely frequently, so wouldn't it be nice to not continually execute another call every time you want it updated?

You need to modify your circuit breaker to support a command that returns an `Observable` that can emit multiple responses. You'll subscribe to this `Observable` to handle each response as it's received. Handling each response as it's returned identifies the execution as being *reactive*.

> **DEFINITION** *Reactive* is an adjective meaning *acting in response to a situation rather than creating or controlling it*. When you're using an `Observable` and listening to results that are emitted from it, you're *acting in response* to each emitted result. An advantage with this approach is that you don't block while waiting for each result to be emitted.

Let's modify your command to provide an `Observable`.

Listing 8.2 `StockObservableCommand`

```
public class StockObservableCommand extends HystrixObservableCommand<String> {     ◁─┐
    private final String stockCode;                                 Specify String as the
                                                             HystrixObservableCommand type.
    public StockObservableCommand(String stockCode) {
        super(HystrixCommandGroupKey.Factory.asKey("StockGroup"));          ◁──┐
        this.stockCode = stockCode;                        Unique key for grouping data
    }                                                        in the Hystrix dashboard

    @Override
    protected Observable<String> construct() {          ◁─────────  Return an
        // Return an Observable that executes an HTTP Request      Observable that
    }                                                             executes a call to
}                                                                 an external service.
```

If you want the command to be executed as soon as an `Observable` is created, you request a hot `Observable`:

```
Observable<String> stockObservable =
➥ new StockObservableCommand(stockCode).observe();
```

Normally, a hot `Observable` will emit responses whether or not there are subscribers, which makes it possible for responses to be lost completely if no one is subscribed. But Hystrix uses `ReplaySubject` to capture those responses for you, allowing them to be replayed to your own listener when you subscribe to the `Observable`.

You could also use a *cold* `Observable` instead:

```
Observable<String> stockObservable =
➥ new StockObservableCommand(stockCode).toObservable();
```

With a cold `Observable`, the execution isn't triggered until a listener has subscribed to it. This guarantees that any subscriber will receive all notifications that the `Observable` has produced.

Which type of `Observable` to use depends on your situation. If a listener can afford to miss some initial data, especially if they're not the first subscriber to an `Observable`, then hot is appropriate. If, however, you want a listener to receive all data, then cold is the better choice.

> **NOTE** Though `HystrixCommand` supports returning an `Observable` from its nonreactive methods, `execute()` and `queue()`, they'll always emit only a single value.

8.3.3 Bulkheads

Bulkheads in software offer a similar strategy to those in ships, by isolating different parts to prevent a failure in one from impacting others. For ships, a failure in a single watertight compartment doesn't spread to others because they're separated by bulkheads.

How does a software bulkhead achieve the same result? By shedding the load that a microservice is experiencing or is about to experience. A *bulkhead* allows you to limit the number of concurrent calls to a component or service, to prevent the network from becoming saturated with requests, which would then increase latency across all requests in the system. Figure 8.7 adds the bulkhead strategy as the next step in your flow.

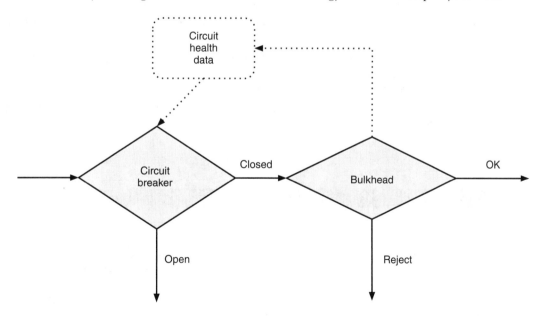

Figure 8.7   Failure mitigation flow with bulkhead

You add a bulkhead after any circuit breaker. There's no need to check the bulkhead if the circuit breaker is Open, because you're in an error state. When you're in a Closed state, the bulkhead prevents too many requests from being executed that could create a network bottleneck.

You may need to call a database service to perform a computation that's extremely intensive and time-consuming, for instance. If you know that the external service can take 10 seconds to respond, you don't want to be sending more than six requests a minute to that service. If you send more than six, your requests are queued for later processing, which causes your microservice to hold up client requests to itself from being released. It's a vicious cycle that can be hard to break, potentially resulting in cascading failures through your microservices. The bulkhead in figure 8.7 performs its checks and indicates whether you're OK to continue processing the request or whether it needs to be rejected.

How would you implement a software bulkhead? Two of the most common approaches are counters and thread pools. *Counters* allow you to set a maximum number of parallel requests that can be active at any one time. *Thread pools* also limit the number of parallel requests that are simultaneously active, but by limiting the number of threads available in a pool for executing requests. For a thread-pool bulkhead, a specific pool is created to handle requests to a particular external service, allowing different external services to be isolated from each other, but also isolated from the thread being used to execute your microservice.

Details of rejected requests are provided to Circuit Health Data so that counters can be updated for use the next time that the circuit breaker status needs to be calculated.

As a software bulkhead, Hystrix provides execution strategies for thread pools (THREAD) and counters (SEMAPHORE). By default, HystrixCommand uses THREAD, and HystrixObservableCommand uses SEMAPHORE.

HystrixObservableCommand doesn't need to be bulkheaded by threads, because it's already executing in a separate thread via the Observable. You can use THREAD with HystrixObservableCommand, but doing so doesn't add safety. If you wanted to run StockCommand in SEMAPHORE, it would look like the following listing.

Listing 8.3 StockCommand using SEMAPHORE

```
public class StockCommand extends HystrixCommand<String> {
    private final String stockCode;

    public StockCommand(String stockCode) {
        super(Setter

    .withGroupKey(HystrixCommandGroupKey.Factory.asKey("StockGroup"))
            .andCommandPropertiesDefaults(
                HystrixCommandProperties.Setter()
                    .withExecutionIsolationStrategy(
```

Using Setter as a fluent interface to define additional configuration for Hystrix

```
        HystrixCommandProperties.ExecutionIsolationStrategy.SEMAPHORE
            )
        )
    );

    this.stockCode = stockCode;
}

    ...

}
```

Set the execution isolation strategy to SEMAPHORE.

The listing illustrates how to set additional configuration for Hystrix to customize the way a particular command behaves. In practice, you wouldn't use SEMAPHORE with HystrixCommand because it doesn't provide any ability to set time-outs on how long an execution should take. Without time-outs, you can easily find yourself with a deadlocked system if the service you consume fails to provide a timely response.

8.3.4 *Fallbacks*

Currently, when your circuit breaker or bulkhead doesn't proceed with the request, an error response is returned. Though that's not great, it's better than your microservice being in a state of waiting until time-out.

Wouldn't it be nice if you could provide a simple response in place of the failure? In some cases, it certainly may not be possible to provide a common response for these situations, but often it's possible and beneficial.

In figure 8.8, you can see fallback handling after Circuit Breaker and Bulkhead on the failure paths. If the microservice your method wants to consume has a fallback handler registered, its response is returned to you. If not, the original error is returned.

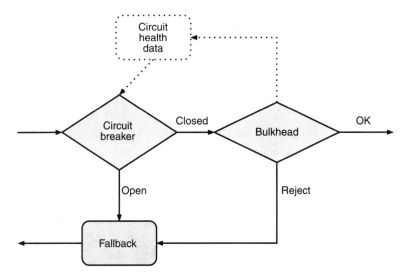

Figure 8.8   Failure mitigation flow with fallback handling

Let's see how to implement a fallback handler for `StockCommand`.

Listing 8.4   `StockCommand` with fallback

```
public class StockCommand extends HystrixCommand<String> {
    ...

    @Override
    protected String getFallback() {
        // Return previous days cached stock price, no network call.
    }
}
```

> Override the default fallback that throws the failure exception.

Implementing a fallback handler is a little different when you're dealing with `Hystrix-ObservableCommand`, but not much.

Listing 8.5   `StockObservableCommand` with fallback

```
public class StockObservableCommand extends HystrixObservableCommand<String> {
    ...

    @Override
    protected Observable<String> resumeWithFallback() {
        // Return previous days cached stock price as an Observable,
  ➥ no network call.
    }
}
```

> Returns an Observable<String> instead of String to match the command response type

8.3.5   *Request caching*

Though not directly mitigating against a failure, *request caching* can prevent bulkhead and other failures from occurring by reducing the number of requests you make on another microservice.

How does it do that? With a request cache, previous requests and their responses can be cached, allowing you to match future requests and return the response from the cache instead. Figure 8.9 shows the request cache sitting in front of other mitigation strategies as it reduces the number of requests that need to pass through any subsequent stages of the flow.

The request cache provides the joint benefits of reducing the number of requests passing through your mitigation flow and increasing the speed with which a response is returned. Enabling the request cache isn't appropriate for all situations but is beneficial when the data being returned doesn't change at all or is unlikely to have changed during the time your microservice completes its task.

This solution is particularly beneficial for reference data or for retrieving a user account, as some examples. It allows your microservice to call out to an external microservice as many times as needed without fear of increasing network traffic. This approach also simplifies the interfaces of your microservices' internal methods and

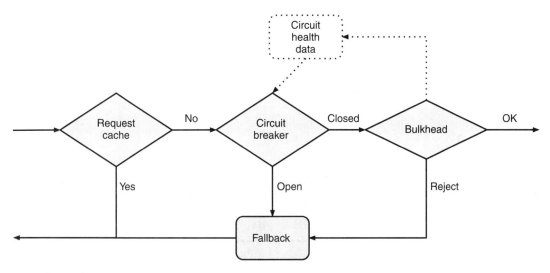

Figure 8.9 Failure mitigation flow with request cache

services, as you no longer need to pass around data in your calls to prevent an additional call. With a request cache, you have no risk of additional calls.

To enable the request cache in Hystrix, you need to do two things. First, you need to activate `HystrixRequestContext` so you have a means of caching responses:

```
HystrixRequestContext context = HystrixRequestContext.initializeContext();
```

This call needs to occur before executing any Hystrix commands. For our situations, you make the first call inside your JAX-RS endpoint method, as you'll see later. Second, you need to define the key to use for caching requests and their responses.

Listing 8.6 `StockCommand` with request cache

```
public class StockCommand extends HystrixCommand<String> {
    private final String stockCode;

    ...

    @Override
    protected String getCacheKey() {
        return this.stockCode;
    }
}
```

> Override key for request cache with the stock symbol you used in your request

8.3.6 *Putting it all together*

In your flow so far, you have a request cache, circuit breaker, bulkhead, and fallback. Figure 8.10 shows how they fit into an actual call.

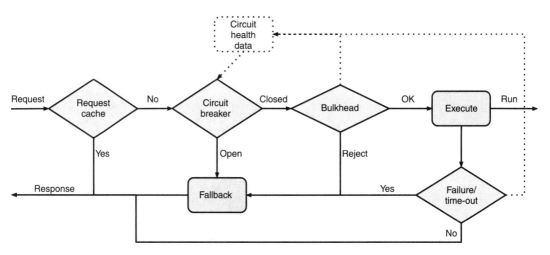

Figure 8.10   Entire failure mitigation flow

Here you add Execute to indicate that you're making the call to an external service. Any failures or time-outs that Execute experiences feed back into the fallback handling, but also provide the failure data to Circuit Health Data. The information is then used by the circuit breaker to determine whether error thresholds have been reached, and the circuit should switch to Open.

Figure 8.11 takes the flow a step further to show how Hystrix provides these features when integrated between your microservice, Service A, and one that you consume, Service B.

As the request enters your Service A method, or endpoint, you create a request and pass it to Hystrix. The request passes through whichever checks have been enabled before being executed on Service B. A response from Service B passes back to

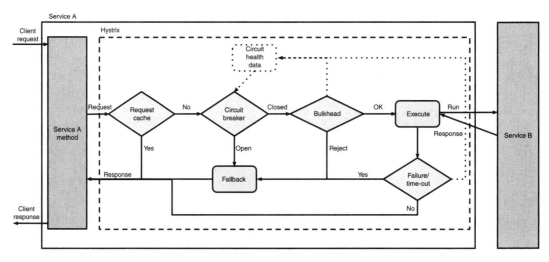

Figure 8.11   Microservice calls with failure mitigation

your Service A method for any required processing before you construct a response for the client.

As you can see, at many points Hystrix can provide a different, or cached, response without needing to call Service B directly. Such a flow provides many benefits in directly reducing failures, but also in reducing the factors that lead to failure. An example is the reduction of microservice load by using a request cache.

Though you've been seeing how Hystrix implements these failure mitigation features, other libraries or frameworks that provide the same features should operate in a similar manner. But the way that other libraries or frameworks implement the required mitigation can differ greatly.

8.3.7 *Hystrix Dashboard*

Awesome—you can now improve the reliability of your microservices in a distributed architecture. But how can you determine whether a particular microservice is continually causing failures? Or whether you need to tune settings to reduce errors and handle additional load?

Sounds like you need a way to monitor how your fault-tolerance library is performing. It just so happens that Hystrix provides SSEs (server-sent events), providing many details about a particular microservice. You can see and analyze everything—the number of hosts running the microservice, requests processed, failures, time-outs, and more.

Hystrix also provides a way to visualize all these events: the Hystrix Dashboard, shown in figure 8.12. The Hystrix Dashboard provides a visual representation of the SSEs that it receives from each registered stream. You'll get to see what a stream is shortly.

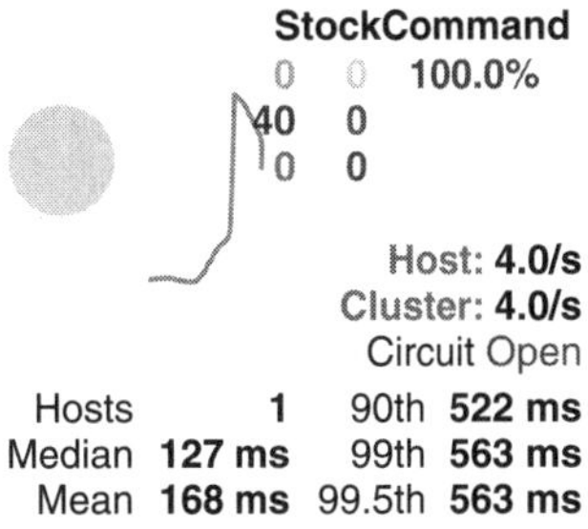

Figure 8.12 shows the information for the Stock-Command. There are many data points in such a small UI, but some of the most crucial are as follows:

- Error percentage in last 10 seconds—100%
- Number of hosts running the microservice—1
- Successful requests in last 10 seconds—0
- Short-circuited requests that were rejected in the last 10 seconds—40
- Failures in last 10 seconds—0
- Circuit is open or closed—Open

StockCommand

0	0	100.0%
40	0	
0	0	

Host: **4.0/s**
Cluster: **4.0/s**
Circuit Open

Hosts	1	90th	**522 ms**
Median	**127 ms**	99th	**563 ms**
Mean	**168 ms**	99.5th	**563 ms**

Figure 8.12 A single circuit from the Hystrix Dashboard

> **TIP** Full details of each metric for a circuit can be found at https://github.com/Netflix/Hystrix/wiki/Dashboard.

Let's see the dashboard in action. Change into the /hystrix-dashboard directory and build the project:

```
mvn clean package
```

then run the dashboard:

```
java -jar target/hystrix-dashboard-thorntail.jar
```

After the dashboard is started, open a browser and navigate to http://localhost
:8090/. For the dashboard to visualize metrics data, it needs to get that data from your
circuit breaker! For a single circuit, you can add the SSE stream directly by adding
http://localhost:8080/hystrix.stream into the main entry box, as shown in figure 8.13.
Click the Add Stream button and then click Monitor Streams. The main page will
load, but until you start your microservice, no SSEs are being received in the stream,
so the visualization won't appear yet.

Change to the /chapter8/stock-client directory and start the microservice:

```
mvn thorntail:run
```

In another browser window, you can access http://localhost:8080/single/AAPL to
request the current stock price details represented by the code AAPL. Any valid stock
code could have been used in the URL path.

If you refresh the page, or make multiple requests in another manner, you can
switch back to the Hystrix Dashboard and see the data on your circuit.

Your stock-client has built-in handling to showcase specific Hystrix functionality.
For instance, every tenth request will throw an exception back to your consuming
microservice, and every second request is put to sleep for 10 seconds to trigger a time-
out. This allows you to see how failures are represented on the dashboard.

To see how request caching works, you can access http://localhost:8080/single/
AAPL/4. Note in the console that only a single request was made to the external service, and each response to the browser has an identical request number.

Figure 8.13 Hystrix Dashboard homepage

To fully see your circuit in action, you need to hit the service many times:

```
curl http://localhost:8080/single/AAPL/?[1-100]
```

This hits your service 100 times in succession, allowing you to monitor the circuit in the dashboard as you see the requests come in. You'll notice a point at which too many errors have occurred, causing the circuit breaker to open. Then you immediately see all remaining requests short-circuited by not calling the microservice and returning the fallback instead. If you wait a few seconds before accessing the service through a browser as before, you then see the circuit-breaker attempt the request, succeed, and revert to Closed again.

Play around with the settings in `StockCommand` to see how the circuit behavior changes. One example, which is present in the book's example code, is to modify `StockCommand` to set the number of threads that should be available to consume the microservice.

Listing 8.7 `StockCommand` with thread configuration

```
super(Setter
    .withGroupKey(HystrixCommandGroupKey.Factory.asKey("StockGroup"))
    .andCommandPropertiesDefaults(
            HystrixCommandProperties.Setter()
                    .withCircuitBreakerRequestVolumeThreshold(10)
                    .withCircuitBreakerSleepWindowInMilliseconds(10000)
                    .withCircuitBreakerErrorThresholdPercentage(50)
    )
    .andThreadPoolPropertiesDefaults(
            HystrixThreadPoolProperties.Setter()       ← Specifies that a single
                    .withCoreSize(1)                     thread must be used
    )
);
```

With the listing 8.7 constructor for `StockCommand`, rerunning your tests shows requests being rejected by `ThreadPool`.

After taking a look at the Hystrix Dashboard, we should all appreciate how crucial such a tool is in our arsenal. Adding Hystrix to your external calls provides a level of fault tolerance to those executions, but it's not foolproof. You need continual real-time monitoring of your microservices to track impending problems and observe failures that could be resolved with tuning of circuit-breaker settings.

If you don't take advantage of what the Hystrix dashboard offers, particularly in terms of real-time monitoring, you won't receive all the benefits of using a fault-tolerant library in your code.

8.4   *Adding Hystrix to your Payment microservice*

You've seen how Hystrix can be implemented and its metrics viewed from a dashboard. Your Stripe microservice isn't super reliable, so let's use Hystrix in Payment to make sure you're not overly impacted by its failures or time-outs!

The previous sections have covered the various pieces Hystrix offers to help with fault mitigation. When adding Hystrix to Payment, you'll take advantage of the full flow that Hystrix provides.

For each of the next sections, you need your Stripe microservice running, so let's start that now. First you need to make sure that a Minishift environment is running and that you've logged into it with the OpenShift client. Then change to the /chapter8/stripe directory and run this:

```
mvn clean fabric8:deploy -Popenshift -DskipTests
```

8.4.1   *Hystrix with the RESTEasy client*

Let's modify Payment from chapter 7 with a `HystrixCommand` for interacting with Stripe.

Listing 8.8 StripeCommand

```
public class StripeCommand extends HystrixCommand<ChargeResponse> {
    private URI serviceURI;

    private final ChargeRequest chargeRequest;

    public StripeCommand(URI serviceURI, ChargeRequest chargeRequest) {
        super(Setter
          .withGroupKey(HystrixCommandGroupKey.Factory.asKey("StripeGroup"))
          .andCommandPropertiesDefaults(
              HystrixCommandProperties.Setter()
                  .withCircuitBreakerRequestVolumeThreshold(10)
                  .withCircuitBreakerSleepWindowInMilliseconds(10000)
                  .withCircuitBreakerErrorThresholdPercentage(50)
          )
        );

        this.serviceURI = serviceURI;
        this.chargeRequest = chargeRequest;
    }

    public StripeCommand(URI serviceURI,
            ChargeRequest chargeRequest, HystrixCommandProperties.Setter
 commandProperties) {
        super(Setter

          .withGroupKey(HystrixCommandGroupKey.Factory.asKey("StripeGroup"))
                    .andCommandPropertiesDefaults(commandProperties)
        );
```

Pass the Stripe URL and **ChargeRequest into the command and set up properties.**

Overloaded constructor allowing Hystrix properties to be set up by caller

```
            this.serviceURI = serviceURI;
            this.chargeRequest = chargeRequest;
        }

        @Override
        protected ChargeResponse run() throws Exception {  ◄
            RestEasyClient client = new RestEasyClientBuilder().build();
            RestEasyWebTarget target = client.target(serviceURI);

            StripeService stripeService = target.proxy(StripeService.class);
            return stripeService.charge(chargeRequest);
        }

        @Override
        protected ChargeResponse getFallback() {
            return new ChargeResponse();
        }
    }
}
```

Equivalent to PaymentServiceResource method in chapter 7, as call is no longer made in JAX-RS Resource

Fallback to empty ChargeResponse if there was a problem.

Now that you have your `StripeCommand`, how different does `PaymentServiceResource` from chapter 7 look?

Listing 8.9 `PaymentServiceResource`

```
@Path("/")
@ApplicationScoped
public class PaymentServiceResource {
    ....

    @POST
    @Path("/sync")
    @Consumes(MediaType.APPLICATION_JSON)
    @Produces(MediaType.APPLICATION_JSON)
    @Transactional
    public PaymentResponse chargeSync(PaymentRequest paymentRequest) throws
⇛ Exception {
        Payment payment = setupPayment(paymentRequest);
        ChargeResponse response = new ChargeResponse();

        try {
            URI url = getService("chapter8-stripe");

            StripeCommand stripeCommand = new StripeCommand(  ◄
                url,
                paymentRequest.getStripeRequest(),
                HystrixCommandProperties.Setter()
                    .withExecutionIsolationStrategy(

    HystrixCommandProperties.ExecutionIsolationStrategy.SEMAPHORE
                    )
                    .withExecutionIsolationSemaphoreMaxConcurrentRequests(1)
                    .withCircuitBreakerRequestVolumeThreshold(5)
            );
```

Instantiate command and set Hystrix properties.

```
                        response = stripeCommand.execute();          ◁──┐ Block on command
                        payment.chargeId(response.getChargeId());       │ execute().
                } catch (Exception e) {
                        payment.chargeStatus(ChargeStatus.FAILED);
                }

                em.persist(payment);
                return PaymentResponse.newInstance(payment, response);
        }

        @POST
        @Path("/async")
        @Consumes(MediaType.APPLICATION_JSON)
        @Produces(MediaType.APPLICATION_JSON)
        public void chargeAsync(@Suspended final AsyncResponse asyncResponse,
                        PaymentRequest paymentRequest) throws Exception {
                Payment payment = setupPayment(paymentRequest);

                URI url = getService("chapter8-stripe");      Instantiate command with
                StripeCommand stripeCommand =                 default Hystrix properties.
                        new StripeCommand(url, paymentRequest.getStripeRequest());  ◁──┘
                stripeCommand
                        .toObservable()
                        .subscribe(              Subscribe to the Observable, passing
                                (result) -> {    success and failure methods.
                                        payment.chargeId(result.getChargeId());
                                        storePayment(payment);
                                        asyncResponse.resume(PaymentResponse.newInstance(payment,
                result)));
                                },
                                (error) -> {
                                        payment.chargeStatus(ChargeStatus.FAILED);
                                        storePayment(payment);
                                        asyncResponse.resume(error);
                                }
                        );
        }
        ....
}
```

Get Observable for command. (annotation pointing to `stripeCommand`)

Your PaymentServiceResource has shown that when expecting only a single response, you're able to easily switch between synchronous and asynchronous execution modes with the same HystrixCommand implementation.

It didn't take much of a refactor from your chapter 7 version to this one, mostly extracting out the code that consumes the external microservice into a new method and class, StripeCommand.

Now that you've refactored your resources, let's run it! Change to the /chapter8/resteasy-client directory and run this:

```
mvn clean fabric8:deploy -Popenshift
```

If the Hystrix Dashboard is still running, head back to the homepage so you can add a new stream. If it's not still running, start it up again as you did earlier in the chapter.

Copy the URL for chapter8-resteasy-client from the OpenShift console, paste it into the text box on the Hystrix Dashboard homepage, and add hystrix.stream as a URL suffix. Click Add Stream and then Monitor Streams.

The Hystrix Dashboard won't show anything immediately because you haven't made any requests yet. To exercise the Payment service, you can execute either single requests or multiple requests, with the latter being easier to see results in the dashboard, especially if their execution can be automated.

With the URL for chapter8-resteasy-client from earlier, you can access the synchronous (/sync) or asynchronous (/async) versions of the service. After starting a series of requests on either, or both, of those endpoints, the Hystrix Dashboard will show all the details of successful and failed requests that have been made.

8.4.2 Hystrix with the Ribbon client

Your RESTEasy client required a little bit of rework to add Hystrix support. Now you'll take a look at what's required for the Ribbon client.

First, you need to update your interface definition for the Stripe microservice so that it takes advantage of Hystrix annotations with Ribbon.

Listing 8.10 StripeService

```
@ResourceGroup(name = "chapter8-stripe")
public interface StripeService {

    StripeService INSTANCE = Ribbon.from(StripeService.class);

    @TemplateName("charge")
    @Http(
            method = Http.HttpMethod.POST,
            uri = "/stripe/charge",
            headers = {
                @Http.Header(
                    name = "Content-Type",
                    value = "application/json"
                )
            }
    )
    @Hystrix(
            fallbackHandler = StripeServiceFallbackHandler.class
    )
    @ContentTransformerClass(ChargeTransformer.class)
    RibbonRequest<ByteBuf> charge(@Content ChargeRequest chargeRequest);
}
```

Adds Hystrix functionality into your Ribbon HTTP request, with a fallback handler

That was easy—only a few extra lines!

> **NOTE** Hystrix annotations are available only for use in combination with Netflix Ribbon.

Right now, the code won't compile because you don't have the class for the fallback handler. Let's add that.

> **Listing 8.11 `StripeServiceFallbackHandler`**

```
public class StripeServiceFallbackHandler implements FallbackHandler<ByteBuf> {
    @Override
    public Observable<ByteBuf> getFallback(
        HystrixInvokableInfo<?> hystrixInfo,
        Map<String, Object> requestProperties) {

        ChargeResponse response = new ChargeResponse();
        byte[] bytes = new byte[0];
        try {
            bytes = new ObjectMapper().writeValueAsBytes(response);
        } catch (JsonProcessingException e) {
            e.printStackTrace();
        }
        ByteBuf byteBuf =
            UnpooledByteBufAllocator.DEFAULT.buffer(bytes.length);
        byteBuf.writeBytes(bytes);
        return Observable.just(byteBuf);
    }
}
```

Implement getFallback() to return whatever you choose in the fallback case.

Create an empty ChargeResponse to use for fallback and convert to byte[].

Write byte[] into ByteBuf that you created on the previous line.

Create an Observable that returns the ByteBuf content as a single result.

The last piece you need is to update `PaymentServiceResource` from chapter 7. But not so! One advantage of using Hystrix with Ribbon when using annotations is that your `PaymentServiceResource` from chapter 7 doesn't need to change at all. A big advantage is that you can easily add Hystrix into an existing microservice that uses Ribbon without refactoring. Simply add an extra annotation and a fallback handler, if needed.

Time to run it! Change to the /chapter8/ribbon-client directory and run this:

```
mvn clean fabric8:deploy -Popenshift
```

As with the RESTEasy client example, you can open a browser and access /sync or /async URLs of the service, using the base URL from the OpenShift console for the service. You can then update the Hystrix Dashboard to use this new stream, execute some requests, and see how the dashboard changes.

As with other examples you've deployed to Minishift, after you're finished, you need to undeploy them to free up the resources:

```
mvn fabric8:undeploy -Popenshift
```

Summary

- Latency and fault tolerance are important when considering deployments to a distributed architecture, as it can adversely affect the throughput and speed of your microservices.

- Your code that consumes microservices can be wrapped with Hystrix to incorporate fault-tolerant features such as fallback, request caching, and bulkheads.
- Hystrix alone is not a panacea for supreme fault tolerance. Real-time monitoring, through a tool such as the Hystrix Dashboard, is crucial to successfully improving overall fault tolerance.

Securing a microservice

In this chapter, you'll expand on previous examples by adding various types of security to them. First you will learn about the different kinds of security that you might need to consider when designing and developing microservices.

9.1 The importance of securing your microservice

Securing your microservice is a critical task that needs to be thought out from the beginning of development. Not doing so early results in greater development time for integrating security later. Why? Not designing for security results in code that might need major refactoring to do so at a later date.

Though not taking security into account before development on a typical Enterprise Java application can easily add months to the development schedule, at least with microservices you usually have a lot less code to be refactored. Even so, isn't it better to design for security up front and save time?

164

9.1.1　Why is security important?

As enterprise developers, we're often called on to develop myriad applications, with the end user of the application varying between internal or external, and sometimes both. Figure 9.1 shows a microservice used by a small group of internal users.

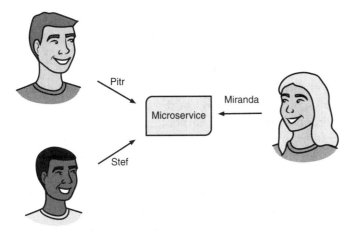

Figure 9.1　Internal users

With these requirements, it'd be fair to determine that you can ignore security, right? Wrong!

Even when you're developing a microservice for internal users only, can you guarantee that the security surrounding your microservice will hold? What happens if, or when, any security barriers preventing external network intrusions are breached?

Figure 9.2 shows how a malicious user, external to the network, would have uninhibited access to a microservice if network security is breached.

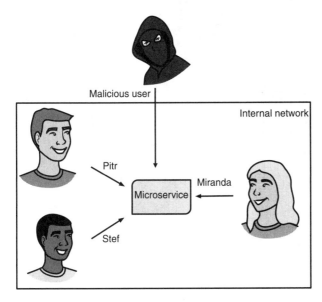

Figure 9.2　Malicious external user

Security is a feature that should never be taken for granted, no matter what precautions might be implemented. A common misconception is that security is infallible, which is certainly not the case.

Looking again at figure 9.2, if you don't consider an internal network secure, you're more inclined to add extra security within your own microservice to prevent unpermitted access to it. If every application or microservice that's purely for internal purposes doesn't include its own security precautions, you've made the security at the boundary of the external network a single point of failure.

That's not even considering the case where you may have a malicious user *within* the internal network, as shown in figure 9.3! Though having an internal malicious user may not be common, this situation can't be discounted. This situation can occur for many reasons: disgruntled employee or corporate espionage the most likely.

Few types of applications are developed that don't need security. Those applications are mostly limited to serving read-only data that's available to the general public already.

That's a fairly narrow definition of an application for which you can ignore security. How many of these are your enterprise's building every day? Probably none! Applications of this type that an enterprise has developed, or will, in its entire lifetime, would be extremely small in number. Static data that's also publicly available doesn't interest an enterprise.

What does all that mean? It means that no application or microservice can ignore security, at all, ever.

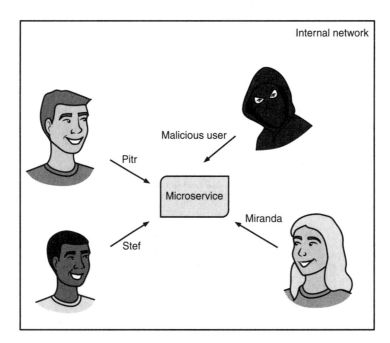

Figure 9.3   Malicious internal user

9.1.2   *What problems does security need to solve?*

Now that you know you need security, what kind of problems do you need to solve? That in itself could be the sole topic for a book! Because you're not looking to re-create *War and Peace* for microservices, you'll focus on the areas that would be of most interest.

Authentication and authorization are the two aspects of security that are the most relevant to microservices for us. Before you delve too deeply, you need to outline what each of these terms means.

Authentication is illustrated in figures 9.1, 9.2, and 9.3. It deals solely with whether a user has the right to access an application or microservice. It doesn't matter where that application or microservice might be hosted, or even whether a user belongs to the enterprise or is external. Authentication is purely concerned with a user being able to access an application.

If a microservice doesn't need to distinguish between users beyond whether or not they're allowed, authentication is all that's needed. But if users who've been authenticated require different levels of access to different parts of an application or microservice, you also need *authorization.*

Figure 9.4 provides an example of user roles that could be used for authorization of a microservice.

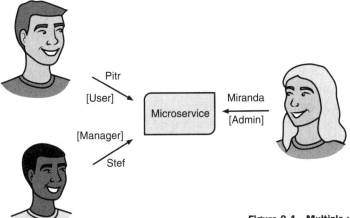

Figure 9.4   Multiple user roles for authorization

You see the roles of Admin, Manager, and User, all fairly typical roles that might be required. Whatever roles might be required for your microservice will vary, potentially from zero to many, depending on the requirements.

An enterprise may also have microservices, as shown in figure 9.5. In this case, you have a microservice administered by an internal user, with the role of Admin. But the User of the microservice is external to the enterprise.

From the perspective of an entire application that may comprise many microservices, you usually need a mixture of authentication and authorization to satisfy security

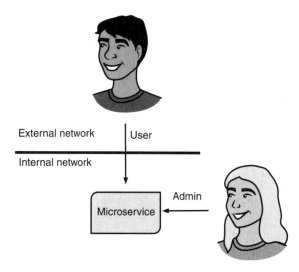

Figure 9.5   Internal and external user roles

requirements. For an individual microservice within an application, you may need to concern yourself with only authentication of a user's request and nothing more.

Whatever your microservice might require—whether it be authentication, authorization, or both—security needs to be considered during design to ensure that it isn't a last-minute concern.

So how do you go about adding security into your microservices? You can certainly develop your own security solution, but that's far from ideal in many situations. You'd have to spend time developing it, maintaining it, and so forth. Developing your own security solution not only results in a delayed start to developing what you want, your microservice, but also creates an additional maintenance burden for future developers.

What you want to do is take advantage of a solid project that's developed and maintained by a large group of developers and that provides the security use cases you need to handle. Though you might have many possible options for such a project available, in this book we'll choose Keycloak.

9.2   *Working with Keycloak*

Keycloak is an open source project providing identity and access management for modern applications and services. Adding authentication to applications and securing services can be achieved with a minimum of fuss.

9.2.1   *Understanding Keycloak's features*

Keycloak provides many features. Here are four most relevant for microservice development:

- *Single-sign on*—Allows users to authenticate against Keycloak rather than each individual application or service. After users log in to Keycloak, they can access any application or service that's authenticated through Keycloak.

- *Social login*—It's super easy to enable social logins with Keycloak! Configure the social network within the admin console and go. No code or application changes are required.
- *User federation*—If your users are registered within LDAP or Active Directory, they can easily be federated with Keycloak. It's also possible to develop your own provider to access your users, if they're in different types of stores, such as a relational database.
- *Standard protocols*—Out of the box, Keycloak provides support for OpenID Connect, OAuth 2.0, and Security Assertion Markup Language (SAML).

Full details on Keycloak and all its features can be found on its website, www.keycloak.org.

9.2.2 Setting up Keycloak

The first thing you need to do is download the Keycloak server for your microservices and applications to integrate with. For our purposes, you have two ways of doing that. You could download a full WildFly distribution customized for Keycloak or download a Keycloak server built with Thorntail. To keep with the microservices way of doing things, choose the Thorntail version. The version you need for our examples is downloadable from http://mng.bz/s6r9.

After downloading, start this version on a separate port so it doesn't interfere with your own microservices:

```
java -Dswarm.http.port=9090 -jar keycloak-2018.1.0-swarm.jar
```

When the server is started, in a browser navigate to http://localhost:9090/auth/. You'll see a screen like the one in figure 9.6.

Welcome to Keycloak

Please create an initial admin user to get started.

Username	
Password	
Password confirmation	
	Create

Documentation | Administration Console

Keycloak Project | Mailing List | Report an issue

Figure 9.6 Setting up the Keycloak Admin user

Enter a username and password for an administrator account on the Keycloak server. Then click Create. Next, click the Administration Console link to see the login screen in figure 9.7.

KEYCLOAK

Username or email

Password

Log in

Figure 9.7   Logging into the Keycloak administration console

Enter the credentials you provided when setting up the administrator account, and then click the Log In button.

Figure 9.8 shows the main screen of the Keycloak administration console. From here, all parts of Keycloak can be modified and adjusted to suit your needs. By default, you're given a Master realm.

Because the Master realm contains the admin user, it's good practice to not use this realm for users who are authenticating with applications or microservices.

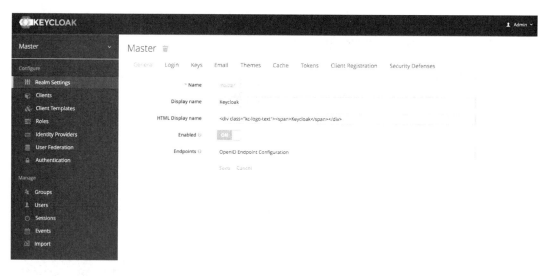

Figure 9.8   Keycloak administration console

Keycloak realms

A Keycloak *realm* manages a set of users, along with their credentials, roles, and groups. Realms are isolated from each other and are responsible for managing only the users they're associated with.

Realms provide a way to segregate groups of users for different purposes. You might have a realm for finance microservices and another realm for people management microservices. This separation ensures that users from each realm remain separate but are managed from a single Keycloak instance.

Depending on your needs, Keycloak is flexible enough to handle any situation that your application or microservice requires. A common requirement for typical application development, but still relevant for microservices, is the need to authenticate a user and use their credentials when calling services.

Figure 9.9 lays out the path a request would take to authenticate a user within a UI.

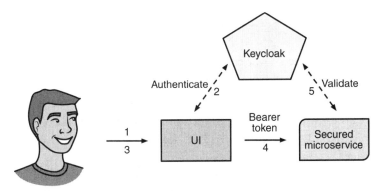

Figure 9.9   User authentication via a UI

The authentication steps are as follows:

1 The user requests to log into the application UI.
2 The UI redirects to Keycloak to perform the login. Keycloak returns tokens that can be used to issue authenticated requests.
3 The user chooses to load a view requiring authentication.
4 A *bearer token* provided by Keycloak is added to the HTTP headers of the request.
5 The token is extracted from the request and passed to Keycloak for validation. If the token is valid, the secured microservice is able to process the request. If the token isn't valid, an HTTP 401 status is returned to indicate that an unauthorized user made a request.

DEFINITION   A *bearer token* is a security token with a special behavioral property. Any party in possession of the token can use it in any way that any other party in possession of the same token could. Using a bearer token doesn't require the holder to prove possession of the cryptographic key.

A slight variation on the preceding process involves one microservice authenticating itself to issue requests against a secured microservice. Figure 9.10 illustrates this variation.

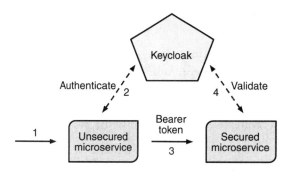

Figure 9.10   **Microservice authentication**

This process differs in that whatever calls the secured microservice doesn't contain or receive an authentication token from a user:

1 The request is received by a microservice that isn't secured.
2 The unsecured microservice authenticates itself against Keycloak.
3 The bearer token is passed in the HTTP headers of the request to the secured microservice.
4 The token is extracted from the request and passed to Keycloak for validation. If the token is valid, the secured microservice can process the request. If the token isn't valid, an HTTP 401 status is returned to indicate that an unauthorized user made a request.

The remainder of this chapter presents examples for both of these scenarios. Let's see how you can use Keycloak to secure some microservices.

9.3   *Securing the Stripe microservice*

In this section, you'll look at how authentication works in the scenario in figure 9.10. Stripe and Payment microservices from chapter 8 will be implemented with security like figure 9.10. The Payment microservice will be based on the RESTEasy client version from that chapter. Let's take a look at the previous scenario, this time with Stripe and Payment; see figure 9.11.

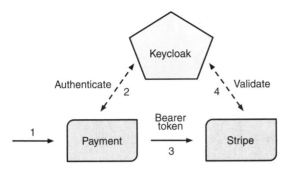

Figure 9.11   Microservice authentication with Stripe and Payment

9.3.1   *Configuring Keycloak*

With your Keycloak server running, the next step is defining a realm for your microservices to associate with.

After you've logged in to the administration console, hover over the Master realm name in the top-left corner to reveal the Add realm button, shown in figure 9.12.

Figure 9.12   Accessing the Add realm button in Keycloak

Click the Add Realm button to open the screen used to create a realm. Figure 9.13 shows this screen.

Figure 9.13   Creating a realm

Click the Select File option to locate cayambe-realm.json from the /chapter9/keycloak directory of the book's code repository. Then click Open.

Figure 9.14 shows the realm you'll create in Keycloak. To perform the import, you need to click Create so that the content of cayambe-realm.json will be imported and a Cayambe realm will exist.

With the Cayambe realm, you're taking advantage of the Keycloak service accounts feature. This feature allows a client to authenticate itself with Keycloak, without any interaction from a user. This feature is super useful for administrative tasks that aren't triggered by a user directly, such as scheduled jobs that still require authentication.

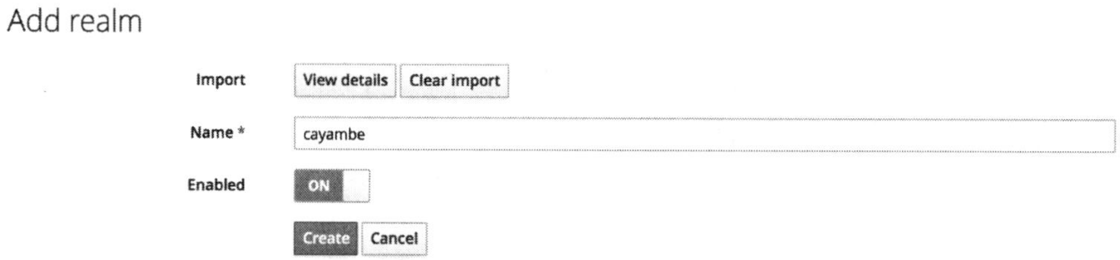

Add realm

Import	View details Clear import
Name *	cayambe
Enabled	ON

Create   Cancel

Figure 9.14 Importing the Cayambe realm

Now that your realm is created, let's look at parts of the JSON you imported so you can see what Keycloak has set up.

Listing 9.1 cayambe-realm.json

```
    "realm": "cayambe",          ◁──── Specifies the realm
    "enabled": true,       ◁──             name to be cayambe
    ...
    "users": [                   Ensures that your realm is        Unique username for
      {                          enabled after being loaded        your service account
        "username": "service-account-payment-service",    ◁──┘    user.
        "enabled": true,
        "serviceAccountClientId": "payment-authz-service",    ◁──┐
        "realmRoles": [                                            Defines the
          "stripe-service-access"                                 clientId that will be
        ]                                                         authenticating with
      }                                                           the service account
    ],
    "roles": {
      "realm": [
        {                                              Defines the stripe-
          "name": "stripe-service-access",             service-access realm role
          "description": "Stripe service access privileges"    ◁──
        }
      ]
    },
    "clients": [
      {                                            Unique clientId for your
        "clientId": "payment-authz-service",    ◁──┘ Payment microservice.
        "secret": "secret",        ◁──
        "enabled": true,                   Secret to be used for authenticating
        "standardFlowEnabled": false,      the service account user.
        "serviceAccountsEnabled": true
      },
      {
        "clientId": "stripe-service",    ◁──   Client ID of the Stripe microservice
        "enabled": true,                       that will be secured.
        "bearerOnly": true    ◁──
      }
    ]
```

The roles that should be assigned to the service account user.

Enables the service account feature of Keycloak for the client

Identifies that the client only validates bearer tokens, but is unable to retrieve them

All the names and IDs you've defined here are unique within the realm you've created but have no meaning by themselves. They're just text.

What's important is that the client ID for a service in the realm matches the specification in the service configuration (which is covered in the next section). With that, your Keycloak server is ready to handle authentication for Stripe and Payment.

9.3.2 Securing the Stripe resource

The first step is to secure the Stripe microservice to ensure that you're accessing Stripe APIs, without appropriate authentication. Once you know that you're properly connecting to the service, you'll add the necessary authentication.

If you take the code from chapter 8, you don't need to modify `StripeResource` to add security. Pretty cool, right? You can add security to an existing RESTful endpoint without modifying its code! How does that work?

Right off the bat you need to let Maven know that you want to use Keycloak with your Thorntail microservice. For that, you need to add a dependency to your pom.xml:

```
<dependency>
  <groupId>io.thorntail</groupId>
  <artifactId>keycloak</artifactId>
</dependency>
```

The only other task is to define where Keycloak is, how it's configured, and what needs protecting. Thankfully, you can do all that from within one file with Thorntail! You add a project-defaults.yml file into the src/main/resources directory of your Stripe microservice with the content shown in the following listing.

Listing 9.2 project-defaults.yml

```
swarm:
  keycloak:
    secure-deployments:
      chapter9-stripe.war:
        realm: cayambe
        bearer-only: true
        auth-server-url: http://192.168.1.13:9090/auth
        ssl-required: external
        resource: stripe-service
        enable-cors: true
  deployment:
    chapter9-stripe.war:
      web:
        security-constraints:
          - url-pattern: /stripe/charge/*
            roles: [ stripe-service-access ]
```

Section defining Keycloak configuration for chapter9-stripe.war deployment

Which realm your deployment uses for authentication—in this case, cayambe

Identify your microservice as bearer-only.

Identify this resource as stripe-service, which corresponds to the Client ID in cayambe-realm.json.

URL of the Keycloak server where the service realm is located. You don't use localhost for when the service is deployed to Minishift.

Section defining deployment-specific configuration for chapter9-stripe.war. This is equivalent to what could be provided as part of web.xml.

Request that /stripe/charge URL patterns from this microservice are protected.

Only users with the role stripe-service-access can successfully execute a request on this microservice.

Now your Stripe microservice is secured from unauthenticated access! Let's give it a try. Change to the /chapter9/serviceauth/stripe directory and run this:

```
mvn thorntail:run
```

Try opening a browser to http://localhost:8080/stripe/charge, and it will indicate *Unauthorized*. Connecting without a bearer token on the HTTP request from the browser results in your request being rejected, because you're not properly authenticated.

To see a little more detail, you can use a browser plugin that shows the HTTP network call or use `curl` from a terminal.

Listing 9.3   Output from `curl` of Stripe

```
$ curl -v http://localhost:8080/stripe/charge

*   Trying ::1...
* TCP_NODELAY set
* Connected to localhost (::1) port 8080 (#0)
> GET /stripe/charge HTTP/1.1              <─── HTTP request headers
> Host: localhost:8080
> User-Agent: curl/7.54.0
> Accept: */*
>
< HTTP/1.1 401 Unauthorized               <─── HTTP response headers
< Expires: 0
< Connection: keep-alive
< WWW-Authenticate: Bearer realm="cayambe"
< Cache-Control: no-cache, no-store, must-revalidate
< Pragma: no-cache
< Content-Type: text/html;charset=UTF-8
< Content-Length: 71
< Date: Sun, 25 Feb 2018 03:22:53 GMT                      Body of HTTP response
<
* Connection #0 to host localhost left intact
<html><head><title>Error</title></head><body>Unauthorized</body></html>  <─┘
```

Now it's easier to see that you're receiving a 401 HTTP response code, indicating you made an unauthorized attempt to access the URL. Now that Stripe is properly secured, how can another microservice access it without receiving user credentials?

You could also have deployed Stripe to Minishift as follows:

```
mvn clean fabric8:deploy -Popenshift
```

9.3.3   *Authenticating in the Payment resource*

The Payment microservice for this chapter is derived from the RESTEasy client in chapter 8. You need to make only a few minor modifications to have it authenticate itself against Keycloak.

To be able to authenticate Payment against Keycloak, you need to add a dependency to the Keycloak Authz Client:

```
<dependency>
  <groupId>org.keycloak</groupId>
  <artifactId>keycloak-authz-client</artifactId>
  <version>3.4.0.Final</version>
</dependency>
```

This dependency provides all the utility classes you need to authenticate with Keycloak. Now you need to define what Keycloak you're interacting with, and which Payment microservice is within the Cayambe realm. For that, you need to create a keycloak.json file within the src/main/resources/ directory.

Listing 9.4 keycloak.json for Payment service

> **The realm your deployment uses for authentication—in this case, cayambe.**

> **URL of the Keycloak server where the cayambe realm is located.**

> **Identify this resource as payment-authz-service, which corresponds to the Client ID in cayambe-realm.json.**

> **The credential that needs to be passed to Keycloak to authenticate this client.**

```
{
  "realm": "cayambe",
  "auth-server-url": "http://192.168.1.13:9090/auth",
  "resource": "payment-authz-service",
  "credentials": {
    "secret": "secret"
  }
}
```

That's all the configuration you need. Next add the code to authenticate with Keycloak. Because you're now using Hystrix, you need to add the authentication handling into `StripeCommand`.

Listing 9.5 `StripeCommand`—`getAuthzClient` method

> **Add a helper method for retrieving the AuthzClient for Keycloak.**

> **If you haven't already created an AuthzClient, proceed.**

> **Create the AuthzClient, which uses the information from keycloak.json to authenticate itself.**

```
private AuthzClient getAuthzClient() {
    if (this.authzClient == null) {
        try {
            this.authzClient = AuthzClient.create();
        } catch (Exception e) {
            throw new RuntimeException("Could not create authorization
client.", e);
        }
    }

    return this.authzClient;
}
```

With `AuthzClient` at your disposal, you can now retrieve an access token that you can add to any request you make to Stripe. To do that, you must modify your `run()`

method from `StripeCommand` by adding a request filter after you have a `Resteasy-Client` instance.

Listing 9.6 `StripeCommand`—run method

Use the AuthzClient to retrieve an access
token from Keycloak, adding a prefix of
Bearer to the token and adding it to a List.

Register an anonymous
ClientRequestFilter for
modifying the HTTP request.

```
protected ChargeResponse run() throws Exception {
    ResteasyClient client = new ResteasyClientBuilder().build();

    client.register((ClientRequestFilter) clientRequestContext -> {
        List<Object> list = new ArrayList<>();
        list.add("Bearer " +
       getAuthzClient().obtainAccessToken().getToken());
        clientRequestContext.getHeaders().put(HttpHeaders.AUTHORIZATION,
 list);
    });

    ResteasyWebTarget target = client.target(serviceURI);

    StripeService stripeService = target.proxy(StripeService.class);
    return stripeService.charge(chargeRequest);
}
```

Add the List you created to the AUTHORIZATION
HTTP header of the request.

That's all you need to do to pass a bearer token on any request you make to Stripe. Pretty simple, right?

9.3.4 *Testing your secured microservice*

Now that you have Stripe and Payment set up, it's time to see all the services running and interacting with each other. If you don't have the Keycloak server and Stripe already running, start them again, ensuring that you deploy Stripe into Minishift.

Then, you need to start Payment by changing to the /chapter9/serviceauth/payment-service directory and running the following:

```
mvn clean fabric8:deploy -Popenshift
```

Open the OpenShift console to retrieve the URL of Payment. Then use the same tools you used in chapters 7 and 8 to execute an HTTP POST against the /sync and /async endpoints. If you try to access the Stripe microservice directly, you'll still receive the HTTP response code 401 indicating you're unauthorized.

To see the HTTP headers for Stripe when you're calling it from Payment, you need to intercept the request or have some other way to output it. In this instance, you'll modify Stripe to output HTTP request and response headers directly.

Let's uncomment the following from project-defaults.yml in /chapter9/service-auth/stripe:

```
undertow:
  servers:
    default-server:
      hosts:
        default-host:
          filter-refs:
            request-dumper:
  filter-configuration:
    custom-filters:
      request-dumper:
        class-name: io.undertow.server.handlers.RequestDumpingHandler
        module: io.undertow.core
```

Restart Stripe and then issue another HTTP POST request on Payment. Within the OpenShift console, locate the Stripe service entry and click the three dots to the right of the pod status. From there, select View Logs, and you should see output logged for Stripe, such as the following:

```
--------------------------REQUEST--------------------------
              URI=/stripe/charge
 characterEncoding=null
     contentLength=63
       contentType=[application/json]
           header=Accept=application/json
           header=Connection=Keep-Alive
           header=Authorization=Bearer

   eyJhbGciOiJSUzI1NiIsInR5cCIgOiAiSldUIiwia2lkIiA6ICJCTTRFT3FlZXU1bGowaWZw
   cHR0aWtEejdnakhsNzBjd2hreGY4c05

   NWU1NIn0.eyJqdGkiOiJmNDIyNmJlYS1hNWE2LTQ0NDgtOTBiZS1kNmI4NGGUwY2FlOWUiLCJ
   leHAiOjE1MTk1MzI0MTksIm5iZiI6MC

   wiaWF0IjoxNTE5NTMyMzU5LCJpc3MiOiJodHRwOi8vMTkyLjE2OC4xLjEzOjkwOTAvYXV0aC
   9yZWFsbXMvY2F5YW1iZSSIsImF1ZCI6I

   nBheW1lbnQtYXV0aoatc2Vydml jZSISInN1YiI6IjljZjAyOTQ5LTgxMzctNGM1Ny04MTY4L
   TVhMz1hMDczMTR1MCISInR5cCI6IkJl

   YXJlciIsImF6cCI6InBheW1lbnQtYXV0aoatc2Vydml jZSISImF1dGhfdG1tZSI6MCwic2Vz
   c21vbl9zdGF0ZSI6Ij15MGM3MTJiLTJ

   kMzItNGZjMi05YWJjLTIxOGFlNTk2MjQwMiIsImFjciI6IjEiLCJhbGxvd2VkLW9yaWdpbnM
   iOltdLCJyZWFsbV9hY2Nlc3MiOnsicm

   9sZXMiOlsic3RyaXBlLXNlcnZpY2UtYWNjZXNzIl19LCJyZXNvdXJjZV9hY2Nlc3MiOnt9LC
   JwcmVmZXJyZWRfdXNlcm5hbWUiOiJzZ
           XJ2aWNlLWFjY291bnQtcGF5bWVudClzZXJ2aWNlIn0.fO-mOqigv661fSj-
   HNtVGixm_63QYw6Y15Yo-
           BpDy7vLNQ5uLnWXLTovkiCnOfB8K1mNlAgWM-h5Nwc7IUCy7MJtMg-
           5L0ts0OOQRknIi42QrEN2kSTvQuTwJCtuhmQqfaV23rpn5SG7hf-
   5RVFnpgq3ElfEMW2fs7Ygnv-
           FlQ1Ls7Ns_uKZ7iH7kpwHl30xvXK_Lid9NXEyZI3e-
```

```
      7DcpFZPvALRt5_xBJOZk2ZfdITBVKxKc3g7r78ndmK1rnC8ar6t8Fplba2pUv_HYrMvthGp6
      XUwALr31qQcAmBS4Oua-
              qRJr2oa7SwSPfkYBsdR_BvPO1rM2R9h8VSYb_5z-A
              header=Content-Type=application/json
              header=Content-Length=63
              header=User-Agent=Apache-HttpClient/4.5.2 (Java/1.8.0_141)
              header=Host=chapter9-stripe:8080
              locale=[]
              method=POST
            protocol=HTTP/1.1
         queryString=
          remoteAddr=/172.17.0.5:47052
          remoteHost=172.17.0.5
              scheme=http
                host=chapter9-stripe:8080
          serverPort=8080
      ------------------------RESPONSE-------------------------
         contentLength=56
           contentType=application/json
              header=Expires=0
              header=Connection=keep-alive
              header=Cache-Control=no-cache, no-store, must-revalidate
              header=Pragma=no-cache
              header=Content-Type=application/json
              header=Content-Length=56
              header=Date=Sun, 25 Feb 2018 04:19:24 GMT
              status=200
      ================================================================
```

9.4   *Capturing user authentication*

To see how you can use user credentials to call a secured microservice, let's secure the new Admin interface for Cayambe.

In this scenario, it's been decided that a few users need the ability to delete categories from the system. That seems reasonable enough. But you don't want everyone with access to be able to delete a category. That certainly wouldn't be an ideal outcome!

To achieve this goal, you need a few code modifications:

1 Secure the HTTP DELETE method on the JAX-RS resource.
2 Integrate with Keycloak for logging a user into the UI.
3 Add a Delete button to the UI for categories in the tree but enable it only when a user has the Admin role.

9.4.1   *Configuring Keycloak*

I didn't show it when you set up the Cayambe realm earlier, but the realm is already set up with what you need for user authentication. Now let's cover the details of the parts specifically about user authentication.

Listing 9.7   cayambe-realm.json

```
"realm": "cayambe",            ◁──      Specifies the realm
...                                     name to be cayambe
"users": [
  {
    "username": "ken",
    ...
    "realmRoles": [            ◁──      Creates a user named ken that has
      "admin",                          the realm roles of user and admin
      "user",
      "offline_access"
    ],
    ...
  },
  {
    "username": "bob",
    ...
    "realmRoles": [            ◁──      Creates a user named bob that
      "user",                           has the realm role of user
      "offline_access"
    ],
    ...
  }
],
"roles": {
  "realm": [                  ◁──      Defines the user and
    {                                  admin realm roles
      "name": "user",
      "description": "User privileges"
    },
    {
      "name": "admin",
      "description": "Administrator privileges"
    }
  ]
},
"clients": [
  {
    "clientId": "cayambe-admin-ui",      ◁──  Client ID for your UI
    "enabled": true,
    "publicClient": true,                ◁
    "baseUrl": "http://localhost:8080",       publicClient indicates that
    "redirectUris": [                         the client has the ability to
      "http://localhost:8080/*"               log in users to Keycloak
    ]
  },
  {
    "clientId": "cayambe-admin-service",  ◁─  Client ID of the JAX-RS
    "enabled": true,                          endpoints that the UI uses.
    "bearerOnly": true
  }
]
```

Base URL of the application.

Now you're ready to move on to the changes your application needs.

9.4.2 *Securing category deletion*

Taking code from the admin directory of chapter 6, you need to make only a few small modifications to secure it as you did with Stripe. Once again, you need to add the Maven dependency for Keycloak in Thorntail:

```
<dependency>
  <groupId>io.thorntail</groupId>
  <artifactId>keycloak</artifactId>
</dependency>
```

Next you configure the integration with Keycloak through project-defaults.yml.

Listing 9.8 project-defaults.yml

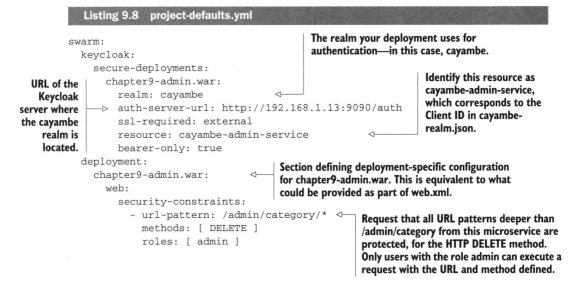

```
swarm:
  keycloak:
    secure-deployments:
      chapter9-admin.war:
        realm: cayambe
        auth-server-url: http://192.168.1.13:9090/auth
        ssl-required: external
        resource: cayambe-admin-service
        bearer-only: true
  deployment:
    chapter9-admin.war:
      web:
        security-constraints:
          - url-pattern: /admin/category/*
            methods: [ DELETE ]
            roles: [ admin ]
```

The realm your deployment uses for authentication—in this case, cayambe.

Identify this resource as cayambe-admin-service, which corresponds to the Client ID in cayambe-realm.json.

URL of the Keycloak server where the cayambe realm is located.

Section defining deployment-specific configuration for chapter9-admin.war. This is equivalent to what could be provided as part of web.xml.

Request that all URL patterns deeper than /admin/category from this microservice are protected, for the HTTP DELETE method. Only users with the role admin can execute a request with the URL and method defined.

That's as far as you need to go to secure the deletion of categories over REST, but you'll take this a step further to provide details about who is doing the deleting.

By adding the Keycloak dependency from Thorntail, you can retrieve details of the user making a request in the microservice. That's nice for being able to audit who is doing what, though for our purposes you're going to print out the information to the console.

Listing 9.9 `CategoryResource`

```
@DELETE
@Produces(MediaType.APPLICATION_JSON)
@Path("/category/{categoryId}")
@Transactional
public Response remove(
        @PathParam("categoryId") Integer categoryId,
        @Context SecurityContext context) throws Exception {
```

Inject the JAX-RS SecurityContext as a method parameter. This gives you access to security information from the HTTP request.

```
    String username = "";
```
**Check if the User Principal is of type
KeycloakPrincipal, which is what you expect.**
```
    if (context.getUserPrincipal() instanceof KeycloakPrincipal) {
        KeycloakPrincipal<KeycloakSecurityContext> kp =
            (KeycloakPrincipal<KeycloakSecurityContext>)
     context.getUserPrincipal();
```
Retrieve the User Principal into a KeycloakPrincipal.
```
        username = kp.getKeycloakSecurityContext().getToken().getName();
    }
```
**From the token on the HTTP request, get the
username of the user who initiated the request.**
```
    try {
        Category entity = em.find(Category.class, categoryId);
        em.remove(entity);
        System.out.println(username + " is deleting category with id: " +
 categoryId);
    } catch (Exception e) {
```
**Print a simple audit message stating
who is deleting which address.**
```
        return Response
                .serverError()
                .entity(e.getMessage())
                .build();
    }

    return Response
            .noContent()
            .build();
}
```

9.4.3 Authenticating the user in a UI

Now that your RESTful endpoint is secure for category deletion, you can make the functionality available from the application UI. To see the changes you've made to the UI, look in the /chapter9/admin_ui/ui directory of the code for the chapter.

In this situation, you've chosen to include the JavaScript that Keycloak provides by adding an NPM dependency into package.json for `keycloak-js`. You could also download the appropriate JavaScript from the server directly, from http://localhost:9090/auth/js/keycloak.js.

As with your Java-based services, you need a keycloak.json file to configure our connection to the Keycloak server.

Listing 9.10   keycloak.json for Admin UI

```
{
  "realm": "cayambe",
  "auth-server-url": "http://192.168.1.13:9090/auth",
  "ssl-required": "external",
  "resource": "cayambe-admin-ui",
  "public-client": true
}
```

This code should now be quite familiar to you, because it covers the typical requirements for connecting to Keycloak. It defines `cayambe-admin-ui` as the resource you specified earlier as your Client ID, within the cayambe-realm.json file you imported into Keycloak.

With the keycloak.json file in place, you can initialize your connection to Keycloak.

Listing 9.11   keycloak-service.js

**Import the Keycloak object from
the keycloak-js NPM module.**

**Create the Keycloak object and
tell it where keycloak.json is
for configuration.**

```
import Keycloak from 'keycloak-js';

const keycloakAuth = Keycloak('/keycloak.json');
keycloakAuth.init({ onLoad: 'check-sso' })
  .success((authenticated) => {
    // Handle successful initialization
  })
  .error(() => {
    // Handle failure to initialize
  });
```

**Initialize Keycloak with check-
sso, which checks only whether
a user is currently logged in.**

**If you successfully connected to Keycloak,
you're passed an authenticated parameter to
let you know whether a user is authenticated.**

As part of the `success()` handling from listing 9.11, you want to set variables that you'll need later. One of those is to retrieve the URL for logging into Keycloak, because you need to add the URL into the UI:

```
this.auth.loginUrl = this.auth.authz.createLoginUrl();
```

You can then pass that value into your ReactJS component for the header of the page, so that you can provide a link to log in:

```
<li className="dropdown">
  <a className="dropdown-toggle nav-item-iconic"
 href={this.props.login}>Login</a>
</li>
```

`this.props.login` is set to the value of the Keycloak login URL, which you set on `this.auth.loginUrl`. You also want to add information into the header of the page about the current logged-in user, and provide a way for that user to log out as well. It'll be an exercise for you to explore the JavaScript and see how that works.

The last piece is to provide a button in the UI to delete a category. `CategoryList-Container`, a ReactJS component, will set a Boolean value for the `adminRole` property to indicate whether the user has that role.

Then you just need HTML code to enable and disable a button based on this property:

```
<button disabled={!this.props.adminRole} className="btn btn-danger"
 onClick={() => this.props.onDelete(category.id)}>Delete</button>
```

That's most of the UI work done, except for passing the token you have for an authenticated user into any request that needs it. Let's do that now.

You need to modify the ReactJS action you have for `delete` to set the token on a request, just as you did in the Payment microservice earlier. The process is similar in JavaScript.

Listing 9.12   Delete admin category

Imports an NPM module
to assist in HTTP calls

Defines the root URL of the
RESTful endpoint for the
address microservice

```
import axios from 'axios';
const ROOT_URL = 'http://localhost:8081';

if (store.getState().securityState.authenticated) {
    store.getState().securityState.keycloak.getToken()
        .then(token => {
            axios.delete(`${ROOT_URL}/admin/category/${id}`, {
                headers: {
                    'Authorization': 'Bearer ' + token
                }
            })
                .then(response => {
                    // Handle success response
                })
                .catch(error => {
                    // Handle errors
                });
        })
        .catch(error => {
            dispatch(notifyError("Error updating token", error));
        });
} else {
    dispatch(notifyError("User is not authenticated", ""));
}
```

Checks
whether
there's an
authenticated
user

Retrieves an authenticated
token from keycloak-service.js

Defines the HTTP
DELETE request you
want to execute

Sets the token you received
from keycloak.getToken() into an
authorization header for the request

Did you forget how a UI and Keycloak interact? Let's take another look in figure 9.15.

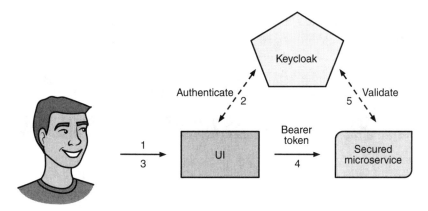

Figure 9.15   User authentication via UI

Anytime the UI calls `delete` on your RESTful endpoint, a token, if present, will be set on the request. For now, no other request from the UI will pass a token, but if there was a need to secure additional endpoints or to log information about the user making a request, then it could be added in a similar manner.

9.4.4   *Testing that the new UI and service all work*

It's time to take the new UI for a spin. If Keycloak isn't still running, start it with the command you used earlier in the chapter. Start the RESTful endpoints for your Admin service, change to /chapter9/admin_ui/admin, and run this:

```
mvn thorntail:run
```

Finally, you can run the UI! You want to simulate a production build, so you need a separate command to build and then start the UI:

```
mvn clean install
java -jar target/chapter9-ui-thorntail.jar
```

Now you can navigate to http://localhost:8080 and you'll see the main page of the application, shown in figure 9.16.

Figure 9.16   Cayambe Admin screen

You can see your categories, as before, but now you also have a Login link in the top-right corner, and a disabled Delete button for each category.

Clicking Login, you're redirected to Keycloak to authenticate yourself. Enter bob as the username and `password` for the password. You're redirected back to your application and you're now authenticated, as shown in figure 9.17.

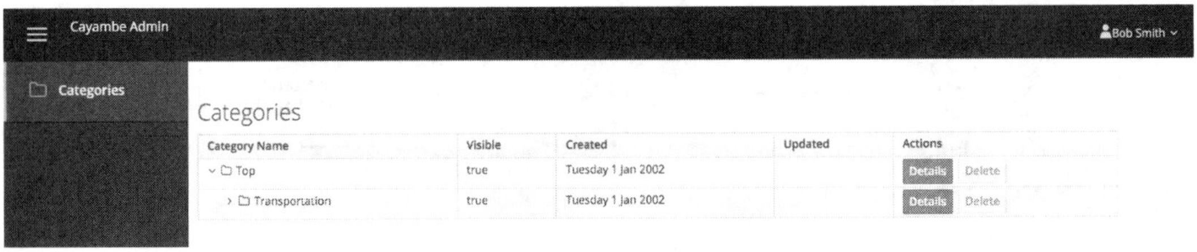

Figure 9.17   Cayambe Admin when logged in with the User role

Although you're authenticated, the Delete button is still disabled. Because Bob has only the User role, you're not permitted to delete categories.

To see how to delete a category, let's log out from Bob by clicking the user details in the top-right corner, and then select Logout from the options.

Now let's log in as ken with the same password as before; see figure 9.18.

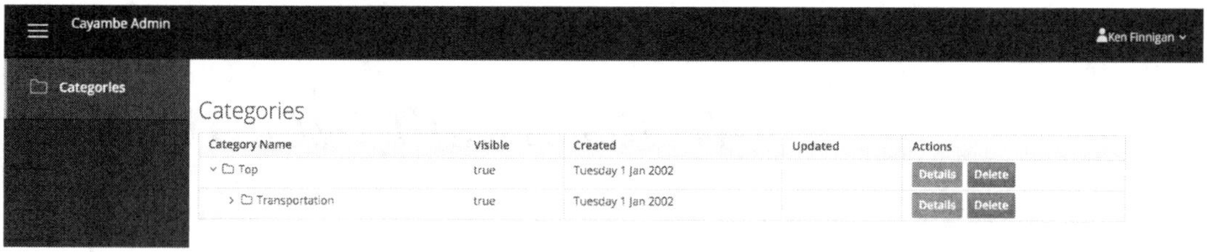

Figure 9.18   Cayambe Admin when logged in with the Admin role

The Delete button is now bright red, indicating it's available for you to use. Clicking it deletes the category you choose, and you'll see that category removed, as well as a message letting you know the category was successfully deleted.

I didn't cover a lot of ReactJS code in this chapter, such as the code to check the token validity and to refresh it when it's expiring. Please take a look at all the JavaScript code available for the application in the source code for the book.

Summary

- Securing your microservices is critical, regardless of whether they're intended for internal users only. You can't predict all the types of malicious users who may attempt to do harm through your microservices.
- Keycloak can accept bearer tokens, provide an authorization client, and provide easy configuration for securing your microservices.
- You can authenticate against Keycloak without a user, which is essential for microservice-to-microservice calls when the recipient is secured.
- You can integrate Keycloak into an application UI to provide authentication, and pass tokens to RESTful endpoints that are secured.

10

Architecting a microservice hybrid

This chapter covers

- Running the Cayambe monolith
- Integrating microservices into Cayambe with a hybrid approach
- Modifying Cayambe to integrate your microservices
- Running the integrated Cayambe in a hybrid cloud

This chapter starts by showing you the old Cayambe and how to get it running locally. Then, after covering some theory on using the hybrid approach to integrating your microservices, you'll revisit the architecture you're looking to achieve for the new Cayambe. Next, you'll dive into implementing the hybrid approach, with the microservices you've developed throughout the book so far. Finally, you'll take your revitalized Cayambe monolith, along with the required microservices, and get them all running in the cloud.

10.1 The Cayambe monolith

Figure 10.1 provides a reminder of the Cayambe homepage from a user's perspective.

Figure 10.1 Cayambe homepage

Cayambe (https://sourceforge.net/projects/cayambe/) is described as a "J2EE E-Commerce Solution using Java Servlets & JSP & EJB." It was built on JDK 1.2 and uses Apache Struts v1. The existing code, which was last updated 15 years ago and can be found at http://cayambe.cvs.sourceforge.net/viewvc/cayambe/, was downloaded and imported to the code repository for this book under /cayambe.

I faced initial challenges in finding compatible versions of Apache Struts, as well as making the necessary changes for it to compile on JDK 8! I resolved some minor bugs as well, to ensure that the basic UI was as functional as possible (as much as possible, given that I wasn't involved in Cayambe's creation).

> **NOTE** The changes required to compile and run the original Cayambe code are beyond the scope of this book. But you can see the changes by viewing the Git commit history of the code at http://mng.bz/4MZ5.

Figure 10.2 provides a detailed view of the layers of code that Cayambe currently has architected. You start with JavaServer Pages (JSP) for the UI; these pages interact with Struts forms and actions. In turn, they interact with a layer of delegates that communicate with the Enterprise JavaBeans (EJB) that are present in what is referred to as the *backend* because it doesn't involve user-facing code. Finally, the EJBs execute calls on the Data Access Objects (DAOs) that provide persistence to the database.

Figure 10.2 provides a great view into the many layers that are present within Cayambe, as well as which pieces of each layer interact with the others. For instance,

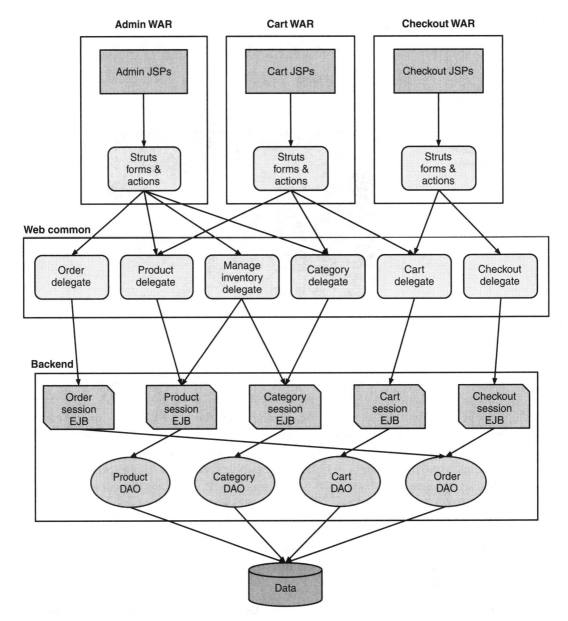

Figure 10.2   Cayambe code structure

you can see that Struts forms and actions for both the Admin WAR and Cart WAR use
the same delegate classes for Category and Product. Though such a situation is typical
of older code, you should use design tools such as DDD (Domain-Driven Design),
which was discussed in chapter 1, to separate the domain model of administration
from a user placing an order. You likely would want particular pieces of data for

Category and Product present that are applicable to only administrators of the site, but not to a user trying to place an order.

10.2 Running the Cayambe monolith

Running Cayambe locally requires these prerequisites:

- WildFly 11.0.0.Final which you can download from http://mng.bz/uZdC
- MySQL Connector for Java which you can download from https://dev.mysql.com/downloads/connector/j/
- A running MySQL Server, whether locally or in a Docker container

10.2.1 Database setup

With a running MySQL server, you can now set up the database and load data.

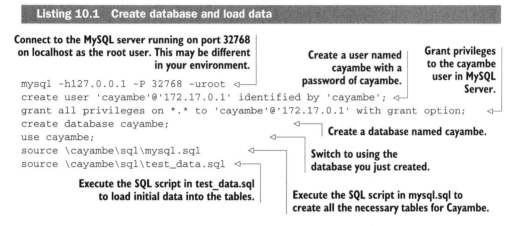

Listing 10.1   Create database and load data

Connect to the MySQL server running on port 32768 on localhost as the root user. This may be different in your environment.

Create a user named cayambe with a password of cayambe.

Grant privileges to the cayambe user in MySQL Server.

```
mysql -h127.0.0.1 -P 32768 -uroot
create user 'cayambe'@'172.17.0.1' identified by 'cayambe';
grant all privileges on *.* to 'cayambe'@'172.17.0.1' with grant option;
create database cayambe;
use cayambe;
source \cayambe\sql\mysql.sql
source \cayambe\sql\test_data.sql
```

Create a database named cayambe.

Switch to using the database you just created.

Execute the SQL script in test_data.sql to load initial data into the tables.

Execute the SQL script in mysql.sql to create all the necessary tables for Cayambe.

With these steps, you now have a database ready for use with Cayambe. The next task is to configure WildFly to be able to access the database you just set up.

10.2.2 WildFly setup

After you've extracted the WildFly 11.0.0.Final download into a directory of your choosing, you need to provide some setup so that WildFly knows where the MySQL driver can be found. To do that, you create /modules/system/layers/base/com/mysql/main inside the location where WildFly was extracted.

Inside the directory you just created, copy the MySQL connector for Java JAR file that you downloaded earlier. In the same directory, create this file.

Listing 10.2   MySQL driver module.xml for monolith

```
<?xml version="1.0" encoding="UTF-8"?>
<module xmlns="urn:jboss:module:1.3" name="com.mysql">

  <resources>
```

Sets the module name to be com.mysql, matching the directory structure you created

```
            <resource-root path="mysql-connector-java-5.1.43-bin.jar"/>    ⟵──┐
        </resources>
        <dependencies>                                  ⟵──────────┐
            <module name="javax.api"/>
            <module name="javax.transaction.api"/>
        </dependencies>
    </module>
```

Path to the MySQL connector for Java JAR. Your JAR may require a different version in the name.

Some dependencies that are required for JDBC drivers in WildFly

What you've done here is create a JBoss module definition that's used by WildFly. JBoss Modules is an open source project at the core of WildFly's management of class-loaders, and the separation of classes between classloaders to prevent clashes. For this example, you don't need to understand how JBoss Modules does what it does. All you need to know is how to create a new module, as you did here, for adding JDBC drivers into WildFly.

Finally, you need to tell WildFly about the new database driver and define a new data source that Cayambe can use to talk to the database. All WildFly configuration is present in standalone.xml. You need to locate standalone.xml inside /standalone/configuration/ of the WildFly installation and then open the file for editing. Locate the section for the datasource's subsystem and replace the entire section with the following content.

Listing 10.3 standalone.xml snippet

Existing ExampleDS datasource present in WildFly. It hasn't been altered.

```
<subsystem xmlns="urn:jboss:domain:datasources:5.0">
    <datasources>
        <datasource jndi-name="java:jboss/datasources/ExampleDS"
            pool-name="ExampleDS" enabled="true" use-java-context="true">    ⟵──┐
            <connection-url>jdbc:h2:mem:test;DB_CLOSE_DELAY=-
⟹ 1;DB_CLOSE_ON_EXIT=FALSE</connection-url>
            <driver>h2</driver>
            <security>
                <user-name>sa</user-name>
                <password>sa</password>
            </security>
        </datasource>
        <datasource jta="true" jndi-name="java:/Climb" pool-name="MySqlDS"
⟹ enabled="true" use-ccm="true">
            <connection-url>jdbc:mysql://localhost:32768/cayambe</connection-url> ⟵─┐
            <driver-class>com.mysql.jdbc.Driver</driver-class>
            <driver>mysql</driver>
            <security>
                <user-name>cayambe</user-name>    ⟵──┐
                <password>cayambe</password>
            </security>
            <validation>
                <valid-connection-checker
                    class-name="org.jboss.jca.adapters.jdbc.extensions.mysql
⟹ .MySQLValidConnectionChecker"/>
                <background-validation>true</background-validation>
```

Climb datasource for Cayambe made accessible under JNDI name java:/Climb

mysql is the name of the driver definition, which is added at the end of the listing.

MySQL connection URL to database. Needs to be modified for your environment.

Security credentials you created in MySQL for the database

```
            <exception-sorter class-
        name="org.jboss.jca.adapters.jdbc.extensions.mysql
➥ .MySQLExceptionSorter"/>
          </validation>
        </datasource>
        <drivers>                                    ┐  Existing h2 driver
          <driver name="h2" module="com.h2database.h2">  ◁─┘  for ExampleDS
            <xa-datasource-class>org.h2.jdbcx.JdbcDataSource</
➥ xa-datasource-class>                          ┐  mysql driver definition, which
          </driver>                              │  points to the com.mysql
          <driver name="mysql" module="com.mysql">  ◁─┤  module you created earlier
            <xa-datasource-
        class>com.mysql.jdbc.jdbc2.optional.MysqlXADataSource</
➥ xa-datasource-class>
          </driver>
        </drivers>
      </datasources>
    </subsystem>
```

That's all you need to do to configure WildFly to work with Cayambe.

10.2.3 *Running Cayambe*

You're almost ready to start Cayambe and see it running. But first you need to build the EAR deployment. Figure 10.3 reminds you of what Cayambe looks like from a deployment perspective, which you first saw in chapter 2.

Cayambe EAR

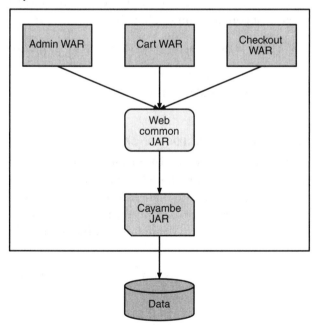

Figure 10.3 Cayambe monolith deployment

Cayambe uses EAR (Enterprise Application aRchive) as the means of packaging the deployment. EAR allows Cayambe to include multiple WARs in addition to common JAR libraries that can be shared.

> **NOTE**   Though EARs were the preferred method for packaging a Java EE deployment, WAR deployments are more common at present. That's not to say that EARs aren't still being used, either by choice or legacy code, but EAR usage is less prevalent than it was.

To build Cayambe, you need to change to the /cayambe directory of the book's code and run the following:

```
mvn clean install
```

Maven will construct each of the JARs and WARs that the project code resides within, and then package it into an EAR for you to deploy. After that construction is complete, copy /cayambe-ear/target/cayambe.ear into /standalone/deployments of the WildFly installation.

Now start WildFly, including your deployment, by running this command from the root of the WildFly installation:

```
./bin/standalone.sh
```

Lots of messages are output to the console as WildFly starts, and then your deployment is started. WildFly is ready to accept traffic to Cayambe after the messages stop, and you should see a message that contains content like this:

```
WFLYSRV0025: WildFly Full 11.0.0.Final (WildFly Core 3.0.8.Final) started in
↪ 6028ms
```

You can access the user site at http://localhost:8080, and the administration site at http://localhost:8080/admin.

10.3   *Cayambe hybrid—monolith with microservices*

In chapter 1, you learned about the Hybrid pattern for monoliths, whereby an existing monolith can have existing functionality migrated to a microservice environment. This pattern allows those pieces of the monolith that require higher scalability or performance to be efficiently separated, while not requiring the entire monolith to be rebuilt to make improvements. Let's revisit what a monolith using the Hybrid pattern might look like; see figure 10.4.

> **NOTE**   In this particular instance, you won't be using a gateway that fronts all your microservices.

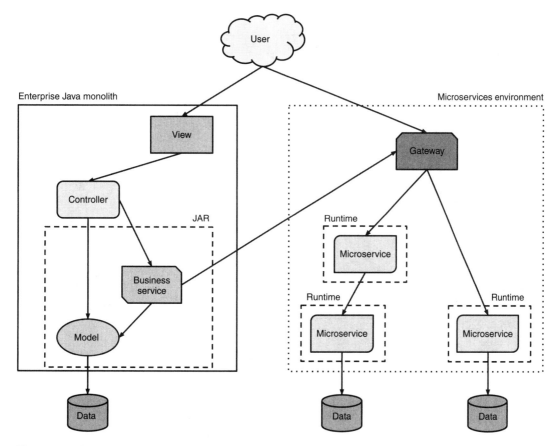

Figure 10.4 Enterprise Java and microservices hybrid architecture

There are certainly benefits to being able to split a monolith into pieces, while also separating out where those pieces might be deployed. Although doing so adds overhead, at least in terms of network calls and performance, the advantages often outweigh any downsides. This is especially true when those advantages revolve around key aspects, such as continuous delivery and release cadence.

In chapter 2, you developed a new administration UI, as well as RESTful endpoints for interacting with the data. In chapter 7, you introduced a separate microservice for processing card payments, to make it easier to integrate with external systems. Finally, in chapter 9, you added security to your administration UI, which was originally created in chapter 2.

How does it all fit together? Figure 10.5 represents the proposed architecture of the Cayambe hybrid monolith. You'll combine large pieces of the original monolith with new microservices that you've developed throughout the book. This architecture has certainly come a long way from where it started, but you still have some work ahead.

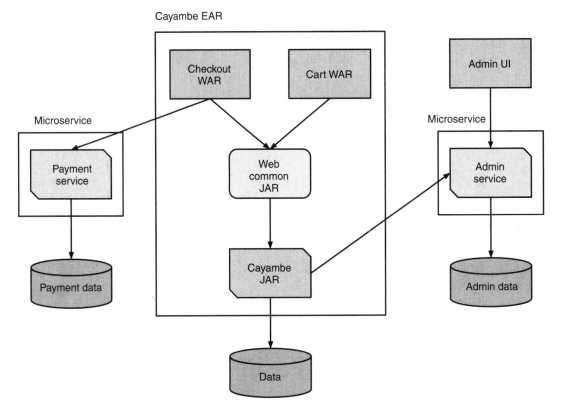

Figure 10.5   Proposed Cayambe hybrid monolith

So what exactly did you do in figure 10.5? You wanted to integrate the Payment micro-service for processing card payments during the checkout process, and you wanted the UI to retrieve category information from Admin instead of storing the data itself. In addition to the new microservices, you also replaced the UI for administration with a new one, so you can remove the old one from Cayambe.

Let's look at the requirements for each integration. All the code for the Cayambe hybrid monolith and its microservices is present within the book's code in /chapter10.

10.3.1 Integrating the Payment microservice

As a result of integrating the Payment microservice (and, in particular, because you're using an external payment provider—in this case, Stripe), you no longer need to store your customers' credit card information. This is a huge benefit because the rules and restrictions around storing credit card information can be difficult to enforce, and off-loading that responsibility to a company specializing in that area is easier.

Because you don't need to store that information, let's remove it from the `billing_info` table of Cayambe. You modify /sql/cayambe/mysql.sql so that the fol-lowing columns are removed:

- name_on_card
- card_type
- card_number
- card_expiration_month
- card_expiration_year
- authorization_code

You replace all those columns with a single column for card_charge_id. In changing what you're storing in the database, you also need to update classes that passed those values around.

Listing 10.4 OrderDAO

```
public class OrderDAO {
    public void Save(OrderVO orderVO)
    {
    ...

        StringBuffer sqlBillingInfo = new StringBuffer(512);
        sqlBillingInfo.append("insert into billing_info ");
        sqlBillingInfo.append("(order_id,name,address1,address2,city,state,
➥ zipcode,country,name_on_card,");
        sqlBillingInfo.append("card_charge_id,phone,email) ");          ◁─┐
        sqlBillingInfo.append("values ('" );
        sqlBillingInfo.append(orderId);
        sqlBillingInfo.append("','");
```
Remove existing card columns from the select statement and add card_charge_id.

```
    ...

        sqlBillingInfo.append(orderVO.getBillingInfoVO().getCountry());
        sqlBillingInfo.append("','");
        sqlBillingInfo.append(orderVO.getBillingInfoVO().getCardChargeId()); ◁─┐
        sqlBillingInfo.append("','");
```
Remove calls to set the values for the removed columns, and replace them with getCardChargeId() for the new field.

```
    ...
    }
    ...

    public OrderVO getOrderVO( OrderVO orderVO )
    {
    ...
            b.setCardChargeId( rs.getString("billing_info.card_charge_id") ); ◁─┐
    ...
    }
}
```
Remove retrieval of old card data columns and add one for card_charge_id.

Here you modify OrderDAO that interacts directly with the database for storing and retrieving the data for an order. Because you've modified methods that were on BillingInfoVO, you now need to make changes there as well, as shown in listing 10.5.

Listing 10.5 BillingInfoVO

```
public class BillingInfoVO implements Serializable {

    private Long billingId = null;
    private Long orderId =  null;
    private String name = null;
    private String address = null;
    private String address2 = null;
    private String city = null;
    private String state = null;
    private String zipCode = null;
    private String country = null;
    private String phone = null;
    private String email = null;

    private String cardToken = null;      ◁────
    private String cardChargeId = null;

    . . .

    public void setCardToken ( String _cardToken ) { cardToken = _cardToken; }  ◁─┘
    public String getCardToken () { return cardToken; }

    public void setCardChargeId ( String _cardChargeId ) { cardChargeId =
➥ _cardChargeId; }
    public String getCardChargeId () { return cardChargeId; }
}
```

> **Replace nameOnCard, cardType, cardExpirationMonth, cardExpirationYear, and authorizationCode with cardToken and cardChargeId. cardToken is used to pass a token from the UI, which you'll see shortly.**

> **Remove getter and setter methods for the previously mentioned fields, and add them for cardToken and cardChargeId.**

Now that you've modified the data objects that you're passing around, let's add the code needed to call the Payment client proxy from inside the Cayambe monolith.

To be able to send and receive the JSON and have it converted to objects, you need ChargeStatus, PaymentRequest, and PaymentResponse. To make it easy, you've copied these files from the Payment microservice, so you have them. Next you need an interface that represents Payment.

Listing 10.6 PaymentService

```
@Path("/")
public interface PaymentService {
    @POST
    @Path("/sync")                                      ◁────
    @Consumes(MediaType.APPLICATION_JSON)               ◁────
    @Produces(MediaType.APPLICATION_JSON)
    PaymentResponse charge(PaymentRequest paymentRequest);  ◁──┐
}
```

> **You're using the /sync endpoint on the Payment microservice.**

> **RESTful endpoint will consume and produce JSON.**

> **Method to be proxied that will call Payment.**

That's all you need in order to define the external Payment microservice. Now let's see how you integrate it into the existing Struts code. To be able to process a card transaction before you save the order, you need to modify `SubmitOrderAction` from within /cayambe-hybrid/checkout.

Listing 10.7　`SubmitOrderAction`

```
public class SubmitOrderAction extends Action
{
  public ActionForward perform( ActionMapping mapping, ActionForm form,
      HttpServletRequest request, HttpServletResponse response )
      throws IOException, ServletException
  {
    ...

    OrderActionForm oaf = (OrderActionForm)form;

    try {
      delegate = new CheckOutDelegate();
      OrderVO orderVO = new OrderVO();
      orderVO = (OrderVO)oaf.toOrderVO();
      orderVO.setCartVO( (CartVO) session.getAttribute("Cart") );
      // Call Payment Service
      ResteasyClient client = new ResteasyClientBuilder().build();
      ResteasyWebTarget target =
        client.target("http://cayambe-payment-service-
  myproject.192.168.64.33.nip.io");
      PaymentService paymentService = target.proxy(PaymentService.class);
      PaymentResponse paymentResponse =
  paymentService.charge(new PaymentRequest()
                          .amount((long) (orderVO.getCartVO().getTotalCost()
  * 100))
                          .cardToken(oaf.getCardToken())
                          .orderId(Math.toIntExact(orderVO.getOrderId())))
        );

      orderVO.getBillingInfoVO().setCardChargeId(paymentResponse.getChargeId());
      delegate.Save ( orderVO );

      CartDelegate cartDelegate = new CartDelegate();
      cartDelegate.Remove( orderVO.getCartVO() );

    } catch(Exception e) {
      forwardMapping = CayambeActionMappings.FAILURE;
      errors.add( ActionErrors.GLOBAL_ERROR, new
  ActionError("error.cart.UpdateCartError") );
    }

  return mapping.findForward( forwardMapping );
  }
}
```

Annotations:
- **Existing Struts Action class for handling order submission**
- **Create a ResteasyClient that calls Payment within OpenShift.**
- **Create a proxy instance of PaymentService.**
- **Call Payment, passing it a PaymentRequest with the amount of the order and the cardToken from Stripe.**
- **Set the chargeId you got back from Payment onto the BillingInfoVO.**

The preceding code will be familiar from chapters 6, 7, and 8, because you used the RESTEasy client proxy generation in those examples as well.

In creating a `PaymentRequest` instance, you called `oaf.getCardToken()`, which contains the card token you need for processing a Stripe request. But you need to update `OrderActionForm` to provide that information for you.

`OrderActionForm` is located in /cayambe-hybrid/web-common. You remove the following fields, and their associated getters and setters:

- `nameOnCard`
- `cardNumber`
- `cardType`
- `cardExpirationMonth`
- `cardExpirationYear`

Finally, you add a field for `cardToken` of type `String`, and the getter and setter for it as well.

Let's modify the checkout page to capture the credit card details, before calling Stripe to retrieve a `cardToken` representing the credit card. For that, you need to update CheckOutForm.jsp inside /cayambe-hybrid/checkout.

Listing 10.8   CheckOutForm.jsp

```
...
<script src="https://js.stripe.com/v3/"></script>        Create a Stripe JavaScript instance,
<script type="text/javascript">                           passing in a publisher key.
  var stripe = Stripe({STRIPE_PUBLISH_KEY});      Initialize the prebuilt UI
  var elements = stripe.elements();                components from Stripe.
...
  var card = elements.create('card', {style: style});
                                                          Set the token ID you
  function stripeTokenHandler(token) {                    received from Stripe onto
    // Insert the token ID into the form so it gets submitted to the server
    var cardToken = document.getElementById('cardToken');   the cardToken element.
    cardToken.value = token.id;

    // Submit the form                              Retrieve the orderForm
    document.getElementById('orderForm').submit();  and submit it.
  };

  document.body.onload = function() {        When the document is loaded, mount the Stripe
    card.mount('#card-element');             card element onto the card-element div.

    card.addEventListener('change', function(event) {
      var displayError = document.getElementById('card-errors');
      if (event.error) {
        displayError.textContent = event.error.message;
      } else {                              Add an event listener
        displayError.textContent = '';       on the UI component
                                             to handle Stripe errors.
```

```
      }
    });

    var form = document.getElementById('orderForm');     ⟵
    form.addEventListener('submit', function(event) {
      event.preventDefault();

      stripe.createToken(card).then(function(result) {     ⟵
        if (result.error) {
          // Inform the user if there was an error.
          var errorElement = document.getElementById('card-errors');
          errorElement.textContent = result.error.message;
        } else {
          stripeTokenHandler(result.token);     ⟵
        }
      });
    });
  };
</script>

<form:form name="OrderForm" styleId="orderForm"
➡ type="org.cayambe.web.form.OrderActionForm"
    action="SubmitOrder.do" scope="request">
...
  <tr>
    <th align="right">
      <label for="card-element">
        Enter card details
      </label>
    </th>
    <td align="left">
      <div id="card-element">     ⟵
        <!-- A Stripe Element will be inserted here. -->
      </div>

      <!-- Used to display form errors. -->
      <div id="card-errors" role="alert"></div>
      <form:hidden property="cardToken" styleId="cardToken"/>     ⟵
    </td>
  </tr>
...
</form:form>
```

Add an event listener for submit onto the orderForm.

Submit event listener asks Stripe to create a token from the card element in the UI.

If Stripe returned success, call the stripeTokenHandler function.

Div to hold the card element Stripe will create for you.

Add a hidden form field to pass the Stripe card token into OrderActionForm.

NOTE The full details of how to integrate UI elements of Stripe into a website can be found at https://stripe.com/docs/stripe-js.

In addition to adding the card capture into the table of the form, you remove all the existing fields that captured each piece of credit card information.

For the preceding CheckOutForm.jsp to work, you also need to modify struts-forms.tld in /cayambe-hybrid/checkout to add styleId to both the form and hidden tags. This allows you to set a name that will be added to the id attribute of the generated HTML element.

That's all the changes you need for the Payment microservice integration. Now it's time to integrate Admin!

10.3.2 Integrating the Admin microservice

To integrate Admin, you want to do something similar to Payment—at least in that you want to provide the classes required to send and receive objects to Admin, as well as to generate a proxy from an interface that represents Admin.

In addition to being able to call Admin, you need to integrate the category retrieval into the Cayambe monolith wherever categories are currently used. In looking at how categories are defined within Cayambe, you notice that categories are a separate database table, and the category/parent relationship is present in a separate table.

You also see that categories are called from various layers within the Cayambe monolith, and that the Category EJB provides many ways to interact with the categories that are split across many Java classes. Such a situation doesn't bode well for a smooth integration of Admin, at least not in the same way that Payment was integrated.

Because the integration would require large code changes across nearly the entire stack, you decide that such an enhancement, though beneficial, has too many risks associated with it. In wanting to be agile and nimble, you don't want to be held up for weeks or months to integrate Admin because you're dealing with problems. These problems could be anything from issues in integrating the actual code, to spending a large amount of time testing the new changes in Cayambe—in addition to regression testing to make sure the changes don't have ripple effects into other parts of the code. It's unfortunate, but sometimes tough decisions like this need to be made for the stability of production code.

So did I just waste large parts of the book for you to write a new UI and service for Admin that you won't use? Far from it! In chapter 11, you'll minimize your risk concerns by using event streaming, allowing you to retain the existing code within the Cayambe monolith but still take advantage of the new Admin UI and microservice.

10.3.3 New administration UI

You've seen the new administration UI, along with its associated microservice, but there's already an administration section inside the Cayambe monolith. You remove the content from /cayambe-hybrid/admin, because you no longer need the existing administration UI. Next you remove all the references to the Admin.war that were present in /cayambe-hybrid/cayambe-ear, as that WAR is no longer a dependency of the EAR and doesn't need to be packaged inside it.

10.3.4 Cayambe hybrid summary

Figure 10.6 provides the complete picture of where you are currently, as well as the remaining pieces that are yet to be developed. You'll add the remaining pieces in chapter 11.

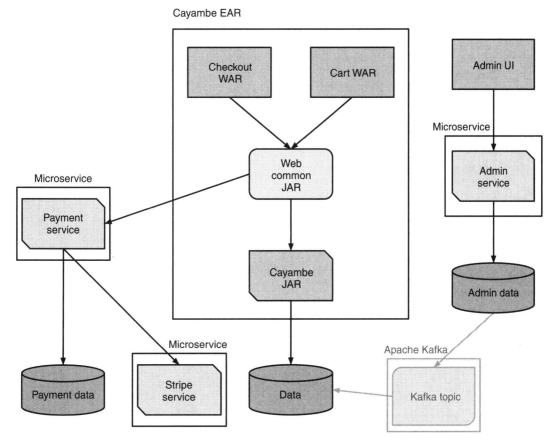

Figure 10.6 Cayambe hybrid monolith

10.4 *Deploying everything to a hybrid cloud*

Because you've converted the Cayambe monolith to a hybrid, deploying everything becomes more complex—but you're also doing everything manually. In a real environment, you'd want the deployments to be automated to make the process even simpler.

This section covers all the pieces of the Cayambe hybrid that need to be set up, configured, or deployed to run it. The first thing you need to do is have Minishift running. It should also start with a clean OpenShift environment, to remove any services that might be present. You're going to need all the room you can get inside a local OpenShift! So let's delete any existing Minishift VM (virtual machine) you have and start from scratch:

```
> minishift delete
> minishift start --cpus 3 --memory 4GB
```

The main difference from previous executions of Minishift is that you're specifying three virtual CPUs and 4 GB of memory. This is necessary to ensure that you have the capacity to install the services you need for this and the next chapter.

10.4.1 Database

Let's create a MySQL database to store your data! Run `minishift console` and log into the OpenShift console.

Open the default My Project. Click the Add to Project menu item near the top and select Browse Catalog. This provides all the types of prebuilt images that OpenShift can install for you, as shown in figure 10.7.

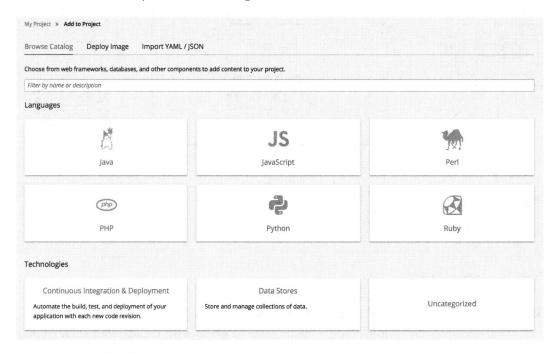

Figure 10.7 Choosing the Browse Catalog option in the OpenShift console

Click the Data Stores box in the bottom row to see the different data stores available. On the Data Stores page that opens, shown in figure 10.8, click the Select button in the MySQL (Persistent) box.

You'll be presented with a page containing configuration for MySQL, most of which can be left with the defaults. The only options you need to set are MySQL Connection Username, MySQL Connection Password, and MySQL Root User Password. Enter values for those fields, make a note of that information, and then click Create.

> **WARNING** Don't use *cayambe* as the MySQL Connection Username, because that would conflict with the user you need to create later.

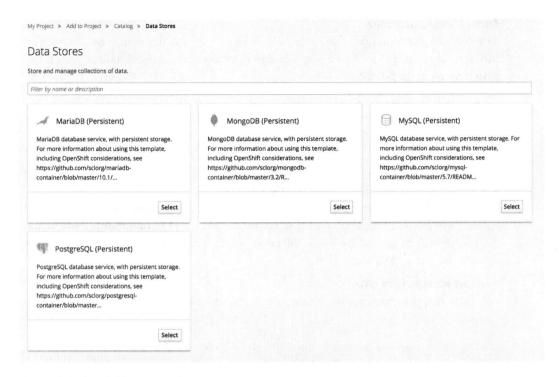

Figure 10.8   OpenShift console—data stores

After a minute or two, a MySQL service will be available in OpenShift. To be able to set up the databases, tables, and data that you need for Cayambe, you need to access the service remotely. Open a terminal window, log in to the OpenShift CLI with `oc login`, and then run `oc get pods`. The command returns a list similar to this:

```
NAME                 READY      STATUS        RESTARTS     AGE
mysql-1-xq98q        1/1        Running       0            2m
```

You need to copy the name of the MySQL pod, mysql-1-xq98q in this case, to connect to it:

```
oc rsh mysql-1-xq98q
```

From inside the pod, you can then run the following to open a command prompt into the MySQL instance:

```
mysql -u root -p$MYSQL_ROOT_PASSWORD -h $HOSTNAME
```

Within the MySQL pod, `$MYSQL_ROOT_PASSWORD` and `$HOSTNAME` are defined as environment variables, so you don't need to remember them to connect to the MySQL instance. Now that you're inside MySQL, let's set up the data you need!

ADMIN MICROSERVICE DATA

The following commands create a `cayambe-admin` user for the admin database, grant the user all privileges to the `cayambe_admin` database, create the database, and finally switch to using that database:

```
create user 'cayambe-admin' identified by 'cayambe-admin';
grant all privileges on cayambe_admin.* to 'cayambe-admin' with grant option;
create database cayambe_admin;
use cayambe_admin;
```

In the context of the `cayambe_admin` database, you can now execute some SQL to create the tables and populate them with initial data.

Open /chapter10/sql/admin/mysql.sql and paste the contents into the terminal window where you're logged into MySQL. You should see SQL statements flash by, and if all went well, no errors! Now that the tables are there, do the same with /chapter10/sql/admin/data.sql to load the data.

PAYMENT MICROSERVICE DATA

You now run a similar set of commands for a `cayambe-payment` user and `cayambe_payment` database:

```
create user 'cayambe-payment' identified by 'cayambe-payment';
grant all privileges on cayambe_payment.* to 'cayambe-payment' with grant
➥ option;
create database cayambe_payment;
use cayambe_payment;
```

Now open /chapter10/sql/payment-service/mysql.sql and paste the contents into the terminal window where you're logged into MySQL. That should create the two tables you need and set an initial value for the ID sequence generator that JPA needs.

CAYAMBE MONOLITH DATA

Finally, run a similar set of commands for the `cayambe` user and database:

```
create user 'cayambe' identified by 'cayambe';
grant all privileges on cayambe.* to 'cayambe' with grant option;
create database cayambe;
use cayambe;
```

Open /chapter10/sql/cayambe/mysql.sql and paste the contents into the terminal window, which will create all the tables for the Cayambe monolith. Then copy the contents of /chapter10/sql/cayambe/test_data.sql to load the initial test data.

10.4.2 Security

You already have a Keycloak server that you set up as part of chapter 9, so you're going to reuse that:

```
/chapter9/keycloak> java -Dswarm.http.port=9090 -jar keycloak-2018.1.0-
➥ swarm.jar
```

Open http://localhost:9090/auth/ and log into the administration console. Select the Clients option from the left navigation menu. From the list of available clients, click cayambe-admin-ui to open its details. All you need to do is update the three URLs that specify where your new administration UI is running, by changing the port from 8080 to 8090.

10.4.3 *Microservices*

Now it's time to start deploying the microservices to OpenShift.

ADMIN MICROSERVICE

Because the Admin microservice was brought across from previous chapters, you don't need to do anything to it other than deploy it!

```
/chapter10/admin> mvn clean fabric8:deploy -Popenshift
```

After this microservice is deployed, you should see it within the OpenShift console.

STRIPE MICROSERVICE

As with Admin, you don't need to do anything in the Stripe code, so you just deploy it:

```
/chapter10/stripe> mvn clean fabric8:deploy -Popenshift
```

PAYMENT MICROSERVICE

Next, you need to deploy Payment, which is done in the same way as the others:

```
/chapter10/payment-service> mvn clean fabric8:deploy -Popenshift
```

10.4.4 *Cayambe hybrid*

Now you're ready to set up a WildFly application for the Cayambe hybrid. You can reuse the WildFly 11 and MySQL connector JAR downloads from earlier in the chapter and unpack them into a new directory.

After they're all extracted, create a directory structure that matches /wildfly-11.0.0 .Final/modules/system/layers/base/com/mysql/main. Into that directory, copy the JAR file for MySQL Connector, and create a module.xml file with the following content.

> **Listing 10.9 MySQL driver module.xml for hybrid**

```xml
<?xml version="1.0" encoding="UTF-8"?>
<module xmlns="urn:jboss:module:1.3" name="com.mysql">

  <resources>
    <resource-root path="mysql-connector-java-5.1.43-bin.jar"/>      ◁──┐
  </resources>
  <dependencies>
    <module name="javax.api"/>
    <module name="javax.transaction.api"/>
  </dependencies>
</module>
```

The particular version referenced here needs to match the file you copied into the directory.

Next you need to provide WildFly with the information it needs to configure the data-source for Cayambe. Open /wildfly-11.0.0.Final/standalone/configuration/standalone .xml, and replace the current datasource's subsystem config with the following.

Listing 10.10   standalone.xml

```xml
<subsystem xmlns="urn:jboss:domain:datasources:5.0">
  <datasources>
    <datasource jndi-name="java:jboss/datasources/ExampleDS" pool-
name="ExampleDS"
        enabled="true" use-java-context="true">
      <connection-url>jdbc:h2:mem:test;DB_CLOSE_DELAY=-
1;DB_CLOSE_ON_EXIT=FALSE</connection-url>
      <driver>h2</driver>
      <security>
        <user-name>sa</user-name>
        <password>sa</password>
      </security>
    </datasource>
    <datasource jta="true" jndi-name="java:/Climb" pool-name="MySqlDS"
enabled="true" use-ccm="true">
      <connection-url>jdbc:mysql://localhost:53652/cayambe</connection-url>
      <driver-class>com.mysql.jdbc.Driver</driver-class>
      <driver>mysql</driver>
      <security>
        <user-name>cayambe</user-name>
        <password>cayambe</password>
      </security>
      <validation>
        <valid-connection-checker
          class-name="org.jboss.jca.adapters.jdbc.extensions.mysql
.MySQLValidConnectionChecker"/>
        <background-validation>true</background-validation>
        <exception-sorter class-
      name="org.jboss.jca.adapters.jdbc.extensions.mysql
.MySQLExceptionSorter"/>
      </validation>
    </datasource>
    <drivers>
      <driver name="h2" module="com.h2database.h2">
        <xa-datasource-class>org.h2.jdbcx.JdbcDataSource</
xa-datasource-class>
      </driver>
      <driver name="mysql" module="com.mysql">
        <xa-datasource-
      class>com.mysql.jdbc.jdbc2.optional.MysqlXADataSource</xa-datasource-
class>
      </driver>
    </drivers>
  </datasources>
</subsystem>
```

Listing 10.10 is virtually identical to listing 10.3, except for one difference: the port number for the MySQL instance for Cayambe is set to 53652. You might be wondering what that port number is from, because it's not a standard MySQL port. Well, you're going to define that port by forwarding the `mysql` service port within OpenShift so you can access it:

```
oc port-forward {mysql-pod-name} 53652:3306
```

> **NOTE** If an existing forwarded port is shut down, or your machine is rebooted, you'll have to rerun this command before WildFly will be able to find the database.

10.4.5 *Cayambe EAR*

Now that WildFly is set up, let's deploy the modified Cayambe hybrid EAR to it. First you need to build it!

```
/chapter10/cayambe-hybrid> mvn clean install
```

After it's built, copy /cayambe-hybrid/cayambe-ear/target/cayambe.ear into /wildfly-11.0.0.Final/standalone/deployments. Now you start WildFly:

```
/wildfly-11.0.0.Final/bin/standalone.sh
```

With WildFly started, it's now possible to try out the Cayambe UI by opening http://localhost:8080.

10.4.6 *Admin UI*

The last piece to get running is the new administration UI, because you already have the Admin microservice running from earlier.

For the most part, the code is the same as that you used in chapter 9, with two small modifications. You adjusted the port that the UI runs on to be 8090, so it didn't clash with the main UI, and you also modified ROOT_URL in /chapter10/admin-ui/app/actions/category-actions.js to be the URL shown in the OpenShift console for cayambe-admin-service.

> **NOTE** Be sure to remove the trailing slash from the URL.

It's time to start the administration UI:

```
/chapter10/admin-ui> mvn clean package
/chapter10/admin-ui> npm start
```

Summary

- You set up and ran the Cayambe monolith to show the code as it was before you made any modifications.

- You integrated the microservices that you'd developed throughout the book into Cayambe, making the necessary modifications to Cayambe to make the integration possible.
- You learned that although you might want to integrate a microservice (in this case, Admin), sometimes doing so can add too much risk, so other options need to be considered.
- You deployed the handful of microservices and the Cayambe hybrid and had them all functioning together.

Data streaming
with Apache Kafka

In chapter 10, you put together the Cayambe hybrid, combining the slimmed-down monolith with your new microservices. This chapter simplifies the access of administration data in the Cayambe hybrid by switching it to use data streaming.

First you'll learn about data streaming and how it can benefit developers and architects alike. Taking those lessons, you'll develop a data-streaming solution for the Cayambe hybrid from the previous chapter, completing the journey from monolith to hybrid.

11.1 What can Apache Kafka do for you?

Before delving into Apache Kafka, the solution you're going to use for recording and processing data streams, you need some background on data streaming. Otherwise,

211

what Apache Kafka does and how it works will be completely foreign to you as an Enterprise Java developer.

11.1.1 Data streaming

Data streaming doesn't just refer to the way Netflix gets its movies to play on all your devices. It also refers to a continuously generated stream of data from potentially thousands of sources; each piece of data, or record, is small in size and is stored in the sequence that it was received. That may seem like a lot of buzzwords, but data streaming is still relatively new, and new ways to use it are always being conceived.

What kinds of data apply to data streaming? In a nutshell, pretty much any type of data could be useful in the context of data streaming. Common examples include measurements from vehicle sensors, real-time share prices from the stock market, and trending topics from social networks and sites.

A common use case for data streaming occurs when you have a lot of data, or records, and you want to analyze it for patterns or trends. It may well be that large amounts of the data can be completely ignored, and only key pieces of data are pertinent. It's also possible for the same set of data records to have different purposes, dependent on which system might be consuming it! For instance, an e-commerce site that captures a stream of page-visit events can use the same data not only to record the number of pages a user visits before purchasing, but also to analyze the number of views each page is getting across all users. This is the beauty of data streaming: you can solve different problems with the same set of data.

Figure 11.1 illustrates how data is received as a stream.

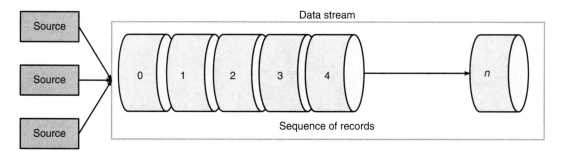

Figure 11.1   Data-streaming pipes

The data for a particular type is received from potentially many sources, and is added to the end of the stream, or pipe, in the order it was received by the system that's responsible for recording the data stream. There's no concept of inserting a particular record at a given point in the stream. Everything is added to the end as it's received.

Though you have several options for recording and processing data streams, for this chapter you'll focus on Apache Kafka, so let's take a look at it now.

DEFINITION To clarify the terminology used throughout this chapter, the terms *data streaming*, *data streams*, and *streaming* all refer to the same thing: the process of streaming data from a source for capture.

11.1.2 *Apache Kafka*

Apache Kafka (https://kafka.apache.org/) was originally developed by LinkedIn in 2010 to be the core for its central data pipeline. Currently, the pipeline processes upward of 2 trillion messages a day! In early 2011, Apache Kafka was proposed as an open source project at Apache, and it moved out of the incubation phase in late 2012. In the space of a few years, many enterprises are using Apache Kafka, including Apple, eBay, Netflix, Spotify, and Uber.

What is Apache Kafka? It's is a distributed streaming platform. What do I mean by *distributed* here? Apache Kafka can partition data from a single data stream across multiple servers within a cluster. In addition, each partition is replicated across servers for fault tolerance of that data.

There are many ways to configure Apache Kafka, in terms of how it's distributed and its level of fault tolerance, but those topics are beyond the scope of this chapter. For full details, take a look at the Apache Kafka documentation at https://kafka.apache.org/documentation/.

As a streaming platform, the key capabilities that Apache Kafka provides are as follows:

- Publish and subscribe to streams of records.
- Store streams of records in a fault-tolerant, durable manner.
- Process streams of records as they happen.

At its core, Apache Kafka is a distributed commit log: it doesn't notify sources that a piece of data has been recorded in the stream until it's committed to the log. Being distributed, as I mentioned before, refers to each commit in the log, or stream, being spread across partitions and replicated.

Another way of describing Apache Kafka is as a database with no clothes: the data is at the forefront and not hidden. Databases, at their core, use a commit log, as Apache Kafka does, to track changes and as a means of recovering from server failures to reconstitute the database. With Apache Kafka, the clothes of the database (tables, indexes, and so forth) have been stripped away, leaving just the commit log. This makes Apache Kafka infinitely more consumable and accessible than regular databases.

Apache Kafka also uses semantics that are familiar to Enterprise Java developers that have integrated with messaging systems. There are *producers*, which generate records or events that are added to the stream, equivalent to the multiple sources present in figure 11.1 previously. Each stream of records is referred to as a *topic*, and anything that reads records from the stream is a *consumer*. Figure 11.2 shows how producers and consumers integrate with Apache Kafka.

In addition, *connectors* enable databases, or other systems, to be sources of records being sent to Apache Kafka. Finally, *stream processors* have the ability to stream records

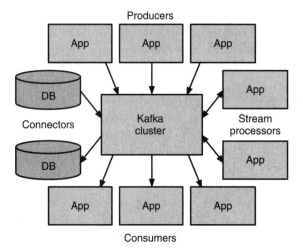

Figure 11.2   **Apache Kafka integrations (reproduced from https://kafka.apache.org/intro.html)**

from one or more topics, perform some type of transformation on the data, and then output it to one or more different topics.

WHAT IS A RECORD?

Now that you understand some of the pieces that make up Apache Kafka, let's define what a *record* means. Each record within a stream consists of a key, a value, and a timestamp. The key and value are straightforward in terms of their purpose, but why is a timestamp needed? The timestamp is crucial to Apache Kafka knowing when a record was received (which will become even more critical when we cover partitions).

You also need to be aware of additional concepts about records before continuing. Each record is *immutable* within the data stream: you can't edit, modify, or remove a record from the data stream after it's been added. All you can do is provide update records for the same key that sets a different value.

Figure 11.3 expands on the stream from figure 11.1, showing possible records for a real-time stream of share prices. In figure 11.3, you can see that there's no single record for the key RHT. There are currently three, all with different values. This is the immutability of the data stream. If the stream weren't immutable, there likely would be a single record with key RHT that's continually updated with a new value.

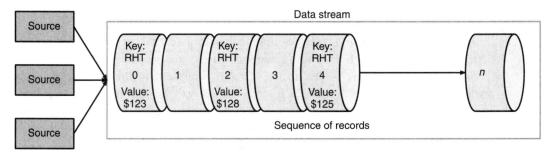

Figure 11.3   **Immutable data stream**

A big advantage with immutable data streams is that you have a history of change for the same key. Certainly in some situations, you might be concerned with only the current value of something. But far more often, knowing the history and being able to determine change over time is critical.

Records are also *persisted*: the log is retained on the filesystem, allowing the records to be processed at any point in the future. Having said that, limits exist on how long a record is retained. Each record is persisted only so long as is allowed by the retention policy on that particular topic. A topic could be defined to retain records indefinitely, presuming disk space isn't an issue, or it could be purged after a few days, whether or not it has been consumed by anything.

HOW DO TOPICS WORK?

Topics in Kafka relate to a category, or type, of record that can be published and consumed. For instance, you'd use one topic for real-time share prices and a separate topic for measurements from vehicle sensors.

Each topic is divided into one or more partitions, across one or more servers within the Kafka cluster. A *partition* is a single logical data stream, or topic, such as those you saw in figures 11.1 and 11.3, that's split into multiple physical data streams.

Figure 11.4 shows a partition. Partitioning of a topic increases the parallelism that can be achieved when writing or reading from a specific topic. The figure illustrates a single topic that's split into three partitions. Each partition represents an ordered and immutable sequence of records that's continually appended to, creating a structured log of change events within a data stream. Each record in a given partition is assigned a sequential ID number known as the *offset*. The offset uniquely identifies a record within a specific partition.

A critical point with Kafka records that developers need to be especially mindful of is the definition of the key to be associated with a record. If the key isn't truly unique within the context of the business, there's the danger of overlap between key and timestamp combinations—especially as Kafka guarantees that all records with the same key are placed on the same partition, ensuring that all records for a key are stored in sequence on a single partition.

Figure 11.5 shows how producers and consumers interact with a topic partition.

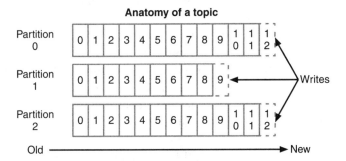

Figure 11.4   Topic partitions (reproduced from https://kafka.apache.org/intro.html)

As mentioned previously, producers always write new records to the very end of a partition. Consumers typically process records sequentially, but are able to specify at which offset they begin processing. For instance, in figure 11.5, Consumer B may have begun reading from offset 0 and is now processing offset 11. Consumer A is at offset 9 but may have begun reading records from that offset only and not from 0.

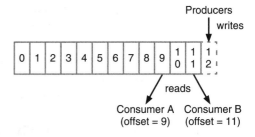

Figure 11.5   Topic producers and consumers (reproduced from https://kafka.apache.org/intro.html)

Figure 11.5 introduces some concepts regarding consumers that are worth elaborating on, so you're familiar with what they can do:

- Consumers can start reading a topic from any offset, including from the very beginning, offset 0.
- Consumers can be load balanced by specifying a consumer group when reading records.
- A *consumer group* is a logical grouping of multiple consumers, ensuring that each record is read by only a single consumer within the same consumer group.

11.2   *Simplifying your monolith architecture with streaming*

Figure 11.6 is a brief reminder of what has been developed and integrated so far with the Cayambe hybrid. The grayed-out piece is to be completed in this chapter and links the Admin and Cayambe databases, via an Apache Kafka topic, to remove the need for the Cayambe database to manage categories directly. This makes it possible to simply feed the data from one database to another.

Without data streaming in figure 11.6, you have a few alternatives:

- Modify the Cayambe JAR to retrieve records from the Admin database. Quite apart from it being bad data design to have different services interacting with the same database, you found in chapter 10 that such a change in this case would require a lot of code changes to accomplish.
- Develop a scheduled job to extract all the records from the Admin database, and then clear out and insert those records into the Cayambe database. This is simpler to implement but does result in periods where the data is out of sync, and also where the data in Cayambe would be unavailable when the job to run it is executing. Depending on how frequently the data changes, this may be an acceptable solution, though having any scheduled downtime is far from ideal.
- Modify the Admin microservice to also update the records within the Cayambe database. Though this would be easier to implement than the first option, this solution is prone to problems around transactions and knowing whether both updates were successful. It would require the Admin microservice to be a lot smarter about succeeding or failing, and how to handle failures appropriately in one of the database calls to roll back the other.

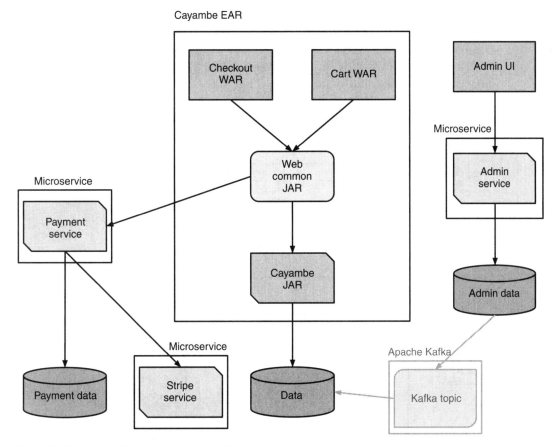

Figure 11.6 Current Cayambe hybrid monolith

To properly support the model in figure 11.6, you want to be able to convert the database change events into records in Kafka for you to process. Such a solution has the least impact on the Admin microservice while still enabling you to consume its data. What you need is a connector for Kafka that can do this for you.

Are any tools available that would make that possible? Why, yes, there are! Debezium is an open source project for streaming changes out of databases into Kafka.

> **NOTE** Debezium is a distributed platform for change data capture. You can start Debezium, point it at your databases, and react to each insert, update, or delete that's made on those databases in completely separate applications. Debezium allows you to consume database row-level changes, without any impact or changes to applications that currently perform those database updates directly. A huge benefit with Debezium is that any applications or services consuming the database changes can be taken down for maintenance without losing a single change. Debezium is still recording the changes into Kafka, ready for consumption when the services are available again. Full details on Debezium can be found at http://debezium.io/.

To gain a better understanding of Apache Kafka, data streaming, and how they can be integrated into your microservices, you aren't going to implement Debezium for the Cayambe hybrid in this chapter. I'll leave that as an additional exercise for you.

For the Cayambe hybrid, you're going to directly produce events into Apache Kafka, and then consume them on the other side. Figure 11.7 shows the changes you're going to make to the architecture, in support of showing more details of the way Apache Kafka works.

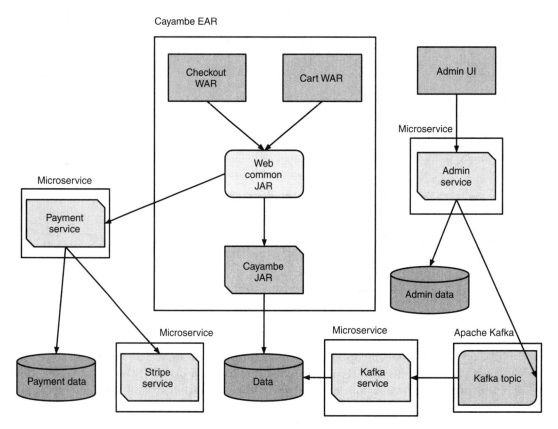

Figure 11.7   Cayambe hybrid monolith

You're adding code to the Admin microservice to produce events that will be sent to an Apache Kafka topic. Then you have a Kafka microservice to consume those events and update the Cayambe database with the changes.

You're still going to use data streaming to move the data you need from one place to another, though not using something like Debezium will be a bit less efficient in terms of real production use, but beneficial to understand what's going on.

11.3 *Deploying and using Kafka for data streaming*

Before looking at implementing the microservices to integrate with Kafka, let's get Kafka up and running on OpenShift! If you don't have Minishift running already, let's start it now just as you did in chapter 10:

```
> minishift start --cpus 3 --memory 4GB
```

11.3.1 *Kafka on OpenShift*

After Minishift is up and running, start the OpenShift console and log in. In your existing project, click Add to Project and then click Import YAML/JSON.

Paste into the text box the contents of /chapter11/resources/Kafka_OpenShift .yml, some snippets of which are in this listing.

Listing 11.1 Kafka OpenShift template

```
apiVersion: v1
kind: Template
metadata:
  name: strimzi              ◁──┘  strimzi is the name of the application
  annotations:                     that will appear within OpenShift.
    openshift.io/display-name: "Apache Kafka (Persistent storage)"
    description: >-
      This template installs Apache Zookeeper and Apache Kafka clusters. For
      more information
        see https://github.com/strimzi/strimzi
    tags: "messaging,datastore"
    iconClass: "fa pficon-topology"
    template.openshift.io/documentation-url:
      "https://github.com/strimzi/strimzi"
message: "Use 'kafka:9092' as bootstrap server in your application"
...
objects:
- apiVersion: v1
  kind: Service
  metadata:
    name: kafka               ◁── Defines the kafka service
  spec:
    ports:
    - name: kafka
      port: 9092              ◁──┐ kafka service will be
      targetPort: 9092            available on port 9092.
      protocol: TCP
    selector:
      name: kafka
    type: ClusterIP
  ...
- apiVersion: v1
  kind: Service
  metadata:
    name: zookeeper           ◁── Defines the zookeeper service
  spec:
```

```
  ports:
  - name: clientport
    port: 2181
    targetPort: 2181
    protocol: TCP
  selector:
    name: zookeeper
  type: ClusterIP
...
```

◁─── **zookeeper service is available on port 2181.**

Hold on there, what's ZooKeeper doing there? It wasn't mentioned before! That's right, it wasn't mentioned before. ZooKeeper is an implementation detail because it's used internally by Kafka as a distributed key/value store. It's not something you need to interact with. You're seeing it here because you're acting as operations staff to set up Kafka for yourself.

/chapter11/resources/Kafka_OpenShift.yml was originally copied from http://mng.bz/RqUn, but was modified to have only a single Kafka broker instead of three. As a result, it doesn't support topic replication, but your OpenShift instance needs fewer resources to run Kafka!

After you've pasted the contents of the modified file into the pop up, click Create and then Continue to see a form where you can specify different default values. For now, leave those as they are and click Create at the bottom of the page. OpenShift will now provision a Kafka cluster with a single broker, which you can see from the main console page under the strimzi application.

> **WARNING**   It can take a little time to complete the downloading of the necessary Docker images and then start the containers. Don't be concerned if the Kafka cluster fails initially if ZooKeeper isn't running yet. Given time, it'll restart, and everything will be running as expected.

After all the pods are started, open a terminal window and log into the OpenShift client, if you're not already. You need to retrieve all the OpenShift services to find the URL for ZooKeeper:

```
> oc get services
NAME                 CLUSTER-IP       EXTERNAL-IP   PORT(S)    AGE
kafka                172.30.225.60    <none>        9092/TCP   5h
kafka-headless       None             <none>        9092/TCP   5h
zookeeper            172.30.93.118    <none>        2181/TCP   5h
zookeeper-headless   None             <none>        2181/TCP   5h
```

From the list, you can see the ZooKeeper URL is 172.30.93.118. Head back to the OpenShift console and select Applications and then Pods from the menu options. This provides a list of the running pods in OpenShift. With a single broker, there should be only a single kafka-* pod. Click that Pod and then select the Terminal tab, and you should see something similar to figure 11.8.

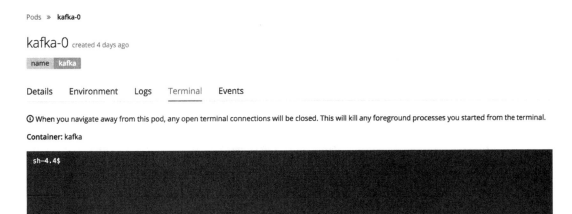

Figure 11.8   OpenShift pod terminal

To use Kafka, you need to create a topic for your records. Let's do that within the Terminal tab:

```
./bin/kafka-topics.sh --create --topic category_topic --replication-factor
  1 --partitions 1 --zookeeper 172.30.93.118:2181
```

You use a Kafka script to create a topic named `category_topic` that has only a single partition and a single replication. You specify only single replication and partition because you have a single broker in the cluster. For instance, if you had three brokers in the cluster, you could use three partitions and a replication factor of 2.

11.3.2   Admin microservice

Now that Kafka is running and your topic is created, it's time to modify the Admin microservice to produce events onto the topic!

To assist in integrating your Enterprise Java code with Kafka, you'll use a library that converts the *pull* approach of Kafka into a *push* approach. This library is still in its infancy but is easy to use because it removes a lot of the boilerplate code that's required when using the Kafka APIs directly. It's written as a CDI extension and is available as Maven artifacts for you to consume. The code is available at https://github.com/aerogear/kafka-cdi.

What's the advantage of converting Kafka's *pull* approach into a *push* one? It's beneficial for those of us more familiar with Enterprise Java development, where with the CDI programming model we're able to listen for events and perform an action when we receive one. This is what the Kafka library we're using brings for us, the ability to listen for events every time a new record is written to a topic, just as if it were a CDI event listener.

The first thing you need to do is update the pom.xml of the Admin microservice to use the new dependency:

```
<dependency>
  <groupId>org.aerogear.kafka</groupId>
  <artifactId>kafka-cdi-extension</artifactId>
  <version>0.0.10</version>
</dependency>
```

Next you modify `CategoryResource` to connect with the Kafka topic, and produce records to be appended onto it.

Listing 11.2 `CategoryResource`

Identifies the Kafka server you're connecting to. You can use environment variables for the host and port because you're deploying the microservice into the same OpenShift namespace as Kafka.

```
@Path("/")
@ApplicationScoped
@KafkaConfig(bootstrapServers =
  "#{KAFKA_SERVICE_HOST}:#{KAFKA_SERVICE_PORT}")
public class CategoryResource {
...
    @Producer
    private SimpleKafkaProducer<Integer, Category> producer;
...
    public Response create(Category category) throws Exception {
...
        producer.send("category_topic", category.getId(), category);
...
    public Response remove(@PathParam("categoryId") Integer categoryId,
        @Context SecurityContext context) throws Exception {
...
        producer.send("category_topic", categoryId, null);
...
    }
}
```

Inject a CDI producer that accepts an Integer as key and Category as value.

create() was modified to call send() after the new Category was created. It indicates the topic you're sending the record to, along with the key and value.

remove() was modified in a similar manner. The main difference with create() is that you're passing a null value because there's no longer a valid value.

With the changes made to the Admin microservice, you can now deploy it! Before deploying the microservice, you need to have Keycloak running, because your microservice uses it to secure the delete endpoint. To do that, you need to run this:

```
/chapter9/keycloak> java -Dswarm.http.port=9090 -jar
  keycloak-2018.1.0-swarm.jar
```

If the database files haven't been removed from the directory, Keycloak should start up and remember all the settings you've installed previously. With Keycloak running again, you can now deploy Admin:

```
/chapter11/admin> mvn clean fabric8:deploy -Popenshift
```

After the microservice is up and running, you can use the new Administration UI, or via HTTP requests directly with Postman, to update and delete categories. How do you know the Admin microservice is correctly putting records onto the Kafka topic? You don't have anything consuming those records!

Thankfully, Kafka provides a consumer you can use in a console to see the contents of a topic. In the OpenShift console, you go back to the kafka-* pod, as you had before, and select the Terminal tab. On the command line, run the following:

```
./bin/kafka-console-consumer.sh --bootstrap-server 172.30.225.60:9092 -
➥ from-beginning --topic category_topic
```

Alternatively, you could connect to the kafka-* pod and run the command remotely:

```
oc rsh kafka-<identifier>
./bin/kafka-console-consumer.sh --bootstrap-server 172.30.225.60:9092 -
➥ from-beginning --topic category_topic
```

You used the IP address and port of the Kafka service from the list of OpenShift services you retrieved earlier to specify where Kafka is located. Next you tell the script you want to consume all records from the beginning, which is the same as saying from offset 0. Finally, you give it the name of the topic. If all has worked OK, you should see a record appear for each change you made through the Admin microservice.

We've covered the producing side of the Kafka topic. Now let's look at the consuming side.

11.3.3 Kafka consumer

All the code for the Kafka consumer is in the /chapter11/kafka-consumer/ directory of the book's code. As with the producer, you add the kafka-cdi-extension dependency to the pom.xml. The remainder of the pom.xml contains the usual Thorntail plugin and dependencies, and the fabric8 Maven plugin for deploying to OpenShift. You also specify a MySQL JDBC driver dependency so you can update the records within the Cayambe database.

For connecting to the Cayambe database, you need to define a DataSource.

Listing 11.3   project-defaults.yml

```
swarm:                                    Name of the
  datasources:                            DataSource in
    data-sources:                             JNDI.        Uses the module created
      CayambeDS:              ◁─────────────────           from the MySQL JDBC
        driver-name: mysql          ◁─────               driver dependency
        connection-url: jdbc:mysql://mysql:3306/cayambe   ◁───  URL to the MySQL
        user-name: cayambe                                      database instance
        password: cayambe                                       on OpenShift
        valid-connection-checker-class-name:
```

Credentials for the Cayambe database

```
          org.jboss.jca.adapters.jdbc.extensions.mysql.MySQLValidConnectionChecker
```

```
        validate-on-match: true
        background-validation: false
        exception-sorter-class-name:
    org.jboss.jca.adapters.jdbc.extensions.mysql.MySQLExceptionSorter
```

Finally, you create a class to process the records from the Kafka topic, as you receive them.

Listing 11.4 `CategoryEventListener`

As you did on the producer, you define the Kafka host and port for the configuration.

The JNDI name for the CayambeDS that you created with project-defaults.yml. It's used by getDatasource(), so you can update the Cayambe database with changed Categories.

@Consumer identifies the method as accepting Kafka topic records, and provides the necessary configuration to wire it up to the Kafka API. It defines the name of the topic you want records from, the type of the key, a unique consumer group identifier, and that you want the offset to start at the beginning of the topic.

```
@ApplicationScoped
@KafkaConfig(bootstrapServers =
  "#{KAFKA_SERVICE_HOST}:#{KAFKA_SERVICE_PORT}")
public class CategoryEventListener {

    private static final String DATASOURCE =
        "java:/jboss/datasources/CayambeDS";

    @Consumer(topics = "category_topic", keyType = Integer.class,
            groupId = "cayambe-listener", offset = "earliest")
    public void handleEvent(Integer key, Category category) {
        if (null == category) {
            // Remove Category
            executeUpdateSQL("delete from category where category_id = " + key);
            // Remove from Category Hierarchy
            executeUpdateSQL("delete from category_category where category_id = " +
    key);
            executeUpdateSQL("delete from category_category where parent_id = " +
    key);
        } else {
            boolean update = rowExists("select * from category where category_id = "
    + key);
            if (update) {
                // Update Category
                executeUpdateSQL("update category set name = '" + category.getName()
                    + "' header = '" + category.getHeader()
                    + "' image = '" + category.getImagePath()
                    + "' where category_id = " + key);
            } else {
                // Create Category
                executeUpdateSQL("insert into category (id,name,header,visible,image)
    values("
                        + key + ",'" + category.getName() + "', '"
                        + category.getHeader() + "', " +
    (category.isVisible() ? 1 : 0)
                        + ", '" + category.getImagePath() + "')");
```

Execute the SQL to remove the category.

Method to receive the Kafka record, with parameters for the key and value types to be passed

Execute the SQL to remove the category from the category hierarchy, either as a child or parent.

Execute SQL to determine if a row for a category ID already exists. Determines whether you're updating or inserving a record.

Execute SQL to update the fields on a category in the database.

Execute SQL to insert the new category into the database, and insert it into the category hierarchy.

```
          executeUpdateSQL("insert into category_category (category_id,
➥ parent_id)"
                          + " values (" + category.getId() + "," +
➥ category.getParent().getId() + ")");
      }
    }
  }

  private void executeUpdateSQL(String sql) {          ◁──┐ Method to handle SQL
    Statement statement = null;                            update execution.
    Connection conn = null;

    try {
      conn = getDatasource().getConnection();
      statement = conn.createStatement();
      statement.executeUpdate(sql);
      statement.close();
      conn.close();
    } catch (Exception e) {
    ...
    }
  }
boolean rowExists(String sql) {          ◁──┐ Method to check if a Category
    Statement statement = null;               row exists in the database.
    Connection conn = null;
    ResultSet results = null;

    try {
      conn = getDatasource().getConnection();
      statement = conn.createStatement();
      results = statement.executeQuery(sql);
      return results.next();
    } catch (Exception e) {
    ...
    }
    return false;
  }

  private DataSource getDatasource() {          ◁──┐ Method for retrieving the
    if (null == dataSource) {                        DataSource from JNDI.
      try {
        dataSource = (DataSource) new InitialContext().lookup(DATASOURCE);
      } catch (NamingException ne) {
        ne.printStackTrace();
      }
    }
    return dataSource;
  }

  private DataSource dataSource = null;
}
```

CategoryEventListener registers a method to listen to the Kafka events, by defining
the key type, value type, which topic you're processing, a consumer group, and that

you want to process all records in the stream from the beginning. When you receive a Kafka record, you then determine whether you need to remove a category, the value is `null`, or whether we're processing a new or updated record.

To distinguish between update and new categories, you execute an SQL statement on the existing categories in Cayambe to see whether this record exists. If it does, it's an update record; if it doesn't, it's a new one.

If you didn't want the overhead of running an SQL statement to determine whether you're dealing with an update or a new category, you could change the value type for the records in Kafka to be an enclosing object. The `Category` instance, the current value, can be a field on a new type, with a flag to indicate the type of change event that's being dealt with.

Now that you've finished developing the Kafka consumer, you're ready to see it all working in unison! But before you deploy the Kafka consumer you just created, to see the visual changes as they happen, it's worth starting up the Cayambe hybrid from chapter 10 with the following:

```
/wildfly-11.0.0.Final/bin/standalone.sh
```

With Cayambe started, open a browser and navigate around the category tree. You should notice that any changes you made through the Admin microservice aren't visible, which makes sense because you haven't activated the process to update the Cayambe database with any changes. So let's start your Kafka consumer now:

```
/chapter11/kafka-consumer> mvn clean fabric8:deploy -Popenshift
```

When the pod becomes operational, it should process all the records that are present on the Kafka topic, because you specified for it to begin at the earliest offset on the topic. You can open the logs of the service and see the console statements that were printed for each record processed.

With the records processed by the Kafka consumer, go back to the Cayambe UI and refresh the page. When navigating through the category tree and finding categories that were changed through the Admin microservice, you'll notice that they're now updated or removed based on what you did earlier.

You've successfully decoupled the data between the two systems so that one owns the data, the Admin microservice, and the other consumes a copy of it in a read-only manner. As an added benefit, as long as the Kafka producers and consumers are functioning, the data never becomes stale.

11.4   *Additional exercises*

As discussed earlier in the chapter, for an additional exercise, try converting the Cayambe hybrid to use Debezium to process database entries directly, instead of by you producing records within the Admin microservice.

This will also provide another benefit over the current solution, as the category hierarchy can be completely reconstructed from the Kafka topic records whenever needed. The hierarchy will contain records for all the initial inserts you did to load the database initially, as well as any insertions, updates, and removals that have occurred since then.

Summary

- Data streaming simplifies an architecture by enabling separate components or microservices to remain decoupled, while still using the same data.
- You can use data streaming with Apache Kafka to share data among microservices and applications without the need for REST calls to retrieve it.

NOTE Additional details on developing microservices with Spring Boot can be found in the appendix.

appendix
Spring Boot microservices

Throughout the book, we've focused on developing microservices for Enterprise Java with Thorntail. This appendix provides details on developing microservices with Spring Boot. Included are snippets from *Spring Boot in Action* by Craig Walls (Manning, 2015). If you're particularly focused on Spring Boot microservices, taking a look at this book for further details would be worthwhile (see www.manning.com/ books/spring-boot-in-action).

Anatomy of a Spring Boot project

This section contains snippets from section 2.1.1 of *Spring Boot in Action*, outlining the parts of a Spring Boot application and its requirements.

Examining a newly initialized Spring Boot project

Figure 1 illustrates the structure of a Spring Boot reading-list project.

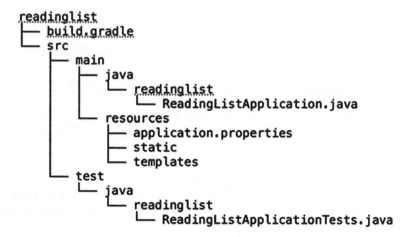

Figure 1   Structure of reading-list project

The first thing to notice is that the project structure follows the layout of a typical Maven or Gradle project. The main application code is placed in the src/main/java branch of the directory tree, resources are placed in the src/main/resources branch, and test code is placed in the src/test/java branch. At this point, you don't have any test resources, but if you did, you'd put them in src/test/resources.

Digging deeper, you'll see a handful of files sprinkled about the project:

- *build.gradle*—The Gradle build specification
- *ReadingListApplication.java*—The application's bootstrap class and primary Spring configuration class
- *application.properties*—A place to configure application and Spring Boot properties
- *ReadingListApplicationTests.java*—A basic integration test class

The build specification contains a lot of Spring Boot goodness to uncover, so I'll save inspection of it until last. Instead, we'll start with ReadingListApplication.java.

Bootstrapping Spring

The ReadingListApplication class serves two purposes in a Spring Boot application: configuration and bootstrapping. First, it's the central Spring configuration class. Even though Spring Boot autoconfiguration eliminates the need for a lot of Spring configuration, you'll need at least a small amount of Spring configuration to enable autoconfiguration. As you can see in this listing, there's only one line of configuration code.

Listing 1   ReadingListApplication

```
package readinglist;

import org.springframework.boot.SpringApplication;
import org.springframework.boot.autoconfigure.SpringBootApplication;

@SpringBootApplication                              ◁── Enable component-scanning
public class ReadingListApplication {                   and autoconfiguration.

  public static void main(String[] args) {
    SpringApplication.run(ReadingListApplication.class, args);    ◁── Bootstrap the
  }                                                                   application.

}
```

@SpringBootApplication enables Spring component scanning and Spring Boot autoconfiguration. In fact, @SpringBootApplication combines three other useful annotations:

- *Spring's* @Configuration—Designates a class as a configuration class using Spring's Java-based configuration. Although you won't write a lot of configuration in this book, you'll favor Java-based configuration over XML configuration when you do.

- *Spring's* @ComponentScan—Enables component scanning so that the web controller classes and other components you write will be automatically discovered and registered as beans in the Spring application context. Later in this appendix, you'll write a simple Spring MVC controller that will be annotated with @Controller so that component scanning can find it.
- *Spring Boot's* @EnableAutoConfiguration—This humble little annotation might as well be named @Abracadabra because it's the one line of configuration that enables the magic of Spring Boot autoconfiguration. This one line keeps you from having to write the pages of configuration that would be required otherwise.

In older versions of Spring Boot, you'd annotate the ReadingListApplication class with all three of these annotations. But since Spring Boot 1.2.0, @SpringBootApplication is all you need.

As I said, ReadingListApplication is also a bootstrap class. There are several ways to run Spring Boot applications, including traditional WAR file deployment. But for now, the main() method here enables you to run your application as an executable JAR file from the command line. It passes a reference to the ReadingListApplication class to SpringApplication.run(), along with the command-line arguments, to kick off the application.

Even though you haven't written any application code, you can still build the application at this point and try it out. The easiest way to build and run the application is to use the bootRun task with Gradle:

```
$ gradle bootRun
```

The bootRun task comes from Spring Boot's Gradle plugin. Alternatively, you can build the project with Gradle and run it with Java at the command line:

```
$ gradle build
...
$ java -jar build/libs/readinglist-0.0.1-SNAPSHOT.jar
```

The application should start up fine and enable a Tomcat server listening on port 8080. You can point your browser at http://localhost:8080 if you want, but because you haven't written a controller class yet, you'll be met with an HTTP 404 (Not Found) error and an error page. Before this appendix is finished, though, that URL will serve your reading-list application.

You'll almost never need to change ReadingListApplication.java. If your application requires any additional Spring configuration beyond what Spring Boot autoconfiguration provides, it's usually best to write it into separate @Configuration-configured classes. (They'll be picked up and used by component scanning.) In exceptionally simple cases, though, you could add custom configuration to ReadingListApplication.java.

Testing Spring Boot applications

The Initializr also gives you a skeleton test class to help you get started with writing tests for your application. But ReadingListApplicationTests, shown in the following listing, is more than just a placeholder for tests. It also serves as an example of how to write tests for Spring Boot applications. @SpringApplicationConfiguration loads a Spring application context.

Listing 2   ReadingListApplicationTests

```
package readinglist;

import org.junit.Test;
import org.junit.runner.RunWith;
import org.springframework.boot.test.SpringApplicationConfiguration;
import org.springframework.test.context.junit4.SpringJUnit4ClassRunner;
import org.springframework.test.context.web.WebAppConfiguration;

import readinglist.ReadingListApplication;

@RunWith(SpringJUnit4ClassRunner.class)
@SpringApplicationConfiguration(                      ⟵  Load context via
        classes = ReadingListApplication.class)          Spring Boot.
@WebAppConfiguration
public class ReadingListApplicationTests {

  @Test                                    ⟵  Test that the
  public void contextLoads() {                context loads.
  }

}
```

In a typical Spring integration test, you'd annotate the test class with @ContextConfiguration to specify how the test should load the Spring application context. But in order to take full advantage of Spring Boot magic, the @SpringApplicationConfiguration annotation should be used instead. As you can see in listing 2, ReadingListApplicationTests is annotated with @SpringApplicationConfiguration to load the Spring application context from the ReadingListApplication configuration class.

ReadingListApplicationTests also includes one simple test method, contextLoads(). It's so simple, in fact, that it's an empty method. But it's sufficient for the purpose of verifying that the application context loads without any problems. If the configuration defined in ReadingListApplication is good, the test will pass. If any problems exist, the test will fail.

You'll add some of your own tests as we flesh out the application. But the contextLoads() method is a fine start and verifies every bit of functionality provided by the application at this point.

Configuring application properties

The application.properties file given to you by the Initializr is initially empty. This file is optional, so you could remove it completely without impacting the application. But there's also no harm in leaving it in place.

You'll definitely find opportunity to add entries to application.properties later. For now, however, if you want to poke around with application.properties, try adding the following line:

```
server.port=8000
```

With this line, you're configuring the embedded Tomcat server to listen on port 8000 instead of the default port 8080. You can confirm this by running the application again.

This demonstrates that the application.properties file comes in handy for fine-grained configuration of the stuff that Spring Boot automatically configures. But you can also use it to specify properties used by application code.

The main thing to notice is that at no point do you explicitly ask Spring Boot to load application.properties for you. By virtue of the fact that application.properties exists, it will be loaded and its properties made available for configuring both Spring and application code.

Spring Boot starter dependencies

This section provides information about the Spring Boot starters and how they're used.

Using starter dependencies

To understand the benefit of Spring Boot starter dependencies, let's pretend that they don't exist. What kind of dependencies would you add to your build without Spring Boot? Which Spring dependencies do you need in order to support Spring MVC? Do you remember the group and artifact IDs for Thymeleaf, or any external dependency? Which version of Spring Data JPA should you use? Are all of these compatible?

Uh-oh. Without Spring Boot starter dependencies, you have some homework to do. All you want to do is develop a Spring web application with Thymeleaf views that persists its data via JPA. But before you can even write your first line of code, you have to figure out what needs to be put into the build specification to support your plan.

After much consideration (and probably a lot of copy-and-paste from another application's build that has similar dependencies), you arrive at the following dependencies block in your Gradle build specification:

```
compile("org.springframework:spring-web:4.1.6.RELEASE")
compile("org.thymeleaf:thymeleaf-spring4:2.1.4.RELEASE")
compile("org.springframework.data:spring-data-jpa:1.8.0.RELEASE")
compile("org.hibernate:hibernate-entitymanager:jar:4.3.8.Final")
compile("com.h2database:h2:1.4.187")
```

This dependency list is fine and might even work. But how do you know? What kind of assurance do you have that the versions you chose for those dependencies are even compatible with each other? They might be, but you won't know until you build the application and run it. And how do you know that the list of dependencies is complete? With not a single line of code having been written, you're still a long way from kicking the tires on your build.

Let's step back and recall what it is you want to do. You're looking to build an application with these traits:

- It's a web application.
- It uses Thymeleaf.
- It persists data to a relational database via Spring Data JPA.

Wouldn't it be simpler if you could specify those facts in the build and let the build sort out what you need? That's exactly what Spring Boot starter dependencies do.

Specifying facet-based dependencies

Spring Boot addresses project dependency complexity by providing several dozen starter dependencies. A *starter dependency* is essentially a Maven POM that defines transitive dependencies on other libraries that together provide support for a certain functionality. Many of these starter dependencies are named to indicate the facet or kind of functionality they provide.

For example, the reading-list application is going to be a web application. Rather than add several individually chosen library dependencies to the project build, it's much easier to simply declare that this is a web application. You can do that by adding Spring Boot's web starter to the build.

You also want to use Thymeleaf for web views and persist data with JPA. Therefore, you need the Thymeleaf and Spring Data JPA starter dependencies in the build.

For testing purposes, you also want libraries that will enable you to run integration tests in the context of Spring Boot. Therefore, you also want a test-time dependency on Spring Boot's test starter.

Taken altogether, you have the following five dependencies that the Initializr provides in the Gradle build:

```
dependencies {
    compile "org.springframework.boot:spring-boot-starter-web"
    compile "org.springframework.boot:spring-boot-starter-thymeleaf"
    compile "org.springframework.boot:spring-boot-starter-data-jpa"
    compile "com.h2database:h2"
    testCompile("org.springframework.boot:spring-boot-starter-test")
}
```

As you saw earlier, the easiest way to get these dependencies into your application's build is to select the Web, Thymeleaf, and JPA check boxes in the Initializr. But if you didn't do that when initializing the project, you can certainly go back and add them by editing the generated build.gradle or pom.xml.

Via transitive dependencies, adding these four dependencies is the equivalent of adding several dozen individual libraries to the build. Some of those transitive dependencies include such things as Spring MVC, Spring Data JPA, and Thymeleaf, as well as any transitive dependencies that those dependencies declare.

The most important thing to notice about the four starter dependencies is that they're only as specific as they need to be. You don't say that you want Spring MVC; you simply say that you want to build a web application. You don't specify JUnit or any other testing tools; you just say that you want to test your code. The Thymeleaf and Spring Data JPA starters are a bit more specific, but only because there's no less-specific way to declare that you want Thymeleaf and Spring Data JPA. The four starters in this build are only a few of the many starter dependencies that Spring Boot offers.

In no case did you need to specify the version. The starter dependencies' versions are determined by which Spring Boot version you're using. The starter dependencies themselves determine the versions of the various transitive dependencies that they pull in.

Not knowing what versions of the various libraries are used may be a little unsettling to you. Be encouraged to know that Spring Boot has been tested to ensure that all of the dependencies pulled in are compatible. It can be liberating to just specify a starter dependency and not have to worry about which libraries and which versions of those libraries you need to maintain.

But if you must know what you're getting, you can always discover that from the build tool. In the case of Gradle, the `dependencies` task will give you a dependency tree that includes every library that your project is using and their versions:

```
$ gradle dependencies
```

You can get a similar dependency tree from a Maven build with the `tree` goal of the dependency plugin:

```
$ mvn dependency:tree
```

For the most part, you should never concern yourself with the specifics of what each Spring Boot starter dependency provides. Generally, it's enough to know that the web starter enables you to build a web application, the Thymeleaf starter enables you to use Thymeleaf templates, and the Spring Data JPA starter enables data persistence to a database by using Spring Data JPA.

But what if, in spite of the testing performed by the Spring Boot team, there's a problem with a starter dependency's choice of libraries? How can you override the starter?

Overriding starter transitive dependencies

Ultimately, starter dependencies are just dependencies like any other dependency in your build. You can use the facilities of the build tool to selectively override transitive dependency versions, exclude transitive dependencies, and certainly specify dependencies for libraries not covered by Spring Boot starters.

For example, consider Spring Boot's web starter. Among other things, the web starter transitively depends on the Jackson JSON library. This library is handy if you're building a REST service that consumes or produces JSON resource representations. But if you're using Spring Boot to build a more traditional human-facing web application, you may not need Jackson. Even though including it shouldn't hurt anything, you can trim the fat off of your build by excluding Jackson as a transitive dependency.

If you're using Gradle, you can exclude transitive dependencies like this:

```
compile("org.springframework.boot:spring-boot-starter-web") {
  exclude group: 'com.fasterxml.jackson.core'
}
```

In Maven, you can exclude transitive dependencies with the <exclusions> element. The following <dependency> for the Spring Boot web starter has <exclusions> to keep Jackson out of the build:

```
<dependency>
  <groupId>org.springframework.boot</groupId>
  <artifactId>spring-boot-starter-web</artifactId>
  <exclusions>
    <exclusion>
      <groupId>com.fasterxml.jackson.core</groupId>
    </exclusion>
  </exclusions>
</dependency>
```

Conversely, maybe having Jackson in the build is fine, but you want to build against a different version of Jackson than what the web starter references. Suppose that the web starter references Jackson 2.3.4, but you'd rather use version 2.4.3. Using Maven, you can express the desired dependency directly in your project's pom.xml file like this:

```
<dependency>
  <groupId>com.fasterxml.jackson.core</groupId>
  <artifactId>jackson-databind</artifactId>
  <version>2.4.3</version>
</dependency>
```

Maven always favors the closest dependency, meaning that because you've expressed this dependency in your project's build, it'll be favored over the one that's transitively referred to by another dependency.

Similarly, if you're building with Gradle, you can specify the newer version of Jackson in your build.gradle file like this:

```
compile("com.fasterxml.jackson.core:jackson-databind:2.4.3")
```

This dependency works in Gradle because it's newer than the version transitively referred to by Spring Boot's web starter. But suppose that instead of using a newer version of Jackson, you'd like to use an older version. Unlike Maven, Gradle favors the newest version of a dependency. Therefore, if you want to use an older version of Jackson, you have to express the older version as a dependency in your build and exclude it from being transitively resolved by the web starter dependency:

```
compile("org.springframework.boot:spring-boot-starter-web") {
  exclude group: 'com.fasterxml.jackson.core'
}
compile("com.fasterxml.jackson.core:jackson-databind:2.3.1")
```

In any case, be cautious when overriding the dependencies that are pulled in transitively by Spring Boot starter dependencies. Although different versions may work fine, a great amount of comfort can be taken from knowing that the versions chosen by the starters have been tested to play well together. You should override these transitive dependencies only under special circumstances (such as a bug fix in a newer version).

Now that you have an empty project structure and build specification ready, it's time to start developing the application itself. As you do, you'll let Spring Boot handle the configuration details while you focus on writing the code that provides the reading-list functionality.

Developing a Spring Boot application

In listing 3, you'll further develop a Spring Boot application, with content from section 2.3.1 of *Spring Boot in Action*.

Focusing on application functionality

One way to gain an appreciation of Spring Boot autoconfiguration would be for me to spend the next several pages showing you the configuration that's required in the absence of Spring Boot. But several great books on Spring could show you that, and showing it again wouldn't help you get the reading-list application written any quicker.

Instead of wasting time talking about Spring configuration, know that Spring Boot is going to take care of that for you, so let's see how taking advantage of Spring Boot autoconfiguration keeps you focused on writing application code. I can think of no better way to do that than to start writing the application code for the reading-list application.

Defining the domain

The central domain concept in your application is a book that's on a reader's reading list. Therefore, you'll need to define an entity class that represents a book. Listing 3 shows how the Book type is defined.

Listing 3   The Book class

```java
package readinglist;

import javax.persistence.Entity;
import javax.persistence.GeneratedValue;
import javax.persistence.GenerationType;
import javax.persistence.Id;

@Entity
public class Book {

  @Id
  @GeneratedValue(strategy=GenerationType.AUTO)
  private Long id;
  private String reader;
  private String isbn;
  private String title;
  private String author;
  private String description;

  public Long getId() {
    return id;
  }

  public void setId(Long id) {
    this.id = id;
  }

  public String getReader() {
    return reader;
  }

  public void setReader(String reader) {
    this.reader = reader;
  }

  public String getIsbn() {
    return isbn;
  }

  public void setIsbn(String isbn) {
    this.isbn = isbn;
  }

  public String getTitle() {
    return title;
  }

  public void setTitle(String title) {
    this.title = title;
  }

  public String getAuthor() {
    return author;
  }

  public void setAuthor(String author) {
    return author;
```

```
  }

  public void setAuthor(String author) {
    this.author = author;
  }

  public String getDescription() {
    return description;
  }

  public void setDescription(String description) {
    this.description = description;
  }
}
```

As you can see, the `Book` class is a simple Java object with a handful of properties describing a book and the necessary accessor methods. It's annotated with `@Entity` designating it as a JPA entity. The `id` property is annotated with `@Id` and `@Generated-Value` to indicate that this field is the entity's identity and that its value will be automatically provided.

Defining the repository interface

Next you need to define the repository through which the `ReadingList` objects will be persisted to the database. Because you're using Spring Data JPA, that task is a simple matter of creating an interface that extends Spring Data JPA's `JpaRepository` interface:

```
package readinglist;

import java.util.List;
import org.springframework.data.jpa.repository.JpaRepository;

public interface ReadingListRepository extends JpaRepository<Book, Long> {

  List<Book> findByReader(String reader);
}
```

By extending `JpaRepository`, `ReadingListRepository` inherits 18 methods for performing common persistence operations. The `JpaRepository` interface is parameterized with two parameters: the domain type that the repository will work with, and the type of its ID property. In addition, I've added a `findByReader()` method through which a reading list can be looked up, given a reader's username.

  If you're wondering about who will implement `ReadingListRepository` and the 18 methods it inherits, don't worry too much about it. Spring Data provides a special magic of its own, making it possible to define a repository with just an interface. The interface will be implemented automatically at runtime when the application is started.

Creating the web interface

Now that you've defined the application's domain and have a repository for persisting objects from that domain to the database, all that's left is to create the web frontend. A Spring MVC controller like the one in the following listing will handle HTTP requests for the application.

Listing 4   `ReadingListController`

```java
package readinglist;

import org.springframework.beans.factory.annotation.Autowired;
import org.springframework.stereotype.Controller;
import org.springframework.ui.Model;
import org.springframework.web.bind.annotation.PathVariable;
import org.springframework.web.bind.annotation.RequestMapping;
import org.springframework.web.bind.annotation.RequestMethod;

import java.util.List;

@Controller
@RequestMapping("/")
public class ReadingListController {

  private ReadingListRepository readingListRepository;

  @Autowired
  public ReadingListController(
          ReadingListRepository readingListRepository) {
    this.readingListRepository = readingListRepository;
  }

  @RequestMapping(value="/{reader}", method=RequestMethod.GET)
  public String readersBooks(
      @PathVariable("reader") String reader,
      Model model) {

    List<Book> readingList =
        readingListRepository.findByReader(reader);
    if (readingList != null) {
      model.addAttribute("books", readingList);
    }
    return "readingList";
  }

  @RequestMapping(value="/{reader}", method=RequestMethod.POST)
  public String addToReadingList(
          @PathVariable("reader") String reader, Book book) {
    book.setReader(reader);
    readingListRepository.save(book);
    return "redirect:/{reader}";
  }

}
```

`ReadingListController` is annotated with `@Controller` in order to be picked up by component scanning and automatically registered as a bean in the Spring application context. It's also annotated with `@RequestMapping` to map all of its handler methods to a base URL path of "/".

The controller has two methods:

- `readersBooks()`—Handles HTTP GET requests for /{reader} by retrieving a Book list from the repository (which was injected into the controller's constructor) for the reader specified in the path. It puts the list of Book into the model under the key books and returns readingList as the logical name of the view to render the model.

- `addToReadingList()`—Handles HTTP POST requests for /{reader}, binding the data in the body of the request to a Book object. This method sets the Book object's reader property to the reader's name, and then saves the modified Book via the repository's save() method. Finally, it returns by specifying a redirect to /{reader} (which will be handled by the other controller method).

The readersBooks() method concludes by returning readingList as the logical view name. Therefore, you must also create that view. I decided at the outset of this project that we'd be using Thymeleaf to define the application views, so the next step is to create a file named readingList.html in src/main/resources/templates with the following content.

Listing 5   readingList.html

```html
<html>
  <head>
    <title>Reading List</title>
    <link rel="stylesheet" th:href="@{/style.css}"></link>
  </head>

  <body>
    <h2>Your Reading List</h2>
    <div th:unless="${#lists.isEmpty(books)}">
      <dl th:each="book : ${books}">
        <dt class="bookHeadline">
          <span th:text="${book.title}">Title</span> by
          <span th:text="${book.author}">Author</span>
          (ISBN: <span th:text="${book.isbn}">ISBN</span>)
        </dt>
        <dd class="bookDescription">
          <span th:if="${book.description}"
                th:text="${book.description}">Description</span>
          <span th:if="${book.description eq null}">
                No description available</span>
        </dd>
      </dl>
    </div>
    <div th:if="${#lists.isEmpty(books)}">
```

```
    <p>You have no books in your book list</p>
  </div>

  <hr/>

  <h3>Add a book</h3>
  <form method="POST">
    <label for="title">Title:</label>
      <input type="text" name="title" size="50"></input><br/>
    <label for="author">Author:</label>
      <input type="text" name="author" size="50"></input><br/>
    <label for="isbn">ISBN:</label>
      <input type="text" name="isbn" size="15"></input><br/>
    <label for="description">Description:</label><br/>
      <textarea name="description" cols="80" rows="5">
      </textarea><br/>
    <input type="submit"></input>
  </form>

  </body>
</html>
```

This template defines an HTML page that is conceptually divided into two parts. At the top of the page is a list of books that are in the reader's reading list. At the bottom is a form that the reader can use to add a new book to the reading list.

For aesthetic purposes, the Thymeleaf template references a stylesheet named style.css. That file should be created in src/main/resources/static and look like this:

```
body {
    background-color: #cccccc;
    font-family: arial,helvetica,sans-serif;
}

.bookHeadline {
    font-size: 12pt;
    font-weight: bold;
}

.bookDescription {
    font-size: 10pt;
}

label {
    font-weight: bold;
}
```

This stylesheet is simple and doesn't go overboard to make the application look nice. But it serves our purposes and, as you'll soon see, serves to demonstrate a piece of Spring Boot's autoconfiguration.

Believe it or not, that's a complete application. Every single line has been presented to you in this appendix. Flip back through the previous pages, and see if you can find any configuration. Aside from the three lines of configuration in listing 1 (which turns on autoconfiguration), you didn't have to write any Spring configuration.

Despite the lack of Spring configuration, this complete Spring application is ready to run. Let's fire it up and see how it looks.

Spring Boot testing

This section provides information about testing with Spring Boot, by mocking parts of Spring MVC. This section contains content from section 4.2.1 of *Spring Boot in Action*.

Mocking Spring MVC

Since Spring 3.2, the Spring Framework has had a useful facility for testing web applications by mocking Spring MVC. This makes it possible to perform HTTP requests against a controller without running the controller within an actual servlet container. Instead, Spring's Mock MVC framework mocks enough of Spring MVC to make it almost as though the application is running within a servlet container—but it's not.

To set up a Mock MVC in your test, you can use `MockMvcBuilders`. This class offers two static methods:

- `standaloneSetup()`—Builds a Mock MVC to serve one or more manually created and configured controllers
- `webAppContextSetup()`—Builds a Mock MVC using a Spring application context, which presumably includes one or more configured controllers

The primary difference between these two options is that `standaloneSetup()` expects you to manually instantiate and inject the controllers you want to test, whereas `webAppContextSetup()` works from an instance of `WebApplicationContext`, which itself was probably loaded by Spring. The former is slightly more akin to a unit test in that you'll likely use it only for focused tests around a single controller. The latter, however, lets Spring load your controllers as well as their dependencies for a full-blown integration test.

For our purposes, you're going to use `webAppContextSetup()` so you can test the `ReadingListController` as it has been instantiated and injected from the application context that Spring Boot has autoconfigured.

The `webAppContextSetup()` takes a `WebApplicationContext` as an argument. Therefore, you need to annotate the test class with `@WebAppConfiguration` and use `@Autowired` to inject the `WebApplicationContext` into the test as an instance variable. This listing shows the starting point for your Mock MVC tests.

Listing 6 MockMvcWebTests

```
@RunWith(SpringJUnit4ClassRunner.class)
@SpringApplicationConfiguration(
    classes = ReadingListApplication.class)       Enables web
@WebAppConfiguration                              context testing
public class MockMvcWebTests {
```

```
@Autowired                                          Injects
private WebApplicationContext webContext;   <──┘    WebApplicationContext

private MockMvc mockMvc;

@Before
public void setupMockMvc() {
  mockMvc = MockMvcBuilders              <── Sets up MockMvc
      .webAppContextSetup(webContext)
      .build();
  }
}
```

The `@WebAppConfiguration` annotation declares that the application context created by `SpringJUnit4ClassRunner` should be a `WebApplicationContext` (as opposed to a basic non-web `ApplicationContext`).

The `setupMockMvc()` method is annotated with JUnit's `@Before`, indicating that it should be executed before any test methods. It passes the injected `WebApplication-Context` into the `webAppContextSetup()` method and then calls `build()` to produce a `MockMvc` instance, which is assigned to an instance variable for test methods to use.

Now that you have `MockMvc`, you're ready to write test methods. Let's start with a simple test method that performs an HTTP GET request against /readingList and asserts that the model and view meet your expectations. The following `homePage()` test method does what you need:

```
@Test
public void homePage() throws Exception {
  mockMvc.perform(MockMvcRequestBuilders.get("/readingList"))
      .andExpect(MockMvcResultMatchers.status().isOk())
      .andExpect(MockMvcResultMatchers.view().name("readingList"))
      .andExpect(MockMvcResultMatchers.model().attributeExists("books"))
      .andExpect(MockMvcResultMatchers.model().attribute("books",
          Matchers.is(Matchers.empty())));
}
```

As you can see, a lot of static methods are being used in this test method, including static methods from Spring's `MockMvcRequestBuilders` and `MockMvcResultMatchers`, as well as from the Hamcrest library's `Matchers`. Before diving into the details of this test method, let's add a few static imports so that the code is easier to read:

import static org.hamcrest.Matchers.*;

```
import static
➥ org.springframework.test.web.servlet.request.MockMvcRequestBuilders.*;
import static
➥ org.springframework.test.web.servlet.result.MockMvcResultMatchers.*;
```

With those static imports in place, the test method can be rewritten like this:

```
@Test
public void homePage() throws Exception {
  mockMvc.perform(get("/readingList"))
      .andExpect(status().isOk())
      .andExpect(view().name("readingList"))
      .andExpect(model().attributeExists("books"))
      .andExpect(model().attribute("books", is(empty())));
}
```

Now the test method almost reads naturally. First it performs a GET request against /readingList. Then it expects that the request is successful (isOk() asserts an HTTP 200 response code) and that the view has a logical name of readingList. It also asserts that the model contains an attribute named books, but that attribute is an empty collection. It's all straightforward.

The main thing to note is that at no time is the application deployed to a web server. Instead it's run within a mocked-out Spring MVC, just capable enough to handle the HTTP requests you throw at it via the MockMvc instance.

Pretty cool, huh? Let's try one more test method. This time you'll make it a bit more interesting by sending an HTTP POST request to post a new book. You should expect that after the POST request is handled, the request will be redirected back to /readingList and that the books attribute in the model will contain the newly added book. The following listing shows how to use Spring's Mock MVC to do this kind of test.

Listing 7 `MockMvcWebTests`

```
@Test
public void postBook() throws Exception {
mockMvc.perform(post("/readingList")                        ◁── Performs
        .contentType(MediaType.APPLICATION_FORM_URLENCODED)      POST request
        .param("title", "BOOK TITLE")
        .param("author", "BOOK AUTHOR")
        .param("isbn", "1234567890")
        .param("description", "DESCRIPTION"))
        .andExpect(status().is3xxRedirection())
        .andExpect(header().string("Location", "/readingList"));

Book expectedBook = new Book();           ◁── Sets up
expectedBook.setId(1L);                       expected book
expectedBook.setReader("craig");
expectedBook.setTitle("BOOK TITLE");
expectedBook.setAuthor("BOOK AUTHOR");
expectedBook.setIsbn("1234567890");
expectedBook.setDescription("DESCRIPTION");
                                           Performs
                                           GET request
mockMvc.perform(get("/readingList"))      ◁──
        .andExpect(status().isOk())
        .andExpect(view().name("readingList"))
```

```
        .andExpect(model().attributeExists("books"))
        .andExpect(model().attribute("books", hasSize(1)))
        .andExpect(model().attribute("books",
                    contains(samePropertyValuesAs(expectedBook)))));
}
```

This test is a bit more involved; it's two tests in one method. The first part posts the book and asserts the results from that request. The second part performs a fresh GET request against the homepage and asserts that the newly created book is in the model.

When posting the book, you must make sure that you set the content type to application/x-www-form-urlencoded (with MediaType.APPLICATION_FORM_URLEN-CODED) because that's the content type that a browser will send when the book is posted in the running application. You then use the MockMvcRequestBuilders's param() method to set the fields that simulate the form being submitted. After the request has been performed, you assert that the response is a redirect to /readingList.

Assuming that much of the test method passes, you move on to part 2. First, you set up a Book object that contains the expected values. You'll use this to compare with the value that's in the model after fetching the homepage.

Then you perform a GET request for /readingList. For the most part, this is no different from the way you tested the homepage before, except that instead of an empty collection in the model, you're checking that it has one item, and that the item is the same as the expected Book you created. If so, then your controller seems to be doing its job of saving a book when one is posted to it.

Summary

- Select content from *Spring Boot in Action* covered additional details on developing microservices with Spring Boot.
- Further details on developing Spring Boot microservices can be found in *Spring Boot in Action* (www.manning.com/books/spring-boot-in-action).

index

RELATED MANNING TITLES

The Tao of Microservices
by Richard Rodger

ISBN: 9781617293146
328 pages, $49.99
December 2017

Microservices Patterns
With examples in Java
by Chris Richardson

ISBN: 9781617294549
477 pages, $49.99
October 2018

Spring Microservices in Action
by John Carnell

ISBN: 9781617293986
384 pages, $49.99
June 2017

Microservices in .NET Core
with examples in Nancy
by Christian Horsdal Gammelgaard

ISBN: 9781617293375
344 pages, $49.99
January 2017

For ordering information go to www.manning.com